DATE			

SARNOFF
An American Success

SARNOFF
An American Success
BY CARL DREHER

Quadrangle/The New York Times Book Co.

SARNOFF: *An American Success* is published
posthumously; Carl Dreher died July 13, 1976.

Library of Congress Cataloging in Publication Data

Dreher, Carl, 1896–1976
  Sarnoff, an American success.

  Includes index.
  1. Sarnoff, David, 1891–1971. 2. Radio—
United States—Biography. 3. Television—United
States—Biography. I. Title.
TK6545.S3D73 1976 338.7′61′384540924 [B] 76–50818
ISBN 0–8129–0672–1

CONTENTS

SARNOFF
An American Success

THE DEDICATION

It was a gala yet solemn occasion, the highlight of a life crowded with achievement and now entering its declining phase. The date: September 28, 1967. The place: The David Sarnoff Library, an adjunct of the RCA/David Sarnoff Research Center at Princeton, New Jersey, a few miles south of the university. For the first time, the library—really as much a museum as a library—was opened, not yet to public view, but for some 200 guests invited to do honor to Brigadier General David Sarnoff, chairman of the board of the Radio Corporation of America (now the RCA Corporation) since 1949, but actually the dominant spirit of the company since its founding in 1919.

The composition of this assemblage must have fallen short of what Sarnoff's publicists initially expected, nor did it comport with Sarnoff's status. Almost to a man, the guests were important only in the electronic and allied industries. The only figure of national importance was Dr. Detlev W. Bronk, president of Rockefeller University.

In its January 1975 issue, *Fortune* launched a "Hall of Fame for Business Leadership," initially with "Laureates from Two Centuries," beginning, nonchronologically, with Henry Ford, John D. Rockefeller, and J. Pierpont Morgan; among early achievers, Eli Whitney and George Washington (as much a businessman as a general) and ending with modern notables like Andrew Carnegie and George Eastman. Only fifteen names comprised this tentative roster, and rightfully Sarnoff was among them, though posthumously. At the 1967 ceremony, the master of ceremonies, who presented Sarnoff with the keys to the library and delivered the introductory speech, was Dr. George H. Brown, head of the Research Center and a most estimable scientist-engineer, yet his leading role made the dedication essentially an in-house affair.

This incongruity was tacitly ignored. The library was proudly dedicated, as befits a great corporation. It is, indeed, a place worth visiting, like Monticello, Sarnoff being a kind of electronics Jefferson. But things were changing, and not for the better, Nineteen sixty-six had been a good year for Sarnoff: in his photographs, at least, he appeared as vigorous as ever and those who did not know him might have taken him for a man of sixty rather than seventy-five. Always a relaxed speaker, at the dedication, he showed signs of strain. He was, in fact, nearing the end of his active career. At the end of 1969 he retired because of ill health and was succeeded as board chairman by Robert W. Sarnoff, his eldest son. David Sarnoff died on December 12, 1971.

At the dedication there was no thought of death. Just the same, the installation was a record of the past, however triumphal. "What you will see in this library today represents more than books and photographs and hardware," Sarnoff told his admirers. "It reflects the efforts of more than sixty years and contains the written and graphic evidence of the major events in our fields during this time.

"I have lived them over and over again during the past few years when I was assembling the materials you will find in this library. While there is nothing in this collection that you are not already aware of, perhaps the rising generation may find some interest in reading the documents and reports of what took place—how it all happened."

The rising generation did not. It never does, unless indoctrinated almost from the cradle with bowdlerized images from the past for purposes of social fortification in the present. Although Sarnoff was conservative enough to qualify, as a politician he was undistinguished, and it was not to be expected that the library would become a mecca for devotees of the American way of life. Occasionally, now, the lack of traffic is relieved by groups of children who are herded through the library and given a dose of the Sarnoff legend—by this time a medley of items of genuine historic importance and fables on a par with Parson Weems's story of George Washington and the cherry tree.

Sarnoff was a prolific collector of trophies, scrolls, medals, awards, citations, and other tokens of esteem. Most are housed in a spacious exhibition hall with glass-enclosed, locked bookcases along one wall; opposite, near one end, glass doors open on a patio with an immense stretch of lawn behind it. Except for a cluster of sofas and chairs, the space is occupied by cases containing objects too varied and numerous to catalog here, but one case holds Sarnoff's 26 honorary degrees together with 145 documents—an assortment of awards, appointments, and citations. Other cases hold silver trays, bowls, and wreathes and some singular oddities like a silver galleon presented by British Cable and Wireless Ltd. and a Silver Buffalo Award from the Boy Scouts. The case containing medals and decorations from foreign governments focuses on Sarnoff's appointment as a Commander of the Legion of Honor.

An enclosed gallery reached by steps from the main room gives onto small, windowless rooms containing additional exhibits; one of these, in token of Sarnoff's strong anti-Communist views, includes among memorabilia from Greece, Spain, and South America, and prized relics —a fragment of the Stalin statue destroyed by the freedom fighters in Budapest, and a piece of barbed wire fencing described in an RCA publication release as having come from the Iron Curtain.

A part of the library installation not included in the official description but shown to favored outsiders is the office space and living quarters Sarnoff used when he was staying at the laboratory. The secretary's anteroom is slightly smaller than a vice-president's office at the RCA headquarters in Rockefeller Center, while the General's office, 18 x 30, is considerably larger than the one he occupied at headquarters. The rug is an antique from a demolished Fifth Avenue mansion, and the rest of the furnishings are on the same level of opulence. Sarnoff took extreme care to have everything in the best of taste; thus a margin of less than a foot showing around the rug, had to be stained repeatedly before it was dark enough to satisfy the interior decorator who sought to gratify what she thought would be the General's wishes.

An adjacent bedroom does not equal the grandeur of the office, but the bathroom does. On the other side of the entrance corridor is a dining room seating twelve, with the inevitable telephone out of sight under the General's place at the head of the table. The kitchen is large enough to service a medium-sized restaurant. All the installation lacks is the barber chair Sarnoff kept in his Rockefeller Center suite, another in his five-story townhouse on East 71 Street and, according to some reports, a third in an apartment he maintained in Washington.

The Princeton layout was the closest Sarnoff came to having a country estate and, though it seems grand to the average middle-class visitor, it is not quite up to the status of his corporate position. When he was at Princeton, Sarnoff could be reached, in theory, through the Research Center switchboard, but actually the requirements for communication were the same as at Rockefeller Center; very simple if the secretaries knew you and Sarnoff was willing to talk to you, otherwise impossible.

Although Sarnoff's heart was in the laboratory and he visited it as often as he could, usually with Mrs. Sarnoff, they never stayed overnight. So what might have served as a country home was downgraded to an auxiliary HQ. Sarnoff was so urbanized, so much the corporation man, that except when there was adequate business or personal reason for traveling (he went to Europe every year) his orbit was confined to Rockefeller Center on the south and 71st Street on the north—a distance of slightly over a mile.

Sarnoff's complex legend leaves many questions unanswered: for example, was he justified, at a cost of several million dollars of RCA's money to project his image into the future in this effort at Princeton? I think he was. RCA owed him more than he owed RCA, and the library was one way of collecting the debt. Also he thought—erroneously, as it turned out—that the library would be a permanent public relations asset to the corporation. But even if it adds only to Sarnoff's personal glory, the money was probably as well spent as much of RCA's money over the years, or the money of other corporations of commensurate size and obligations to society. The installation can be invaluable to scholars and journalists interested in communications history and able to make allowances for omission of anything that might be construed as discrediting the central figure. No one can predict what will ultimately come of the violent proliferation of communications, both private and public, that characterized Sarnoff's last years and is still disquieting to some, while exhilarating to others who were in at the beginning of it all. Thus the library has a potential value that awaits future realization.

There are two sides to the collection at Princeton for anyone who knows something of the history of electronic communications and technology, and of Sarnoff's role in creating one of the major social revolutions of the century. The contents of the gleaming glass and chrome cases and the sumptuously bound volumes effectively portray Sarnoff's achievements in corporate management and his genius in the exploitation of electronic technology. Since his role was such a prominent and long-enduring one, the record of his activities takes in aspects of communications history ranging from early marine and transoceanic telegraphy to the latest developments in TV, some of which have nothing to do with broadcasting as the public now knows it. But what is *not* contained in the showcases and bookcases is as important as what is included. The innocent visitor beholds a carefully laundered reproduction of the man and his works. To some extent, this is true of any memorial to the great, but it is aggravated in Sarnoff's case by his lifelong insistence on favorable publicity—whether true, slanted, or false (but plausible).

How did Sarnoff manage to do what he did? He was no Newton, but the great mathematician-physicist's answer, when asked how he had come upon his discoveries, applies just as well to Sarnoff: "Why, by always thinking unto them." Sarnoff rarely allowed himself an idle, unoccupied moment. For him, no cardplaying, no golf, little escape of any kind. The result was a personality of extraordinary amplitude, including unusual self-esteem and self-confidence, vital in exercising leadership. What would have been vanity in a man of ordinary accomplishments was outweighed in his case by industry that matched his pretensions. He constantly brought to bear a whole spectrum of talents, buttressed by an indomitable spirit: clarity of mind in business and the application of technology to business ends, a command of instrumental, get-things-done language, the power of concentration, an ability to strip a problem to its essentials and get at the solution, and a sharp evaluation of men for corporate efficiency. If one or another of these qualities sometimes failed him, his overall batting average was so high that he rose to the top quickly and stayed there no less than fifteen years beyond the customary retirement age.

Of equal importance, Sarnoff had what ordinary businessmen are always talking about because they lack it: "vision." He had the prophetic gift, not in everything—certainly not in politics, but he had it in electronics, and electronics is a very broad field. Almost all his rivals, when they had got hold of a good thing, wanted to hear no more of innovation. They jumped on the radio bandwagon and then were unwilling to take the risks of television. For that matter, why did it fall to the electronics interests to develop television? The movie magnates could have done it—or at least participated—if only they had remembered their experience with sound, which had to be forced on them when they were in the money with silent films. The spirit of entrepreneurial venture had been strong in them at one time; aging, they were ruled by caution, and so finally they were ruled by Sarnoff and a few others with his background and innovative spirit.

Sarnoff was not a gambler. He was willing to venture, but the projects on which he risked RCA's capital and his own career were sure things by the time he had finished investigating, thinking, and planning. If they were sure things it was because he had made them so. And so, if there was an element of public relations bombast when Sarnoff dedicated the library to himself on that sunny September afternoon in 1967, there was also the reality of six decades of productive effort on the part of the man, now old, who wanted his exploits remembered. Almost certainly he had never read Plato, but he knew, as we all know, that time ultimately has its way. But, he wanted something to remain of what had meant so much to him. He had more to conserve, in that sense, than all but a few of his fellow countrymen, and his yearning was the more dramatic because he was an immigrant and the child of immigrants, and when he arrived in the United States he had been a boy struggling for pennies on the wretchedly poor Lower East Side of New York.

THE EMIGRANTS

David was born on February 27, 1891 in Uzlian, a Jewish village, or *shtetl*, of 200 inhabitants in the province of Minsk in western Russia. Minsk was located in the Pale of Settlement, within which the great majority of Jews were confined. The Pale was an extensive region, comprising Lithuania, Byelorussia, Russian Poland, Volhynia, and the Ukraine (but excluding Kiev). Catherine the Great, having acquired some 900,000 Jews by the partitions of Poland in the eighteenth century, in addition to the ones she already had, found her Jews essential for the economy of her western territories, but in the imagination of her counselors they also posed a danger—they might put subversive ideas into the heads of the serfs. The danger was negligible, actually, but in the Pale they could be segregated, mostly in *shtetls*, to survive as best they could as noncitizens, subject to arbitrary discrimination and oppression; the degree varying with the requirements of the czarist state, which was periodically menaced by non-Jewish revolutionists. The Jews served as scapegoats, towards whom the wrath of the oppressed Russian masses could be directed whenever it reached dangerous intensity. The survival of the czarist state in the eighteenth, nineteenth and the early part of the twentieth centuries, shows how long, under the existing levels of technology and communication, a dictatorship can endure.

Measured by the frequency and savagery of pogroms, the last two decades of the nineteenth century were relatively tranquil—a distinction must be made between isolated and organized assaults. The Sarnoffs and their relatives, like other village Jews, were probably less afraid of drunken peasants than the average New Yorker is of muggers. Pogroms, in the sense of systematic beatings, murders, and rapes, did not assume menacing proportions until the early twentieth century, when the tensions of the 1905 revolution were building up. That one was a near miss, followed by World War I and Bolshevism. The Sarnoffs reached the safety of the Lower East Side in 1900 and witnessed these events from afar.

The millions of Jewish emigrants had reason enough to leave when they could. Even during the best periods, they were outsiders, manifested by the fact that few spoke Russian. Rabbis, of course, had command of Hebrew, (corresponding to Latin in Roman Catholic ritual) and laymen had enough Hebrew for the requirements of the synagogue, but Yiddish was the mother tongue of the Russian Jews. Some minor czarist officials who had to deal with Jews spoke Yiddish.

In the thousands of villages like Uzlian, such amenities as telephones, the telegraph, gas, and electric light were entirely unknown; as fate would have it, the foremost entrepreneur in modern communications came from a place where the only communication was by direct word of mouth. In most of the villages, no one had ever seen a ship, and even a train was a novelty; the first time David had the former experience was when he was on his way to America. Even more significant, the typical village Jew completely lacked political understanding. He lived as his ancestors had, in a mini-theocratic state ruled by the local rabbi, and if life was hard, he bore his trials and lived virtuously in the hope of a better life in the herafter. In a country in which czars and their ministers were assassinated or lived in constant danger of assassination, he took no part, did not even know about, the incipient revolts against the tyranny of the government. As a group, the village Jews were almost as cut off from the political convulsions of the country as if they had been inhabitants of another planet.

The former isolation of Uzlian, together with the poverty of the family during their first decade in America, had an important bearing on David Sarnoff's later politics. Since he left Russia at the age of nine, he was not immediately affected, but his parents must have been, and their influence on his development after his bar mitzvah (1904) was apolitical, in contrast to the socialist leanings of many Lower East Side parents at that time.

A posed photograph of David's father, Abraham Sarnoff, shows a handsome bearded man with the high forehead and thoughtful expression of a distinguished rabbi or professor. After the fashion of the time he is seated in an ornately carved armchair; his wife, Leah (née Privin) stands beside him, her hand on his shoulder. She is stout, robust-looking, and by the same token seems more resolute than her husband.

Whatever he looked like, Abraham Sarnoff was neither rabbi nor professor. He was a house painter, but his health was precarious and he could not make a living at it. He had no future in Russia; as it turned out, he had no future in America either. But, like 500,000 other Jews in the 1880–1900 period alone, he emigrated to America where perhaps things would be better; they could hardly be worse. In New York he shared a room with three or four other boarders and nearly starved himself to send back small sums of money, and finally saved enough to pay steerage fare for his wife and three sons. The effort undoubtedly hastened his death.

He had left Uzlian in 1896 when David, the eldest, was five years old. The second son was Lew, the third Morris. Leah, an "American widow," moved back into her parents' home and waited. Her grandmother, a managerial type from whom David may have inherited some of his own talent, arranged for David to live with her brother, a rabbi in a town several hundred miles away, where David would study the Talmud. So, shortly after parting from his father, David went to live with his granduncle, in the region of Borisov; where from dawn to dark, six days a week, in a household without children, he read the version of the Talmud favored by his granduncle until sufficient money had accumulated to bring the family to America.

It has been suggested that David Sarnoff's enforced study of the Talmud as a young boy may have accounted for his powers of intellect and will in late life. This is largely a fanciful view, further distorted by Gentile eagerness to show reverence for Judaic religious lore. Actually, what David read was mainly "ghetto Talmudism," a peculiarly ingrown and sterile product of the oppression and isolation of the Russian Jews, vehemently opposed by the learned. But if not much can be said for the content, which had little lasting influence on Sarnoff since in his adult life he practiced Reform Judaism, it is highly probable that the habit of arduous application for twelve, even fourteen hours a day, was a major factor in molding Sarnoff's character. Life, he was taught by precept and example, was a serious business, calling for hard labor and discipline. That conviction remained with him for seventy years—and deprived him of his childhood both in czarist Russia and America.

Leah Sarnoff and her three sons did have a single political experience just before leaving Russia. In the city of Minsk, en route to the seaport of Libau, they saw a crowd of people gathered for a demonstration of some kind. Eugene Lyons, David Sarnoff's cousin and authorized biographer, quotes Sarnoff's later description of the incident:

> As we watched the surging people, a company of mounted Cossacks came charging down. They called on the crowd to disperse. No one moved. The Cossack leader barked a word of command, and the whole company rode into the wailing mob, lashing out with their long whips and trampling women and children under the hooves of their horses. The sight sickened me and I clung to my mother's skirts.

What Leah Sarnoff and her sons witnessed was a *political* demonstration, perhaps of illegally striking factory workers. No doubt the Cossacks found more satisfaction in beating, raping or murdering Jews —in the Kishinev pogrom 810 Jews were killed and 1,770 wounded— but that was three years later. The Cossacks were not particular: they were cavalrymen who served the czars and their ministers, and their current task was to suppress revolution.

The czar the Cossacks were currently serving was Nicholas II, a monarch of limited mental capacity who, on ascending the throne in 1894, announced he would rule as an autocrat, like his fathers before him. He may have conceived of himself as a male Catherine the Great, but even if he had had her talent, it was a century later. His failure to understand that times had changed cost him his life and the lives of his wife and children.

In 1900, the Sarnoff menage crossed the Atlantic via Liverpool, which was a few dollars cheaper than the direct route. The steamship companies packed steerage passengers into the filthy lower decks like animals, to vomit their way across the ocean for $36. A month or more after leaving Uzlian, the family arrived in Montreal. Carrying what remained of their kosher provisions and the bedding and linens the family had given them, they made their way to Albany by train, thence by Hudson River steamboat to New York where, after some agonizing confusion, they were reunited with the husband and father.

The family went to live in a tenement on Monroe Street, which in later years David occasionally visited to remind himself and his sons of how far they had come. And indeed it was far. The East Side of today, with its oases of low- and middle-income apartments amid modified but still cockroach- and sometimes rat-infested tenements, gives only a faint idea of what Monroe Street was like at the turn of the century. Then there was only a single foul toilet in the hallway for all the tenants on one floor (a variant was a row of privies in the backyard). To make matters even more dismal, the Sarnoff family was reunited in July, during one of the city's worst heat waves. The Lower East Side stank all year round, but it stank worse in summer. It was a slum of slums, containing twice as many people in a given area as the London slums at their worst. A city ghetto in the Promised Land was worse in some respects than a rural ghetto in the old country. But the all-important thing was not the present with its squalor and hardships. Hopes for the future were what counted—and especially hopes for the children.

That was the goal; the means was the "Protestant work ethic." Why Protestant? Where Jews were involved, it was the Jewish work ethic, more comprehensively, the capitalist ethic, an outgrowth of the Industrial Revolution. In czarist Russia it was a phase of the vigorous foreign capitalist development of the country in the later nineteenth and early twentieth centureis, though agriculture still predominated. The Bolsheviks adopted the capitalist work ethic practically unchanged—even intensified.

In this country there were always significant differences between the German Jews and the other Jews. Of the German Jews who came earlier a few were millionaires by the time of the great influx from Russia. They regarded the other Jews with mixed feelings of revulsion and reluctant compassion—but essentially the credo of the two groups was the same and those who made it in business made it by the same means. Moses Rischin quotes an article by Max Cohen, "The Jew in Business," in *The American Hebrew*, May 22, 1891:

> The causes of the remarkable progress made by the Jews in commerce are the simple homely virtues sung in rhythmic prose by [Benjamin] Franklin and [Samuel] Smiles: patient toil; zealous application; intelligence suffused into labor; frugal thrift; and temperance in all things. They had the self-denial to confine their wants to necessities until luxuries could be afforded. Realizing that the same social conditions which enabled others to amass wealth even with the most penurious beginnings to look back upon held similar possibiities for themselves, they did not waste their energies in fruitless fretting at the conditions and fruitless efforts to change them, but devoted themselves to energetic endeavors to utilize them at their best.

Written in the year of David Sarnoff's birth, this is a precise description, translated into adult terms, of his state of mind when he arrived in New York and found his father sick and the family with only a precarious income, often none at all. David recalled later that he asked himself, "If I don't help my family, who will?" Almost immediately he was on the street, hawking Yiddish newspapers. American and Yiddish newspapers alike retailed at a penny apiece, and the newsboys bought them at two for a penny. David brought home the proceeds: meager as they were; a fistful of pennies made a difference—sometimes the difference between the family's eating or not eating.

Next he began to deliver newspapers in the nearby tenements, still at a penny apiece. This meant getting up before dawn, running up and down steep flights of stairs six days a week, and on the seventh day running again to collect six cents, which was not always collectible. Aside from going to school, his life consisted entirely of work. While for several years the newspaper route and selling papers on the street were his basic sources of income, he also ran errands for a butcher, sold candy and soda pop in Yiddish theaters, and picked up a few cents wherever he could. A special and relatively well-paying job was singing as a boy soprano in the synagogue, and occasionally at Jewish weddings.

In 1900, Abraham Cahan, founder and editor of the *Jewish Daily Forward*, reported the complaint of striking vestmakers who appealed to the Law of Moses in their version of Leviticus 6:2: "Thou shalt not withhold anything from thy neighbor or rob him; thou shalt not abide with thee the wages of him that is hired through the night until morning." "So, you see," the vestmakers concluded, "that our bosses who rob us and don't pay us regularly commit a sin, and that the cause of our unions is a just one. What did we come to America for? To bathe in tears and to see our wives and our children rot in poverty? Tears and sighs we had in plenty in the old country."

Such lamentations may have reached young Sarnoff's ears, or he may have read them in the *Forward*, but there was no union for newsboys, and in any case unionism was not his dish. His attitude toward the world was already fixed: when things are wrong, or go wrong, right them for yourself and those dependent on you as best you can by your own exertions. Making allowances for inexperience and meager resources, this principle—in fact, every one of the traits of character that contributed to David Sarnoff's phenomenal success—was already in evidence before he reached his teens. From the beginning, drawing on some inner source of strength, presumably in part hereditary, David taught himself the lesson of courage in the face of adversity. He had no time for despair.

There was more freedom for poor Jews in the East Side ghetto than in Russia; at least there were no Cossacks. However, to suppose that poor Jews escaped from tyranny to a land of liberty would be a gross misconception. By the early 1890s some liberalization in the conditions of workers, Jewish and otherwise, had taken place. "Yellow dog" contracts, forbidding workers to join unions, had been outlawed—but were freely circumvented well into the twentieth century. An antiblacklisting law was on the statute books but was not enforced. The right to strike was limited. The courts permitted strikes for higher wages, but strikes for reduced hours or improved working conditions were punishable as "criminal conspiracy." The fourteen-hour day, the eighty-four-hour week, and malnutrition were still the rule rather than the exception.

There was some regulation of female and child labor and tenement house clothing manufacture, but a single, meagerly paid inspector and one assistant were appointed to oversee the operation of tens of thousands of factories throughout New York City—mainly home workshops in the needle trades. Moses Rischin quotes a teacher's characterization of the Lower East Side as "a community where all the life of a family, eating, sleeping, cooking, working, illness, death, birth and prayer is often crowded into one small room." It might have been more than one room, but the significant term is "working." All the voluminous literature in Yiddish and English focuses on the Jewish East Side as the site of clothing manufacture where a typical family sewed from dawn until late into the night, the total family income coming typically to $9 a week, of which $10 a month went for rent. The immigrants came to New York to be exploited, sometimes by their own *Landsleit*— fellow countrymen and coreligionists. That was their economic function; without it, they would never have been admitted, and with its cessation, immigration was restricted.

The Jews were not unique in this respect, except that their immigration was especially large—in a little more than three decades no less than two million of the Jews of Eastern Europe—mainly Russians but including Polish-Russian, Rumanians, and others—came to the United States.

The Lower East Side tenement clothing factories were an especially horrible instance of man's inhumanity to man, coming close for several decades to Marx's forecast of proletarian labor's "immiseration," limited only by the necessity to keep the proletariat propagating itself for future generations of exploitation. In the early 1900s, stable unions were still exceptional in the clothing trades, but home sweatshops became fewer and were replaced by more efficient large factories. This is probably why the Sarnoff flat on Monroe Street never functioned as a tenement clothing factory, with David as one of the operators. His mother did piecework sewing at starvation wages, but David went into the streets, to his ultimate advantage and that of the growing family. Abraham Sarnoff, sick as he was, had sired two more children, a boy and a girl, before he succumbed. It was not unusual: the tenements teemed with children.

It was the immigrant parents who deserved the most credit for whatever success their children achieved. David Sarnoff was eloquently revealing of both an excruciating social situation and of his own feelings when he spoke to an audience of the Hebrew Immigrant Aid Society in 1959, after thanking the members for an award they had given him:

> I wish there were some award for the myriad nameless Jewish immigrants—our parents and grandparents—who never attained celebrity but who have provided a substantial part of the bone and flesh and robust spirit of our community. I often marvel at their courage in pulling up roots in the old country and their sacrifices in sinking new roots in the American soil. It is too easy to forget how hard were their lives and how bravely they met their challenge.
>
> It seems to me that no one who is not himself an immigrant, or the child of immigrants, can quite comprehend the magnitude of their adventure or the pathos of their transplantation. When I arrived in America I was nine years old; so I remember—how well I remember!—what it is like to find oneself in a strange new world.
>
> As an immigrant boy, I was tossed into the bewildering whirlpool of a metropolitan slum area, to sink or swim. I started my business career, at once, by selling newspapers on the sidewalks of New York. I learned the hard way what a helping hand, a sympathetic word, a reasonable opportunity can mean in giving hope to a new arrival in this wonderful land.

To no one were David Sarnoff's remarks on this occasion more pathetically applicable than to his own father. Abraham Sarnoff's life was blameless, short, and sad. The only mark he left in history was through his children, but he did not see them grow to maturity or even make a start toward emergence from the ghetto. He died around the time when David got his first job—as a messenger boy at $5 a week. He was in his grave long before the beginning of David's triumphal rise to the top echelons of the great industry he helped to found. His mother at least witnessed the beginnings of the ascent of her first born into the ranks of the successful, although she could never understand the means by which he rose—wireless communication was something completely outside her experience.

The Lower East Side was not an out-and-out jungle; like many other Jewish families, the Sarnoffs received assistance from Jewish charities. Prominent Christians, like Henry Codman Potter, the Episcopal Bishop of New York, exerted themselves to imporve the condition of the East Side poor. Tenement squalor was interspersed with settlement houses—the University Settlement, with Seth Low of Columbia University as president; the College settlement, founded by Smith College women; the Henry Street Settlement of Lillian Wald and Mary Brewster, particularly vital because it provided a visiting nurse service; and several others. Most important in young Sarnoff's life was the Educational Alliance, originally the Hebrew Institute. The Alliance was of inestimable service in adapting immigrants to American ways. It provided a library, class rooms and meeting rooms, an auditorium seating 700, a gymnasium, shower baths, a roof garden, and other facilities. Adults and children were taught English, civics, American history, English literature, and a variety of cultural subjects. The curriculum included classes for aspiring poets, an art course founded by the painter Henry McBride, and sculpture, with Jacob Epstein among the teachers. The Alliance probably contributed as much to David Sarnoff's education as the public schools did, and in later life he repaid it.

The Alliance was not exclusively Jewish. Al Smith, four-time governor of New York, was one of its alumni. Nor was it exclusively civic and cultural; it graduated some of the leading boxers of the day, including the dentist Abe Attell, world featherweight champion, 1908–1912. Sarnoff was not among the amateur boxers, or the gymnasts, or the Boy Scouts (not yet organized under that name) who camped overnight at the foot of the Palisades and swam in the Hudson. He had neither the time nor the inclination for such diversions.

Instead, he confined himself to what promised to be useful to him

—the instrumental things. He made amazing strides in learning English and already as a young man had a better command of it than the great majority of college graduates. In an Educational Alliance debate on the topic, "Resolved: the United States should grant independence to the Philippines," David's team—representing the "Paul Revere Club"—defended the affirmative and won.

As a child actor, David was less precocious. In an Alliance pageant he had a walk-on part with a single line: "Cleanliness is next to godliness." He rehearsed the five words for weeks, with matching gestures, but when the moment for his entrance came before an audience including relatives, friends, and neighbors, he stood in the spotlight, paralyzed, opened his mouth and not a word came out. Thirty-five years later, on the same stage, Sarnoff, something of a showman in later life, recounted the story and delivered his line, gestures and all.

Some of the accounts of incidents in Sarnoff's early life are not nearly as well founded—the story of the purchase money for the newsstand, for instance. When David was thirteen, he rightly concluded that if he could acquire a newsstand, the problem of the family's support would be solved. By that time Lew and Morris were old enough to take turns with David in tending the stand, and when they were at school their mother could fill in. Also their father might be able to help, even if he was too weak to work at his trade. After considerable research David found a suitable stand, including a delivery service, at the corner of Tenth Avenue and 46th Street.

But where could he get the $200 the owner demanded? According to one possibly apocryphal account, the family managed to borrow the money, but tradition credits a far more moving story. In this version, a nice middle-aged woman, apparently a social worker, having heard that David had been supporting his family and needed $200 to buy the newsstand, visited the Sarnoff home, talked to David about his plans, handed him $200 in cash, and left without giving her name and address. Nor was it clear whether the money was a loan or gift. David did, however, remember her face and met her twenty years later at the home of the copper magnate and philanthropist, Adolph Lewisohn. She did not recognize Sarnoff, and when he reminded her of the incident, she burst into tears, then told him she had represented a wealthy man who liked to help people anonymously. She had investigated, found David a worthy object of philanthropy, and her employer had provided the needed funds. She and Sarnoff became friends, and he now took the place of the still-anonymous original donor—bread cast upon the waters.

Whatever the truth of the matter, there is no question that the acquisition of the newsstand represented a turn in the Sarnoff family's fortunes. Not that it lightened David's burden: winter and summer he would get up at 4 A.M., pick up the heavy bundles of newspapers and complete deliveries before the school bell; from school he would rush to pick up the papers for afternoon delivery, run up and down stairs in an Irish neighborhood where the tough kids were not partial to Jewish boys, so that he often made his way from one tenement to another via the roofs to avoid getting beaten up on the street.

Under the circumstances, it is astonishing that David did well at school, for, indeed, he was a bright student. If his father had been in good health, no doubt David would, like other bright New York boys, have gone on to Townsend Harris Hall, the three-year preparatory school of the College of the City of New York, and to the college itself. But that was out of the question for David. He had to find a job. In retrospect, his life was more the result of foresight and planning than most lives are; but pure chance led him to a job with the Marconi Company and a career in communications, in which he proved that lack of higher education was not an insuperable handicap in building up a great corporate enterprise. In his case, the effect was the very opposite—he got a seven-year start by going into business immediately after finishing elementary school.

3

DOTS AND DASHES

In 1906, and for many years afterward, just north of where Sixth Avenue and Broadway crisscross at 34th Street, there stood a building of considerable floor area, though only a few stories in height. The architecture was Manhattan Romanesque and the exterior was a brown-orange stucco. The building was a landmark, known to New Yorkers as the headquarters of James Gordon Bennett's *Herald*. In honor of the paper and its publisher, the little triangular park south of the building was called Herald Square.

Since David Sarnoff had been in the newspaper business, although only on the retail delivery end, in his boyish fancies he pictured himself as a newspaper reporter, perhaps even an editor or publisher in time. With only a minimal education, he was well aware that all he could expect at the outset was a job at the very bottom. Why he chose the *Herald* has not been established—maybe because the building's architecture was so conspicuously different from anything else in midtown. At any rate, it was there that David, fifteen years old, dressed in his one good suit, came to look for work.

He entered the lobby, too nervous to consult the building directory or ask about the employment office. He saw a man behind a window and assumed he must be connected with the newspaper. He asked the man for a job—any job.

"I don't know about the *Herald*," the man said, "but we can use another messenger boy in our shop." David had not noticed that the office belonged to the Commercial Cable Company, which rented space from the *Herald*. He knew now he was in the wrong place; he could hear the clicking of telegraph sounders coming from behind the window where the man sat.

The job would pay $5 a week and 10 cents an hour for overtime. David took it.

Anyone of the millions who currently believe more or less firmly in the influence of astrology on human affairs might regard the outcome of the boy's venture as preordained. By sheer chance he had blundered into the office of an undersea cable company, beginning his career in telegraphy with an organization that in years to come would face competition from the Marconi Company and subsequently from the Radio Corporation of America. Yet, if David had gotten that job with the *Herald*, it is possible he would eventually have landed in wireless telegraphy anyway, for Bennett was a pioneer in that field, too. In 1899 he had engaged Guglielmo Marconi to report the international yacht races off New York harbor; in the following year he sponsored a Marconi wireless installation on the Nantucket lightship. Currently the *Herald* was operating its own New York City station at the Battery— call letters OHX—for communication with ships and broadcasting news, election returns and so on via marine wavelengths—all in Morse, of course. The call letters and wavelength were arbitrarily chosen; there was no law regulating wireless telegraphy, and anybody could go on the air with any call letters and on any frequency he chose. Amateurs often had no idea of the frequency on which they were operating. At any rate, David Sarnoff was now a messenger boy for a cable company, and he was never to be reporter, editor or publisher, although in later life he was to have close contacts with the press at all levels.

David Sarnoff did not intend to remain a messenger boy for very long, but his employment was even shorter than he had anticipated. He carried out his duties faithfully, delivering telegrams by bicycle, and did not dishonor the uniform, but he was fired, not exactly for his Judaism —the Commercial Cable Company had no special interest in that— but because of the obligations it entailed. He was a member of the synagogue choir—although with the onset of puberty that job, too, was shortly to end—but when Rosh Hashanah and Yom Kippur came around, he was still employed as a boy soprano. When David asked the office manager for three days' leave without pay and insisted, he was told to turn in his uniform and his bike. Telegrams had to be delivered, Jewish holidays or no.

The dismissal, though unavoidable, was a blow. But in David's short service with the cable company, he had become a telegrapher on his own. The Herald Square office was connected by wire with the main Commercial Telegraph office at 20 Broad Street. At times this circuit was extremely busy, and the sounders, actuated by telegraph keys, clattered at both ends. (A telegraph key is a form of switch which can be closed and opened rapidly by hand to form the dots and dashes of the Morse code.) David was fascinated by a means of communication altogether novel to him and was eager to acquire a skill that might provide an opportunity for promotion from the lowly estate of messenger boy.

At any rate, David invested his earliest messenger-boy earnings in a $2 telegraph practice set. He found he had a talent for telegraphy and in a short time could send and receive at moderate speeds, gradually working up to a receiving speed at which he could read the Herald Square-Broad Street traffic. Over this circuit a wireline friendship developed between David and an experienced Broad Street operator named Jack Irwin. This was not unusual; many operators chatted by telegraph in idle periods, addressing each other as OM ("Old Man") and never meeting face to face. (Later, when RCA was operating transatlantic circuits between Chatham, Massachusetts, and Stavanger, Norway, inconclusive romances developed between some of the female operators on the Norwegian end and the male operators on the American end, with exchange of photographs by mail and telegraphic messages ending in "Love" when the circuits were idle.) All that Irwin knew about David was that he was a messenger boy and had acquired telegraphic skill in a remarkably short time. Then, suddenly, David disappeared from the circuit.

Vainly scanning the help-wanted columns, David thought of Jack Irwin, and Irwin, meeting David for the first time, had a bright idea. There might just be an opening for a junior operator at the Marconi Company (the full name was the Marconi Wireless Telegraph Company of America) which was arousing some vocational curiosity among wire telegraphers. From his own contact on the Herald Square-Broad Street circuit, Irwin was convinced David was already a competent young operator. Anyway, what could Sarnoff lose?

The Marconi Company was then a struggling organization engaged in a highly speculative enterprise—transatlantic and marine communications—with precarious hopes for the future based on inadequate present facilities. David had heard of wireless but had only the vaguest idea of its technology and prospects. Few were interested enough to remember that in 1901, after erecting a transmitter, high-powered for its time, at Poldhu, Cornwall, Guglielmo Marconi had traveled to Newfoundland with a few assistants and, using an antenna carried aloft by a kite, had received the letter "S." For the first time the Atlantic was spanned by wireless telegraphy, although one-way and with no attempt at actual communication.

Marconi's subsequent experience was a dramatic demonstration of corporate shortsightedness. The Anglo-American Telegraph Company had—or claimed to have—a charter giving them exclusive rights to erect and operate stations for telegraphic communication between Newfoundland and places elsewhere. Wireless telegraphy had never entered the Anglo-American officials' heads, but they notified Marconi that he was violating their charter with his experiments. If he did not dismantle his apparatus and stop what he was doing immediately, they would have the law on him. Since Marconi had proved the possibility of transatlantic wireless communication, though only in the most rudimentary form, and had no desire to waste time and money in litigation, he complied with the order.

Obviously it would have been wiser for the cable company to try to establish cordial relations with the inventor and either enter into a cooperative arrangement with him or make a deal with a competing wireless company or try to develop their own wireless equipment; but they did none of these things. The role they adopted was the easier one of the dog in the manger.

Nothing daunted, Marconi continued his development, with the result that in 1903 felicitations were exchanged between King Edward VII of England and President Theodore Roosevelt via a Marconi station in England and another at South Wellfleet on Cape Cod. The feat made headlines, but reliable commercial communication was something else again. Nor, during the first decade of the century, was any money made in marine wireless—ship-to-ship or ship-to-shore—although there were obvious important applications of the technique to enhance safety at sea and in naval communications. Before the advent of wireless telegraphy, ships had often left port never to be heard of again, and naval vessels had communicated with shore by carrier pigeon.

When David, now still fifteen, came to the American Marconi office at 27 William Street in downtown Manhattan, he looked confident enough despite his firing by American Cable; although he was short and skinny and appeared younger than he was. He told George De Sousa, the Marconi traffic manager, that he had been sent by Jack

Irwin. "Could you use a man as a junior operator?"

De Sousa was a kindly, gentlemanly sort (which was just as well, for he was looking at his future boss). He managed not to smile. Without inquiring into David's ability, he said, "We don't need a man, but we could use a boy—an office boy."

David accepted immediately—he was still in the "any job" class. The pay was $5.50 a week—and no overtime. The date of the hiring was September 30, 1906, and it proved to be of historic importance in the annals of electronics and its expansion into almost innumerable fields of industry and communications. This time the hiring was not succeeded by a firing—as Sarnoff had said at the library dedication, his association with American Marconi and RCA spanned six decades and a few years beyond that, when illness forced his retirement and he was named honorary chairman.

David energetically performed the usual duties of an office boy, including sweeping floors. He also continued practicing as a land-line telegrapher. The Marconi Company had four shore stations: Sea Gate on Coney Island; Sagaponack, near the eastern end of Long Island; Siasconset (pronounced Sconset) on Nantucket Island, Massachusetts, and the Cape Cod station, which had had little success in transatlantic communication and functioned mainly as a marine station. All four were connected to 27 William Street by leased land lines, which kept American Marconi in a chronically unprofitable condition, since the company had only four or six ship installations. For David this was helpful, since light traffic on the land lines enabled him to get in some telegraphing in the intervals of his office-boy duties. He soon became proficient enough so that the regular operator let him handle some of the messages to and from the outlying stations.

David was a quick student in another respect. Included among his duties was filing correspondence—Marconi had to get the most for its $5.50 a week. David was not at all averse to acting as a filing clerk because it enabled him to read the company correspondence—in particular, the interoffice memos. Within a month, he knew more about what was going on at Marconi than any of the employees except those at the very top, like President John W. Griggs, a former governor of New Jersey and attorney general in President McKinley's cabinet. Or E. J. Nally, vice-president and general manager, who had been recruited from the Postal Telegraph Company. The information was to prove valuable later.

Robert H. Marriott, a founder and first president of the Institute of Radio Engineers (1912) knew practically everybody in the fledgling industry from Governor Griggs down to "Davey." In Marriott's *Radio Ancestors*, written many years later, Sarnoff occupies much more space than Griggs. Marriott, one of the "ancestors" himself, was a graduate engineer (Ohio State University, 1897) twelve years older than Sarnoff. "Davey" was known among other Marconi employees as a "Jew boy from the old country whom they had hired as an office boy but who had got the fever to be an operator." Reminiscing further, Marriott remarks, "We had some Jew boy operators in United [United Wireless, insolvent and absorbed by Marconi]. We thought he would drop out and get into dry goods or some kind of banking business."

The "Jew boy" label was not consciously anti-Semitic. "Davey" was well liked in the Marconi organization, and became a protégé of Marriott, who never worked for Marconi. "Jew boy" was merely a stereotype, as a ante-bellum Southern planter might talk benevolently about his "niggers." Old-line Americans had a somewhat patronizing attitude toward immigrants generally. American folklore also required that a "Jew boy" would find his vocation in the garment trades or, if he rose in the world, in investment banking—like Jacob Schiff in Kuhn, Loeb & Company. But "Davey" didn't conform to the stereotype. He graduated to "Dave," then "David," and after a few decades, to "General."

David deceived his employers in one matter that he considered entirely his own business. He was still maintaining his paper route and putting in four hours moonlighting before he arrived, on time and alert, at the Marconi office. But he remained healthy, if somewhat underweight. Later, when his problem was "a tendency to obesity," he had the same seemingly inexhaustible vitality—no minor factor in his success.

Marriott noted also that " 'Davey' hung around (at a shop and stockroom the Marconi Company maintained downtown) and tried to be of assistance to people he thought could help him get what he wanted. He was noticeably clever at finding ways to be helpful."

Not all these ways were technical. Guglielmo Marconi came to the United States often and "Davey" eagerly ran errands for him. Marconi was seventeen years older, but he and the office boy became friendly, in later years intimate. Marconi, an austere-looking Anglo-Italian aristocrat, was an inveterate chaser, and a good many of the errands David ran for him involved delivering candy and flowers to the great inventor's lady friends. For his part, in view of his work schedule, David had little time for girls, and even less money, but he dated as much as he could.

He was able to live a more nearly normal life when he was promoted to the junior operator's job he had wanted in the first place. His salary was raised to $7.50 a week, and he turned the paper route over to his younger brothers. Then another opportunity came along. A ship's operator fell ill just before sailing time and by that time the Marconi officials had enough confidence in their young operator to assign him to the voyage. David had no operator's license, but neither did anyone else. It was not until after 1912, following the *Titanic* disaster, that laws were enacted regulating radio and requiring operators to pass examinations and hold tickets like ships' officers. David had a glorious three-week round-trip voyage to Europe before returning to his operating job at the Marconi head office.

In 1908 Jack Irwin, one of the group who have a place in wireless history because of their early association with Sarnoff, left Commercial Cable and joined Marconi as one of the four operators at Siasconset. When he requested a month's leave of absence, only David volunteered to stand in for him. At that time the offshore islands of Massachusetts were not as popular as they are now; Martha's Vineyard already had a substantial summer population, but Nantucket was farther out at sea —about 30 miles from Yarmouth by ferry—and in the winter Siasconset, on the eastern shore of the island, was downright dismal for people accustomed to city diversions. De Sousa, who had already sized up young Sarnoff as a comer, advised him not to fill in for Irwin, not even for a month; somebody else would be found. The place to be at was headquarters, the center of power and action. Of course he was right, but Sarnoff politely followed his own inclination.

As *he* saw it, the primary necessity was to make up for the gaps in his technical education as soon as possible. In New York he had been reading technical literature and helping out in his spare time at the company's laboratory, but Siasconset could to some extent take the place of a technical high school. The station had a library perfect for Sarnoff's requirements, and when he was not standing the watch or repairing equipment he could study—there would be nothing else to do.

He was seventeen when he arrived at Siasconset. The staff, experienced wireless operators twice his age or older, were somewhat taken aback. They were not rude, only equivocal, and polite to the point of irony. There is a much-reproduced photograph of David at the key, the phones on his head, but he was not trusted at first; one of the older men always monitored his transmitting and receiving. Soon his elders found he was completely competent and let him handle the job by himself. Without having De Sousa's prescience, they realized that they had been joined by someone out of the ordinary.

Sarnoff did not confine himself to the technical library at the station. He got hold of a secondhand bicycle and pedaled the fourteen-mile round trip to the Nantucket village library for cultural and American historical material. At the same time he was taking a correspondence course in high school mathematics—algebra, geometry, and trigonometry. Jack Irwin had had enough of Siasconset and went to sea on one of the Marconi ships; but Sarnoff stayed on, and his stay stretched into eighteen months.

The result was that in 1909, when he was eighteen, Sarnoff was appointed manager—more realistically, chief operator—at Sea Gate. This sounds like a promotion, but monetarily it was not. Starting as an assistant operator at Siasconset, he had earned $60 a month. But he was soon paid the $70 a regular operator was entitled to, of which he kept $30 and sent the rest to his mother. At Sea Gate, by the Marconi Company's reckoning, as manager he was entitled to only $60, presumably because the pleasures of the metropolis were at least theoretically available. Whatever the reason, the general manager, a gentleman of Irish extraction named John Bottomley, who represented the British ownership of American Marconi, so decreed. Sarnoff demurred to no avail. Bottomley rebuked him for his "impudence." Wireless operators had no union; the company decided everything, and the decisions stuck.

By this time, Sarnoff was one of the most expert operators on the Marconi roster, and acknowledged as such by his confreres. He now took some time off as the wireless operator on a sealing ship voyage to the Arctic icefields, an adventure that had little to do with his subsequent rise in the Marconi operating ranks. When he returned to New York, he was appointed manager—and probably sole operator—of the station atop the Wanamaker department store in downtown New York. This station—with call letters MHI—communicated with its twin—MHE—at the Wanamaker store in Philadelphia. The public relations angle was paramount in these installations—Wanamaker's could probably have communicated by wire telephone at less expense. One reason Sarnoff took the job was that he desired to further his education beyond the Siasconset level. The New York assignment enabled him to enroll in a cram evening course in electrical engineering at Pratt Institute. A surviving member of the class of fifty enrolled in the course testifies that only eleven were left at the end, and Sarnoff was one of them.

If that was significant—by now characteristic—the *Titanic* disaster of April 14, 1912, was far more important, not only in future consequences for marine radio, but for Sarnoff's career. And also, it must be said, for the discrepancies between his legendary and actual roles. The wireless aspects of the *Titanic* sinking, as they have come down to us, tend to support Henry Ford's assertion that "history is the bunk." Certainly in industrial history, when a commanding managerial personality has a public relations corps at his service, his press agents are perfectly capable of creating a legend which, endlessly repeated, will firmly establish fancy as fact.

This may seem harmless, but for anyone who has the slightest respect for history, it is intolerable that a distinguished writer like Eric Barnouw in his monumental three-volume history of broadcasting, should be gulled into writing such nonsense as this:

> On an April afternoon in 1912, while on duty at the store [Sarnoff] heard weak signals:"S.S. *Titanic* ran into iceberg. Sinking fast." Sarnoff gave the information to the press and sought further word from distant cracklings. He alerted ships he could not reach: he kept at his key. He established very faint communication with the S.S. *Olympic*, 1,400 miles away.

The fact is that Sarnoff was not on watch. The Wanamaker stations kept store hours. Even if he had been on watch, he could not possibly have heard signals from the *Titanic*, which sank a thousand miles away and hours before he got into the act. When and how he was apprised of the disaster is not clear; it might have been by newsboys hawking "extras" of one or another of the twelve newspapers that were published in New York City at the time. That would have had to be after midnight. Of course, as soon as he got the news, Sarnoff hurried to the station and began his vigil. His sole contribution to the salvage operations was trying to copy in New York names of survivors which the Cunard liner *Carpathia*, the rescue ship, chose to send to authorized Marconi marine stations—Siasconset in particular.

However, most fables contain a grain of truth, and the fable of

Sarnoff's prominent role in the *Titanic* disaster, put together years after the event, contains perhaps two grains, once again revealing his indomitable temperament and his capacity for sustained effort. With the phones glued to his head, he sat up on the Wanamaker roof for seventy-two hours straight, listening, listening, listening, and copying when he could. No doubt he wanted to be of help to the distraught friends and relatives waiting in agony to learn who had survived and who had perished, but he also saw the opportunity to make himself conspicuous and rise into the ranks of management.

Later fictionizing aside, at the time there were two important results. A crowd of curiosity seekers and relatives trying to get news of their loved ones had to be held back by the police, except for the few VIPs who were allowed into the station to peer over Sarnoff's shoulder as he added to the list of names. The hysterical scenes at Wanamaker's were highly gratifying to the Marconi officials. The loss of the *Titanic* was the best thing that had ever happened to the parent company in England and its American subsidiary. Fifteen hundred seven men and women had been lost, but over 700 had survived who, had it not been for Marconi wireless, would have perished from exposure. In two days the stock of the parent company zoomed from $55 to $225 on false reports that all on board were saved and the *Titanic* was proceeding to Halifax under her own steam.

Sarnoff's publicity was on a modest scale at the beginning: neither the *Times* nor the *Herald,* nor any of the other leading newspapers contained any mention of him. Nevertheless the disaster, and the subsequent flood of news and public interest, convinced Sarnoff, still only twenty-one, that personal public relations were second only to talent and application for upward mobility within a corporation—and in staying on top once you got there.

POST-*TITANIC*

Though Sarnoff's career was launched in the classical interaction between an outstanding individual and an organization through which his talents find an outlet, the dominating influence came from the parent company in England, Marconi's Wireless Telegraph, Ltd. More conveniently referred to as "British Marconi," the parent was an early multinational corporation; besides American Marconi, it had subsidiaries in Canada, Belgium, France, Russia, Argentina, and other countries. After the *Titanic* disaster, a great boom in ship installations and shore stations took place; the increase in the value of the parent company's stock was based to a considerable extent on sound expectations of growth. On the other hand, foreshadowing the experiences of the multinationals of the 1960s and later, problems inevitably arose. Although the officers of American Marconi were all Americans, there was no denying that ultimate control was centered in London.

So far as Sarnoff was concerned, for the moment this was of no consequence. After 1912 everything was going for him. Cataloging the virtues of her children, his mother had described David as "the lucky one." And his luck held through most of his life, especially at the crucial transition from wireless operating to the lower ranks of management.

But more than luck was involved. Anybody could have done what Sarnoff did in the aftermath of the *Titanic* disaster—except that nobody else had the necessary initiative and prescience. The brief Wanamaker stardom was indecisive, since the publicity was largely within the company and was not inflated until years later. Still, within the existing limits, it helped. It made Sarnoff stand out among wireless operators in the eyes of the Marconi management, and that had further consequences. Management is always on the outlook for junior executive material to take some of the load off its own shoulders, fill vacancies, and provide new, perhaps profitable, ideas. Also, American Marconi was now unmistakably a growth company, yet one with lagging technology and management. Edward J. Nally was a proven manager in the transoceanic cable field, but his judgment in wireless telegraphy was that of an elderly executive lacking intimate knowledge—"feel"—of a burgeoning technology. The problems were compounded by a patent system designed to evaluate less sophisticated inventions and unable to cope with intricate systems of electronic communications promoted by conflicting interests. The resulting litigation only bred further litigation, in part because the judges who handed down decisions perforce thought in legal—not technical—terms.

Sarnoff was still too young to play a leading part in resolving these problems, but he could be helpful in a subordinate position. At the same time he could learn at least the rudiments of how small business was converted into medium-sized business, and might be headed for big business. However, his present situation required a decision which was to prove crucial. He made the decision himself, but he wanted confirmation and reassurance from an older man—specifically his friend Marriott who, as an experienced engineer, had been helpful to him in the technical end of the business. Mariott was now a government radio inspector, no bonanza, surely, and that might have been a factor in Sarnoff's thinking.

As Marriott tells it, they met for lunch at a cellar restaurant at Broadway and Park Place:

> Pig's knuckles mit sauerkraut and beer or maybe sauerbraten and beer, rye bread, boiled potatoes, or maybe roast beef and German fries, soup, beer, pie with cheese and coffee cost 50 cents and a dime for the waiter. (1913)
>
> Dave began by saying he was going to tell me something I would not like to hear. Then he said he would quit trying to be an engineer. I asked him why. . . . He said: First, because I don't believe I could be as good an engineer as you fellows and, second, because even a good engineer has a small chance to make money. An engineer or scientific experimenter is at the place where money is going out. The place to make money is where money is coming in. . . . I am going to quit trying to be an engineer, therefore, and am going to solicit the sale of contracts and service that will bring money into the company.

At that time Sarnoff needed money and made no bones about it. He was only a few years away from the period when he and his family had been destitute. But once he had become financially secure, money was only incidental. One cannot imagine him pronouncing solemnly, like the traction magnate Edward Stotesbury on the occasion of his eightieth birthday, "I have today achieved my life's ambition. I have just received a letter from my financial advisor telling me that *I am worth a hundred million dollars.*" Stotesbury called a press conference for that. Sarnoff liked publicity, but not that kind. His major impulsions were love of power and, above all, the thrills, however mixed with tribulation, of innovation in industry.

Marriott was understanding. He said he was sorry Dave had changed his mind but had to admit that he had summed up the situation in a few words. What followed was as significant as the decision. With Dave's new job, he was assigned a cubbyhole just big enough for him, a filing cabinet, a visitor, and a hat tree. But the cubbyhole was located at the Marconi headquarters in the Woolworth Building, just outside Mr. Nally's door. Nally called in Dave for all sorts of things, and Dave was always helpful, no longer with getting the bugs out of a receiver in the maintenance shop, but now with executive problems.

"If he had gone in for engineering," Marriott remarks, "he would have been further down the hall . . . Dave slid into one executive position after another." Already he was de facto assistant to the vice president and general manager.

Sarnoff did not spend all his time warming a chair in his cubby hole and waiting for Nally to call on him for advice. The advice would not have been much good if it had been based predominantly on office experience. He spent most of his time on the waterfront. His official position was radio inspector for Marconi ships in New York harbor, a post paralleling that of the federal radio inspectors, like Marriott, who were responsible for seeing to it that departing ships were properly equipped in accordance with legislation passed by Congress following the *Titanic* lesson.

But Sarnoff was not confined in his rounds to Marconi-equipped vessels. He could and did visit foreign-equipped radio "shacks" and compare the installations with those of his own company. His experience as an operator was now paying off. "Hello, Dave," was the greeting when he came aboard, and the operators and Sarnoff, one of their fellowship, would "shoot the breeze." Wireless operators coming ashore after a voyage were like tourists in one respect—they were eager to talk about their experiences on shipboard and shore leave. But these conversations were not idle talk as far as Sarnoff was concerned. Marriott had noted that a 0.5-kilowatt German Telefunken transformer was far smaller than a nominally 10-kilowatt British Marconi transformer —and delivered more power. Sarnoff kept out a sharp eye for such discrepancies and filed the operators' beefs and suggestions for future use. Some he passed on to his superiors; some he kept to himself for the time being. There was a limit to what was welcome and he had to feel his way, striking a balance between what would impress senior officials and what, coming from an aspiring junior, might antagonize them at a time when his power to defend himself might prove insufficient. In effect, he was straddling the traffic department, headed by De Sousa, and the engineering department, with Frederick M. Sammis as chief engineer. De Sousa was no menace; on the contrary, David was his protégé. But Sammis would resent any encroachment on his territory. Yet, in the company's interest and David's own, he had to find fault with some of the Marconi equipment.

Coming from an established cable company, Nally tended to be conservative. Sammis, with British Marconi backing, was similarly inclined. Under these auspices, British Marconi and its subsidiaries were falling behind the exploitation of the available technology. To the extent that Sarnoff had a voice in its decisions, the parent company and its subsidiaries would eventually benefit. He was singularly free of the accretions of corporate inertia and misleading experience. Nor is this just ancient history. Similar conflicts are being fought out daily in the present era of mergers and reorganizations; and today's rising managers, for all that they are better educated and prepared, have much to learn from Sarnoff's career.

To understand the nature of the specific problems confronting the nascent Sarnoff-Nally partnership, we must recall what the term "radio" meant in the early decades of the century, when the art was struggling to become an industry. Today, to most people, "radio" means broadcasting of sound alone, as opposed to television, which transmits both sound and picture. In 1910 broadcasting was unknown, and "radio," stemming from "radiation," was merely an abbreviated synonym for "wireless." The full terms were "radiotelegraphy" and "radiotelephony." Of the latter, there were as yet only rudiments; and "radiotelegraphy" was clumsy, so it was reduced to "radio."

Today radio encompasses an enormous range of communications of the most diverse kind, of which only a small though important fraction —broadcasting—is known to the public. In 1910 and for another decade, "radio" was limited almost entirely to attempts to communicate overseas on long waves (largely 10,000 meters and up) and marine telegraphy, almost all carried on a single wavelength—600 meters. One reason for this crowding was that a distress call would be heard by all ships within range, but the rest of the time the result was savage interference between spark transmitters on ships and ashore, and frayed tempers on the part of all concerned. Amateurs, multiplying faster, as Marriott said, than rabbits or guinea pigs, made things worse; for the most part they were well disciplined, and a surprising number qualified for commercial licenses when regulatory laws were passed. But there was the inevitable fringe of playboys, some of whom would not have recognized an SOS (or the earlier CQD distress signal) if they heard one.

Although pre-*Titanic* radio was in such a chaotic state and only beginning to qualify as a business it had been gestating for more than half a century as a branch of mathematics and physics. The principal names associated with its birth are Michael Faraday (1791–1867) the great British experimenter who discovered electromagnetic induction, from which after a long lapse came generators and motors, electric light, the all-electric kitchen, the motorized factory, and electric power shortages; James Clerk Maxwell (1831–1879) likewise British, a brilliant mathematical physicist who proved light was a form of electromagnetic wave motion and foreshadowed longer waves of the same nature; Heinrich Hertz (1857–1894) a German genius who actually transmitted and received radio waves in the laboratory; and finally Marconi, the Irish-Anglo-Italian who, using these and other preexisting discoveries and devices, put together a primitive communication system late in the nineteenth century.

Until well along in his career, Sarnoff never heard of Faraday, Maxwell, and Hertz. Nor did he need to. All he needed was Marconi and the other engineers—many of them American—who made outstanding contributions to radio as a practical, and eventually profitable, art. Throughout his career Sarnoff was an enterprising businessman, and without the scientist-engineers whose ranks he had left, he would have had nothing to do business with, a fact he fully recognized and acknowledged.

Since so much of the Sarnoff story involves these relationships with engineers, it is illuminating to follow one of the crucial technical developments from its inception to the stage where the entrepreneurs take over and other troubles begin. There are dozens of such progressions to choose from in electronics alone, but the vacuum tube and its derivatives provide an outstanding case. Although for low-power applications the transistor is now preferred, the vacuum tube is probably the seminal invention of the twentieth century. Take it away, and the world as we know it would cease to exist.

The vacuum tube began as a kind of by-blow invention by Thomas A. Edison: the "Edison effect." (In science and technology, "effect" means that something of apparent significance has been observed, but no one can explain what it is or how it works.) In the early 1880s, while trying to find out what made the inside of his incandescent lamps blacken with age, Edison sealed a small piece of metal inside one of the bulbs, with a wire to the outside. He then found out that a small current flowed between this "plate" and the filament, always from the plate to the filament, never in the other direction.

Edison used his discovery to make a special kind of voltmeter for which there was no particular need at the time. He was repelled by invention that lacked practical use, so he took out a patent on what is now called a vacuum-tube voltmeter; or something like it. This disposition followed what seems to be a general law: an inventor is at first capable of applying his invention only in the field in which he is working, which in Edison's case was central station electric power.

The Edison effect was not explained until 1897, when the British physicist J. J. Thomson discovered the electron. Then the puzzle was resolved: the hot filament was boiling off electrons—negatively charged particles—which flowed to the plate. Thus, when plate and filament were externally connected, an electric current flowed inside the bulb from plate to filament; outside the bulb, from filament to plate, completing the circuit.

The physics was now clear, but the commercial complications were only beginning. During the period of mystification, (Sir) J. Ambrose Fleming, a prominent British electrical engineer, had experimented with the Edison effect as a rectifier for changing alternating or bidirectional current into direct or unidirectional current. Fleming became associated with Marconi, and the "Fleming valve" came into use as a detector of wireless oscillations, which are a form of alternating current.

Actually, except for patent purposes, this was a sterile invention. The Fleming valve was not as sensitive as a good crystal detector, which people old enough to have been broadcast listeners at the inception of the great radio craze of the early twenties will remember for its erratic performance. By contrast, the valve was stable, but that was all that could be said for it. It was like an employee who never fails to report for work on Blue Monday, is always punctual and cooperative; all that is wrong with him is that he is incurably dimwitted.

But then, along came Lee De Forest, with a Ph.D. from Yale's Sheffield Scientific School. After some false starts with gas flames as detectors, around 1906 he inserted a third element in the vacuum tube: the "grid," a zigzag wire between filament and plate. It was a stroke of genius; one of several that came upon De Forest, but the outstanding one. The grid converted the tube from a mere rectifier, and not a particularly good one at that, into an amplifier of weak radio signals, a telephone "repeater" or amplifier on wire circuits, an oscillator or generator of radio frequency currents, etc.

It was a multibillion-dollar invention. By means of the "audion," as De Forest called it, the American Telephone & Telegraph Company inaugurated transcontinental wire telephony in 1915; in the same year, with a battery of oscillating audions of their own manufacture, they sent wireless telephone messages from the U.S. Navy station at Arlington, Virginia, to Paris, Hawaii, and other distant places. Ultimately, with some intricate maneuvers by AT&T, De Forest received from them something short of $400,000 for his patent rights, not bad money for those days but far less than the rights were worth for wire telephone use alone.

Between De Forest and American Marconi (later RCA), however, there was a complete stalemate. The courts held that the De Forest audion infringed on the Fleming valve patent, although they also held the audion patent valid. The competing interests were like scorpions in a bottle. It was many years before that conflict was resolved, after several bankruptcies of companies owning the De Forest patents and the absorption of the final one by RCA. Among the exhibits in the David Sarnoff Library is a photograph of De Forest and Sarnoff smilingly shaking hands and a reproduction of a cordial tribute De Forest paid Sarnoff. That was after Sarnoff had become a power in RCA, however; before that, RCA feeling toward De Forest was, for purely commercial reasons, fiercely antagonistic. Everybody in an operating job in Marconi knew the overwhelming superiority of the three-element vacuum tube over any device purporting to fulfill the same functions, but the Marconi management, playing the cards close to their vests, were unwilling to pay De Forest for a license under his audion patents. They figured that they were the bigger scorpion and stayed warily in the bottle.

So it happened that, as long as Sarnoff was a wireless operator, he made use of the equipment Marconi furnished him and the other operators. He never stood a watch with the marvelous capabilities of the audion at his command. After 1912, when ship radio was no longer an option of the owner but, with certain exceptions, was required by law, together with a continuous watch, Sarnoff was no longer an operator. He had been elevated into the junior ranks of management, straddling operation and supervision.

One of the memos Sarnoff wrote to Nally reveals Sarnoff's thinking at this stage, when he was only twenty-three years old; Nally was fifty-five. "It is evident," Sarnoff wrote, "that while an apparatus may have been quite sufficient several years ago and is probably sufficient at present to fulfill all requirements, it is nevertheless well to look forward to the future and this can only be done by frankly discussing the viewpoints of all those who have suggestions to offer. . . ."

Meaning, of course, especially David Sarnoff.

Inevitably, since Sammis was chief engineer and Sarnoff was consistently critical of the company's engineering practices (based largely on British Marconi design), the two came into collision. I happened to be present when a public confrontation occurred. I had been a student of Dr. Alfred N. Goldsmith, one of the three foremost teachers of radio engineering in the country. Since 1916 I had held a commercial operator's license, first class, first grade; in that same year I became a student member of the Institute of Radio Engineers. When I graduated from CCNY in 1917, I was elevated to associate member and operated the stereopticon at the monthly IRE meetings. ("The next slide, please.") I had met Sarnoff and had great respect for him; he was five years older and had been in commercial radio for eleven years, while I was just beginning.

After the presentation of the paper at a meeting in 1918, I had nothing more to do but I was still sitting at the stereopticon, listening to the discussion that always followed the paper. At the front of the auditorium Nan Malkind, the IRE secretary (of whom more later in connection with Sarnoff) was taking stenographic notes of the discussion. Sammis, who had recently resigned his Marconi post, was on his feet, talking, a few feet away from Sarnoff.

I missed what Sammis said, but Sarnoff leaped to his feet. Taking a step toward Sammis, he said angrily, "Are you accusing me of stock jobbing?"

"If the shoe fits, put it on," Sammis snapped.

Two men who were seated between the contestants half-rose, but there was no need. The chairman tapped with his gavel and said, "Order, gentlemen." Still fuming, Sammis and Sarnoff sat down and took no further part in the discussion.

"Stock-jobbing" was a byword in the industry. In 1912, De Forest was fleeced by some stock swindlers and narrowly escaped going to jail with them. Around that time, under the direction of Godfrey Isaacs, American Marconi sold stock for the purpose of building high power transatlantic and transpacific stations—a legitimate financing operation though a premature investment. Apparently Sammis used this stock flotation to attack Sarnoff, but there was nothing to it.

I went home that evening somewhat perturbed. I was an employee of American Marconi, but in the secluded precincts of Dr. Goldsmith's laboratory, and the confrontation was my first experience of the tensions and antagonisms that arise in the normal course of business, more acutely when times are bad, or rapid technological change is occurring. But if I was uneasy, Sarnoff was not. He had already had experienced much of triumph and defeat, and another half century of both—but mostly triumph—was ahead of him.

THE MUSIC-BOX MEMO

The most important thing David Sarnoff did in the thirteen years he spent with the Marconi Company before it became the Radio Corporation of America, was to write a memo to Nally in November 1916, "Subject; Radio Music Box." Although by that time, four years after the *Titanic* episode, Nally relied on Sarnoff for counsel on numerous technical and business matters, this memo was pigeonholed. Nor was Nally alone obtuse: other company officials who read it or learned of its contents considered Sarnoff's proposal a screwball idea to be charitably forgotten.

Sarnoff wrote;

> I have in mind a plan of development which would make radio a 'household utility' in the same sense as the piano or the phonograph. The idea is to bring music into the home by wireless.
>
> While this had been done in the past by wires, it has been a failure because wires do not lend themselves to this scheme. With radio, however, it would be entirely feasible.
>
> For example, a radiotelephone transmitter having a range of say 25 to 50 miles can be installed at a fixed point where the instrumental or vocal music or both are produced. The receiver can be designed in the form of a simple "Radio Music Box" and arranged for several different wavelengths, which should be changeable with the throwing of a single switch or pressing of a single button.
>
> The "Radio Music Box" can be supplied with amplifying tubes and a loudspeaking telephone, all of which can be neatly mounted in one box. The box can be placed on a table in the parlor or living room, the switch set accordingly and the music received. There should be no difficulty in receiving music perfectly when transmitted within a radius of 25 to 50 miles.

Within such a radius there reside hundreds of thousands of families; and as all can simultaneously receive from a single transmitter, there should be no question of receiving sufficiently loud signals to make the performance enjoyable. . . . The use of headphones would be obviated by this method. The development of a small loop antenna to go with each "Radio Music Box" would likewise solve the antenna problem.

The same principle can be extended to numerous other fields as, for example, receiving lectures at home. . . . Baseball scores can be transmitted in the air by the use of one set installed at the Polo Grounds. The same would be true of other cities. The proposition would be especially interesting to farmers and others in outlying districts removed from cities. . . . They could enjoy concerts, lectures, music, recitals, etc. which may be going on in the nearest city within their radius.

The memorandum went on to discuss the prices and profits that might be anticipated. If only one million out of the 15 million families in the United States bought one music box per family, priced at $75 retail, a gross revenue of $75 million would result. In the 1916 accounts of American Marconi, this was a fabulous amount, since only manufacturing and sales costs would have to be deducted. (The income tax, which had been passed in 1913 by a constitutional amendment, was minuscule.) But since the Marconi officials did not have the slightest confidence in the project, none of this was taken into consideration.

Sarnoff's prowess as an industrial prophet has long since been conceded, but a study of all his innovative projects shows that he was not so much an originator as a bold but discriminating selector of partially developed ideas already floating about. And having made his selections, he pressed them hard. The choice was not always happy, but more often than not it was; and once he had satisfied himself he was on the right track, he exerted to the full his ample talents for promotion. However, the "Radio Music Box" was so coldly received that he did not pursue it for the time being. He had a good sense of timing, and it took in the business aspect as well as the technological.

As he had said, the problem of transmitting music had already been solved in principle. On Christmas Eve in 1906, Reginald A. Fessenden, the Canadian-born genius who contributed much to early radio, had transmitted speech and music, including his own violin solo, from his experimental station at Brant Rock, Massachussetts to ships at sea.

During the winter of 1909–1910, De Forest broadcast a performance from the Metropolitan Opera, with Caruso in the cast, but the quality was so atrocious that the performance was never repeated. Earlier, however, he had more success with a less ambitious project; when President Theodore Roosevelt sent an American fleet around the world, two dozen of the ships were equipped with De Forest radio-phones, and enough of them worked often enough so that Admiral Robley D. ("Fighting Bob") Evans became a strong supporter of the equipment.

In May 1914, Sammis had installed a transmitter of the arc type, generating continuous waves suitable for telephony, in the New York Wanamaker station, and Sarnoff and others received speech and music on the S.S. *Antilles* en route to New Orleans when the vessel was 60 miles out of New York. This was not broadcasting, however, but rather point-to-point communication: the idea was to save the expense of a skilled telegrapher by using voice instead of Morse. It did serve to get Sarnoff's mind working along the lines of radiotelephony for "broad-casting," although the term was not coined in the radio sense until several years later.

What has received little attention, however, was that Sarnoff was impelled to pin the idea down in his memo by the existence of an actual broadcasting station on his very doorstep. In November 1916 De Forest had already been broadcasting for several months from Highbridge, New York—not a town, but a locality on the Harlem River in the Bronx—to an audience composed mostly of radio amateurs but also including ship operators at sea or docked in New York Harbor. Although my commercial experience did not begin until 1917, I had had an amateur station with another boy of my age—twelve—in 1908, and in 1916 I had a station of my own, for receiving only, in the Bronx, a few miles from Highbridge, so I got a fairly strong signal from De Forest's transmitter. The quality was quite good, and I used to listen to the station for hours at a time. It broadcast phonograph records, with De Forest himself sometimes officiating as disc jockey, and he was at the microphone when the station broadcast the 1916 election returns. The station also did some remote pickups by telephone lines.

Although I am not impressed by purported technological fatherhood (Edward Teller as the "father" of the hydrogen bomb, etc.) since in the nature of technological innovation every major invention is the culmination of numerous prior inventions (failures, complete or partial, also play an essential part by clearing the ground), I think the title of

De Forest's 1950 book, *Father of Radio* (Chicago: Wilcox & Follett) has more justification than most claims in the field.

And yet, despite the engineering success at Highbridge, nothing much came of De Forest's broadcasts at the time; their sole importance is historical. His audience already had receivers, and the public did not join in a rush to buy, as it did later. There must have been some newspaper publicity, but De Forest's feat attracted less attention than a bizarre murder or a tenement fire tragedy.

Nor was it only a question of timing. Although De Forest was first to come up with a genuine broadcasting station, he never had a chance to commercialize it for reasons implicit in his makeup, connections, and resources. De Forest was not a businessman on a scale approaching his inventive capacity. If he was the engineering father of broadcasting, Sarnoff was the business father, and the detailed extrapolation in his 1916 memo, extending even to the potential revenues, affirms it.

Yet, at the inception, both men suffered the same neglect. Besides, time was running out on the Highbridge venture. Since the summer of 1914, World War I had been raging in Europe, and the United States was preparing to intervene on the Allied side. When we entered the war in April 1917, De Forest's station was shut down along with other nonessential transmitters.

There was an ironical epilogue: De Forest started broadcasting from Highbridge again after the war. I was unaware of this, but Fred Shunaman, a distinguished radio writer and historian, reports it in an article in *Radio-Electronics*, August, 1973. De Forest moved the station to midtown Manhattan, hoping for a wider audience; but the result was no audience at all. The federal radio inspector, Arthur Bachelor, shut him down on the ground he had changed the location of the station without a permit. Mr. Bachelor, whom I got to know well in the course of business later, made it clear that no interference with marine radio would be tolerated, and added that "there is no room in the ether for entertainment." He was an intelligent, fair-minded man and no doubt took his orders from Washington; but neither he nor his superiors nor the Marconi executives had the gift of prophecy David Sarnoff showed in the "Music-Box Memo."

BEGINNING OF A PARTNERSHIP

The lives of David Sarnoff and Edwin Howard Armstrong were inter-twined; much of radio history developed from their relationship, begin-ning with early wireless telegraphy and enduring well into the television era. Yet those lives were about as different as lives could be. Armstrong came of a cultivated Presbyterian household. His father was the Ameri-can representative of the Oxford University Press, and the family lived in a spacious Victorian house in Yonkers, overlooking the Hudson. There was one similarity, though, in the Sarnoff and Armstrong careers; even as boys, both were ambitious and farsighted. Armstrong was in a much better position to plan his life than a poor boy like Sarnoff. When he was fifteen, he informed his parents he intended to be an inventor. *Fortune* wrote in 1948 that Armstrong could indeed qualify as "the greatest American inventor since Edison and the most important of all radio inventors, including Marconi." It was no exaggeration.

As a boy, Armstrong was a wireless amateur. Unlike many old-timers in radio, Sarnoff was never an amateur: there were no amateurs in the ghetto. Armstrong erected a hundred-foot mast in his backyard and climbed it whenever there was a sizable fire in Yonkers, thoroughly unnerving the neighbors. He erected it himself, no doubt with help from brother-amateurs, a coterie which, incidentally, never called themselves "hams"—in amateur and commercial circles alike, a ham was just a bad operator.

Marriott writes: " . . . I believe Edwin Howard Armstrong regards the fact that he was a wireless amateur at an early date as the source of more satisfaction then those academic degrees, medals, and the title of Columbia professor." I knew Armstrong well in the early years and can vouch for the truth of Marriott's statement. I would even add the millions Howard made from his inventions. The memories he kept;

most of the money he spent on further research and invention.

In 1909, when he was eighteen—he and Sarnoff were almost exactly of an age (Armstrong the older by two months)—he went to Columbia for his electrical engineering degree. He got the degree but he was not a good engineering student. There was a reason:—he was interested only in radio. While he was still a junior, he invented what became known as the regenerative circuit, the feedback circuit, the ultra-audion, the oscillating audion—the multiplicity of names reflects the importance of the device—which was also invented by De Forest; but Armstrong knew what he was doing, and De Forest experimented more or less blindly. After patent litigation lasting nineteen years and going up to the Supreme Court not just once but twice, De Forest won, but among radio engineers the credit has gone to Armstrong—by acclamation. Justice Cardozo, who wrote the opinion finally awarding the invention to De Forest, was a great lawyer, but in electronics he and the other justices were lost. When the technical errors in the opinion were pointed out, the opinion was reworded but the conclusion stood.

Earlier, hardly anyone in the industry doubted that Armstrong was the inventor of something sensational—exactly what they didn't know, and Armstrong did not at first enlighten them. Sarnoff went up to Columbia University in January 1914 for a demonstration of the device, which was hidden in a "black box"—perhaps the origin of the term. Stations never before heard in New York, like Glace Bay in Nova Scotia; Clifden, Ireland; Honolulu, and others came in loud and clear. Reporting by memo to Sammis, Sarnoff, signing himself "Chief Inspector," told what he had heard. Sammis forwarded the report to Guglielmo Marconi in London. Marconi answered that nothing remarkable had occurred, since Glace Bay was routinely received in London in daylight.

In London, yes, but, owing to the directional characteristics of the transmitting antenna and the vagaries of radio propagation, not in New York—not even at night, when long distance reception was better. Sarnoff knew intuitively that Armstrong had got hold of something phenomenal, while Marconi and Sammis misdiagnosed the situation because, being older and more experienced and trained as engineers, they doubted the younger man's judgment.

But Sarnoff persisted. At a later test at the Belmar, New Jersey, Marconi receiving station, besides Armstrong and Sarnoff, Roy A. Weagant (a Canadian who later was chief engineer of RCA) and John

H. Morecroft (one of Armstrong's teachers at Columbia) were present. Again the reception was outstanding. Sarnoff concluded his report to Sammis with a sentence that proved to be prophetic: "I believe [Armstrong's] device has tremendous advantages and unless there be other systems of equal merit . . . unknown to me, I am of the opinion that it is the most remarkable receiving system in existence." It not only was then but, *mutatis mutandi,* sixty years later it still is.

At this early period, and for many years afterward Sarnoff and Armstrong were close friends. It was principally radio that kept them together much as, later, it was radio that would drive them apart. Their circumstances otherwise were profoundly different. Sarnoff married an attractive French-born blonde, Lizette Hermant, in 1917. The couple was brought together by their respective mothers, but it was a romantic marriage, Jewish of course on both sides; Sarnoff had never seriously dated any but Jewish girls. In reference to the courtship that culminated in marriage, he made a sardonic remark that circulated in the Marconi Company. "She spoke no English, I spoke no French. What else could we do?"

The Sarnoffs lived in a modest house in Mount Vernon, the least fashionable of the Westchester suburbs. Armstrong was unmarried at the time and lived with his family. Yonkers and Mount Vernon are only a few miles apart and frequently, before the two men went to work, Armstrong would drop in at the Sarnoff house. The Sarnoff boys called him "the coffee man" because, offered breakfast, he always said, "All I want is a cup of coffee."

Armstrong did not marry until 1923, but Sarnoff had something to do with that, too. Having been paid for his inventions in RCA stock, Armstrong was then the company's largest stockholder, or on the way to becoming the largest. He had occasion to visit Sarnoff's office often, and he noticed Sarnoff's secretary, a tall girl from Merrimac, Massachussetts, named Esther Marion MacInnis. Sarnoff was already vice-president and general manager, and a girl didn't get to be his secretary by looks and charm alone. Armstrong was prematurely bald, and a good deal taller than Miss MacInnis, but with his high domed forehead, intent, quizzical gaze, long upper lip, and firm mouth, he was handsome in his way. Handsome enough, at any rate, to deprive Sarnoff of his secretary.

The manner of Armstrong's courtship was in the spirit of the Scott Fitzgerald era. He returned from a European vacation with a Hispano-

Suiza, in which he took Miss MacInnis for a ride on the Long Island Motor Parkway, a private toll road financed by W. K. Vanderbilt that in one respect was the precursor of modern turnpikes:—it had no grade crossings. Instead, it overpassed public roads with a kind of chute-the-chute construction—a sharp upgrade and an equally steep downgrade. The road was 45 miles long, and the challenge was to make it in less than 45 minutes without taking off disastrously at the crossings. According to Miss MacInnis, at one moment on this ride the speedometer read 100 mph.

That was another difference between Armstrong and Sarnoff. Armstrong often appeared to be risking his neck, but the appearance was deceiving. Whether on a radio tower—he was always climbing towers for the joy of climbing—or in driving, he knew exactly what he was doing. In the few years after his marriage when he drove himself, Sarnoff, was an inept driver, at least in Mrs. Sarnoff's view, and she was probably right. He made her nervous, and she was relieved when they moved up to a limousine with a telephone in the back seat and a chauffeur in front.

Armstrong once irritated Sarnoff with his tower climbing after RCA had succeeded American Marconi and was operating a broadcasting station on 42nd Street in New York. The station had two one-hundred-foot steel towers on the roof of a twenty-story building. I was present with Dr. Goldsmith's able assistant, Julius Weinberger, when Armstrong came up to the roof on a summer day, in business clothes, chatted with us for a few minutes, then casually climbed the north tower. He walked around on the crossarm at the top like a construction worker on a steel beam, looking down to the street 400 feet below and obviously enjoying himself. I watched somewhat apprehensively but when he came down I said nothing. Weinberger, however, had been eyeing the aerialist with increasing irritation and, as soon as he came within earshot, he said, "Armstrong, why do you do these damnfool things?"

Dusting his hands with a gesture implying he was getting rid both of the grime from the ladder and the question, Armstrong said, "Weinberger, I do it because the spirit moves me."

Somehow word of Armstrong's antics reached Sarnoff and he told Armstrong to keep off the towers. Armstrong's answer came at the dedication of the station, with Sarnoff the principal speaker. While Sarnoff was holding forth, Armstrong went up on the roof with a photographer and the pair scaled the north tower, which seemed to be Armstrong's favorite. A strap iron ball, representing the world, was mounted some twenty feet above the crossarm. Armstrong climbed up to the ball—he had not done this before—and did a handstand on it in the dark. The photographer remained on the crossarm and took a few flash pictures. Armstrong sent a print to Miss MacInnis and told her to show it to Sarnoff.

That was it. Sarnoff wrote Armstrong a sharp letter barring him from the station. The order remained in force for a few weeks; then Sarnoff relented, but Armstrong never went up on the roof again. The spirit may have moved him, but he knew who was the boss—at least he knew then.

THE DOCTOR

Next to the Sarnoff-Armstrong partnership, the relationship between Dr. Alfred N. Goldsmith and Sarnoff was the essential element in the technical progress of the American Marconi Company and the early Radio Corporation of America. Quite often in those early days I saw them together in more relaxed and revealing contacts than were possible later. Sarnoff was not yet one of the country's foremost managerial personalities; people were not afraid of him, nor felt honored by mere acquaintance with him. In fact, at that stage Goldsmith was the more prominent and influential of the two. We who were his students at Townsend Harris Hall and CCNY always referred to him as "the Doctor," in distinction from run-of-the-mill Ph.D.s on the faculty; Sarnoff likewise called Goldsmith "Doctor," never by his first name, while Goldsmith always called Sarnoff "David."

Yet, while not insignificant, these were superficialities. In subtle ways, one felt the latent strength that would bring Sarnoff to the topmost position in radio; while Goldsmith, though greatly respected and not among engineers alone, lacked both the capacity and the inclination to rise to the presidency of RCA. As Marriott and Sarnoff had agreed, the engineers were down the hall from the general manager's office, the seat of power. A vice-presidency was as far as Goldsmith could get, and during the Depression he was reduced to the peripheral status of consultant, and only later restored to the status of honorary vice-president.

Like Armstrong, Goldsmith had been a student of Michael I. Pupin, the Serbian goatherd who arrived in the United States in 1874 with a red Turkish fez on his head and 5 cents in his pocket—and became professor of electromechanics at Columbia University and a redoubtable inventor. These antecedents impressed Sarnoff, and with good reason. In all the professions, the teacher-pupil, surrogate father-son relationships—when I was in my sixties Goldsmith still referred to me as "one of my boys"—are the means by which civilization—in its technological aspects, not only in engineering but in medicine and the social disciplines—is propagated. Aside from this generational aspect, Goldsmith could serve Sarnoff in the solution of immediate problems: technologically, he knew about all there was to know about radio, both the engineers and the engineering. He was an authority not only in the present but, as head of the research department of the Marconi Company and later of RCA, he was in a position not only to evaluate what was being done, but to foresee the developments that lay ahead.

Just the same, Sarnoff was sometimes ahead of the engineers, ahead even of Goldsmith. Sarnoff's 1916 "Radio Music Box" is a case in point. In 1918 a flotilla of U.S. Navy destroyers equipped with radio telephones was anchored in the Hudson, and several of us in Dr. Goldsmith's lab listened to the messages. The speech was perfectly intelligible but badly broken up by radiotelegraph spark transmission by other vessels. Since we had all listened to De Forest's Highbridge broadcasts of 1916, the thought that radiotelephony might have mass entertainment value reoccurred to us, but the spark interference was so severe that even Dr. Goldsmith was pessimistic. We knew more than Sarnoff—that was the trouble. Within a few years, spark telegraph transmission was obsolete, supplanted by vacuum tube generated continuous waves that could readily be tuned out. Sarnoff may not have foreseen how the interference problem would be solved; he just was confident that it would be. As he said later, he had more confidence in the "scientists"—he meant engineers—than they had in themselves. Justice Oliver Wendell Holmes said that to think great thoughts one must have a heroic mind. The aphorism is as valid in technology as in the cultural realm.

Dr. Goldsmith was a prolific inventor, with 122 U.S. patents to his credit. He was not a nuts-and-bolts type of inventor, however, and Sarnoff, together with the galaxy of RCA administrative engineers, learned what could not be expected of the prophetic, conceptual type of inventor, of which Goldsmith was a prototype. He was speculating about color television while black-and-white was still losing money. The obituaries which appeared in *IEEE Spectrum* after Goldsmith's death on July 1, 1974 noted this characteristic of his and how it fitted in with Sarnoff's plans at various stages in the development of RCA from an impotent subsidiary of Westinghouse and General Electric into a corporation rivaling these giants.

George Brown was a research engineer working at the RCA-Victor plant in Camden, New Jersey, during the Depression. Brown recounts;

> Dr. Goldsmith was a consultant and had come down [from his office in New York] to review the projects going on in the lab. I was so new I didn't have the faintest idea who he was when I sat down to chat with him about my project. . . . He wrote up a report—for General Sarnoff, I guess—about what we were doing. I remember that after we read the report, we decided he wrote reports better than we did. He was really very remarkable in that way, for he could summarize and interpret what we were doing after just a brief chat.

Sarnoff had discerned this ability of Goldsmith's twenty years earlier.

Brown cites an example of Goldsmith's conceptual type of inventing, this one in connection with color television which—again we are dealing in two-decade epochs—was absorbing most of Sarnoff's time and thought in the 1950s, together with frightening amounts of RCA's capital. A cardinal problem with color TV was to discriminate between each of the three beams impinging on the phosphors of the primary colors—red, green, and blue—on the back side of the picture tube. The technique adopted in the fifties was to use a shadow mask which would enable one of the beams to make the red phosphor dots glow while not affecting the blue and the green, which were separately activated by their beams. Brown writes;

> Some inventors work on the nitty-gritty details, but he wasn't that way. He was on a completely different plane, and his inventions would require a great deal of development to get them working. To me that's what made his ideas so interesting. Some people say he didn't invent the shadow mask. Well, if you mean the tube that was eventually built, then he didn't invent it—his patent wasn't remotely workable. . . . I don't think he had the faintest idea how to line up the phosphors, but he still had the basic idea and that's the important thing. It was really a great credit to him.

Sarnoff was not an inventor in any sense, nitty-gritty or conceptual. He hadn't a single patent to his credit. His genius lay in making the right administrative decisions and persisting despite gloomy forecasts of failure. Both he and Armstrong overshadowed Goldsmith; Sarnoff because of his business acumen and unparalleled command presence, Armstrong because he not only had the concepts but embodied them in operational circuits. If that took 50,000 measurements, as it did in one case, 50,000 measurements were made; most of them by Armstrong himself, the rest under his immediate direction. Sarnoff's success was based on four engineers of the first rank, and a dozen or two nearly as indispensable. Of these four, Goldsmith and Armstrong were with him early; a few of the others we will come to later.

In breadth of knowledge and general culture, neither Sarnoff nor Armstrong could hold a candle to Goldsmith. Armstrong had a brilliant mind, but it was confined to engineering; he was admired, also, for his honesty and modesty. Sarnoff was fascinating to talk to, he did wonders with his primary-school education by continuing to learn all his life. That was also Goldsmith's way, but he had a head start through his academic training. The difference between Sarnoff and Goldsmith may be irrelevant from the standpoint of industrial history; from a human viewpoint it is relevant. I can illustrate it best by quoting from a letter the Doctor's secretary for forty years wrote after his death. "Maggie" (Mrs. Robert Euler) wrote:

> The Doctor was a most remarkable and unusual person and I thoroughly enjoyed the years I was in his employ. It was more of an education than a job. His knowledge on all subjects was limitless. Even when we moved down here [to a distant New Jersey suburb] I commuted to New York City—I could not desert him then. . . . I still miss the long hours of dictation which were a challenge rather than a chore to me. One of the Doctor's sayings was that at least we had our memories which *no one* could take from us nor the Government tax! May he be happy wherever he is.

Among all his eulogies and tributes, I doubt that Sarnoff ever got one like that.

THE MAKING OF RCA

World War I brought down the czarist regime in Russia, liquidated the Austro-Hungarian empire, foreshadowed the murder of six million European Jews in World War II and, amid these and other shattering convulsions, effected the transition of American Marconi to the Radio Corporation of America, and thereby the ascent of David Sarnoff from the ranks of middle management to the top echelon of American tycoons. Officially he did not head RCA until thirteen years after its founding; actually, as commercial manager, for all practical purposes he ran it almost from the beginning, directly in some situations, indirectly in others.

With American entrance into the war Sarnoff applied for a commission in the navy. At twenty-six, and holding a responsible job in the largest, most stable of the U.S. wireless companies, he had a valid claim to the grade of lieutenant j.g., in communications. But nothing was forthcoming, and very likely Sarnoff's suspicion that the navy did not welcome Jews as commissioned officers was justified, although several were hired as civilian aides. Called by his draft board, Sarnoff refused to ask for exemption. It took repeated requests from an admiral to keep Sarnoff in the job in which he could best serve the country—staying where he was, in charge of supplying wireless equipment to the armed services, particularly the navy.

Earlier relations between American Marconi and the navy had not been auspicious. The mere fact of foreign control was objectionable, aggravated by American Marconi's refusal to sell equipment. The company's policy was to retain ownership and require both rent and royalty payments—impossible under American law and budgetary procedure. Another difficulty was the refusal of the Marconi companies to allow ships equipped with their apparatus to communicate with ships and land stations otherwise equipped, except under emergency conditions. The result was that the navy resorted to foreign and American companies that were willing to sell their equipment outright and not attempt to restrict intercommunication.

With war imminent, however, Marconi needed the navy and vice versa. Nally went to Washington, taking Sarnoff along, to mend fences. They met with Commander (later Admiral) S. C. Hooper, and agreement was reached on the navy's terms. It could not be otherwise, since American Marconi wished to demonstrate that it really was fully American in spirit and just as patriotic as the competition; also it wanted a share of the lucrative wartime armed services business and to supply equipment for merchant ships running the German submarine blockade under naval escort. So American Marconi became what was sardonically called a "war baby": an industrial corporation whose profits were generated or enhanced by the war. A small research-engineering plant Marconi maintained at Aldene, New Jersey, was expanded into a modern factory, adequate, under pressure, to supply wartime needs.

Sarnoff's role in these negotiations appears to have been one of compromise and moderation, a stance that in industry (although not in politics) he maintained for the rest of his life. He was never intransigent—yet never unnecessarily yielding either. In the present instance he had to balance his obligations to Marconi and his superseding obligations to his country, a country no less dear to him because he had adopted it. And also, so far as possible, to rid American Marconi of the stigma of foreign control.

Beginning with the declarations of war on April 6, 1917, the Marconi transoceanic and marine stations were taken over by the government, represented by the navy. Amateur stations were shut down completely. Operationally, all radio communication, ship-to-shore and intercontinental alike, became a naval responsibility. This arrangement continued all through the war, which ended with the armistice signed in Marshal Foch's railway coach near Compiègne, France on November 11, 1918. And although it was certainly not on the minds of the negotiators assembled at Compiègne, that was also the end of the Marconi Wireless Telegraph Company of America.

The Sarnoff-Nally effort to thoroughly Americanize American Marconi lasted only so long as hostilities lasted. The navy was reasonably well satisfied with Marconi's production during the war and Marconi, as the leading supplier of wireless equipment to the U.S. government, had the unheard of income of $5 million in 1917, when the dollar was worth perhaps ten times as much in buying power as it is today. The navy was likewise satisfied with Sarnoff's services as a negotiator, coordinator and expediter, as attested by a letter of commendation he received from Commander Hooper, head of the Navy Radio Bureau during the war:

> At the beginning of hostilities, this Bureau deemed it of importance to the nation's interest to request that you be denied the privilege of active duty with the troops, as your services were urgently required in connection with the supply of radio equipment to the Fleet. . . . Our constant association throughout this trying time led me to admire your work and your organization tremendously and I came to realize that I could depend upon you above all others.

Gratifying as this acknowledgment must have been, the fact remained that foreign interests held a controlling block of American Marconi's stock. When war broke out in 1914, the British cut the cables between Germany and the United States, and the Germans had to rely on transatlantic wireless circuits of their own for communication between the homeland and the United States. Their large station at Sayville, Long Island carried on a spy service, interspersed with legitimate business, until it was taken over by the navy in 1916. Another German-owned transatlantic station at Tuckerton, New Jersey, suffered the same fate. One way or another, the U.S. Navy controlled wireless communication, long-range and short-range, through the Navy Radio Bureau's operations; but legally British Marconi was still in a dominant position.

With the Allies victorious, the British had a practical monopoly on world communications through their cable network and the parent Marconi Company and its subsidiaries. On the other hand, the United States had emerged from the conflict with relatively minor casualties —about 50,000 Americans lost their lives—and enormous financial and industrial gains. Under these circumstances, British control of world communications was as intolerable as colonial status had become to Americans in the eighteenth century.

Another factor in the situation was the Alexanderson alternator, a property of General Electric. E. F. W. Alexanderson was a Swedish engineer who, following Fessenden's pioneering, had designed and built a generator on the same general principle as the machines one sees in electric power plants all over the world, mostly driven by steam turbines. The electrical section of these turbine generators is called an alternator, since it generates alternating current. The difference was that instead of producing hundreds of thousands of kilowatts at a frequency of 60 cycles per second, the Alexanderson alternator generated only 200 kilowatts in the largest size, but at a frequency of about 20,000 cycles (20 kilocycles). This alternator, with its associated equipment and a large antenna, could span the oceans reliably.

The General Electric Company had spent large sums to develop the Alexanderson machine. Like any other corporation, it wanted to get its money back, plus a profit. In 1915 Marconi himself, accompanied by counsel for British Marconi, had come to the United States to inspect an early model of the alternator. Marconi recognized it as the answer to dependable wireless communication with long waves over long distances. For the time being, since all American wireless equipment was in the hands of the navy, a deal could not be consummated, but in March 1919 officials of British Marconi began negotiations with General Electric for the *exclusive* use of the Alexanderson alternator. Or, if they could not obtain rights barring the system to others, they were prepared to buy twenty-four immediately, fourteen for American and ten for British Marconi, at $127,000 each, an order amounting to over $3 million—real money in those days. And there would be further orders, so that even if the British did not obtain exclusive rights, they would tie up General Electric's production for years to come.

At this point Washington went into action. President Wilson himself had been interested in the future role of the United States in world communications; the transmission of his Fourteen Points from the Marconi-U.S. Navy station at New Brunswick, New Jersey, and the reply from the station at Nauen, Germany, had alerted him to the importance of international wireless telegraphy and was reinforced by advice he received from Rear Admiral W. H. G. Bullard, Commander Hooper's superior officer. As a result of the strain of the peace conference in Paris and his efforts to convert the American people to the idea of American membership in the League of Nations, Wilson suffered a paralytic stroke in October 1919 and had in effect to relinquish the duties of the presidency. The burden of subsequent British Marconi-General Electric negotiations fell on Secretary of the Navy, Josephus Daniels and Franklin D. Roosevelt, still in robust health before his crippling attack of polio in 1921. Daniels would have liked government ownership of radio. It was not incompatable with democracy for communications to be in the hands of the government—England was a case in point. Though under postwar conditions, U.S. stations were still in naval hands, and Daniels and Roosevelt saw no reason why they should not remain so.

If in this respect the outcome was still in doubt, no one in our government wanted the British empire to acquire control of the Alexanderson alternator system and for the United States to be frozen out of that invaluable tool for overseas communications. In *The Electric Word: The Rise of Radio,* Paul Schubert, a pseudonym for Pierre Boucheron, the chief RCA press representative, gives his evaluation of Bullard:

> The Director of Naval Communications . . . Rear Admiral William H. G. Bullard . . . just back from France, was a fighter, a patriot, and a man perhaps better versed in communications, in a broad sense, than anyone else in the Navy. He had been working with radio for years—the Naval Communications Service was in a large measure his creation—and he had come to a deep and passionate belief in the value of American-owned transoceanic radio facilities for American use, not only from a standpoint of defense, but likewise from one of commerce. The reasons for his belief were many, derived for the most part from practical experience, from the episodes of those years that led up to the war.

Bullard and Hooper decided it was their duty to take steps in opposition to the impending Marconi monopoly of American and world radio. A high-level conference was arranged for April 8, 1919, at the General Electric headquarters in New York. Present were Bullard and Hooper representing the Navy; for GE, President E. W. Rice, Jr.; Owen D. Young, vice-president and head of the legal department; and Albert G. Davis, head of the patent department. And where was Sarnoff? He was not yet in those rarefied strata of corporate management, but he was getting close, and Young was to have paramount influence on his subsequent career, as was Davis, though to a lesser extent.

Bullard appealed to the General Electric negotiators not to sell the alternator to the British, leaving the United States helpless to compete in world communications. In the past we had depended largely on foreign countries for submarine cable communications, but now America was coming of age. The GE representatives were impressed, but they had their responsibilities as businessmen—apart from their own sentiments, they owed a duty to their stockholders. Several million dollars of GE investment was at stake. What suggestion did Admiral Bullard have to offer?

Bullard's reply foreshadowed the military-industrial complex but, granting his premises, it made sense. The gist of it was that government and big business must work hand-in-hand to establish American control of American overseas communications. That was the end; the means was the Radio Corporation of America, though not yet called by that name. And although Sarnoff had no role in these deliberations, he adhered to the principle of government-business collaboration in his subsequent career.

It would be wrong to suppose this was the beginning of American imperialism: it had arrived two decades earlier, at the time of the Spanish-American War and the crushing of the Philippine guerrilla rebellion. But now another affirmative step was taken, and it was one Sarnoff in his subsequent career did not neglect.

The chief architect of RCA on the corporate end was GE vice-president Owen D. Young. Like Nally, he and Sarnoff made a team, but Young was a more powerful partner; in the same ratio as GE versus Postal Telegraph or American Marconi. Young was a farm boy from upstate New York and with an early environment totally different from Sarnoff's. He graduated from St. Lawrence University, took his law degree at Boston University and practiced law in Boston, mostly in the public utilities field, where he showed an aptitude for corporate finance that boded well for a lawyer's career. He became GE's chief counsel in 1913.

Young was seventeen years older than Sarnoff, who usually teamed up with older men; or, in reverse, older, already prominent men sized Sarnoff up as someone who would become one of their number and, in the meantime, could be useful to them. However, the difference in age made the partnership unequal when the two first met at the time of the formation of RCA. Young was already close to the top in GE, while Sarnoff was an operating man, preparing for a similar role in RCA but not yet ready to exercise it. Young was too high up to take time out for the journey to England to negotiate for the separation of the British and American Marconi companies; he left that to Nally and Albert G. Davis. What with all the international and financial complications, it took them three months to complete the divorce, but they finally came back with 364,826 shares of American Marconi purchased for GE from the British owners. The way was opened for the formation on December 1, 1919, of the Radio Corporation of America, with Young as chairman of the board, Nally as president pro tem, De Sousa as treasurer, Alexanderson as chief engineer, and Admiral Bullard as an ex officio member of the board for liaison between the government and the company. Sarnoff remained as commercial manager, and when it is said that within some thirty days he was running the company, that again must be understood in an operational sense—he tackled and solved the day-by-day problems. At twenty-eight, he was not yet qualified for membership on the board.

General Electric obviously was in charge in a corporate sense; it had shelled out the money. It had also made its investment at the behest of the government, with no immediate prospect of profit. Naturally profit was the ultimate aim; the government's role, however, was a publicity man's dream, and for many years RCA was plugged as an example of big-business devotion to the highest national ideals. All through the twenties and into the thirties, the patriotic zeal of the RCA founders was the staple of RCA public relations. The PR people made them look as patriotic as Betsy Ross. They were patriotic—no doubt of that—but they were also devout believers in free enterprise and the primacy of profits. They could not have bought out British Marconi without a reasonable prospect of future gain.

The transaction might, however, have had an unintended side-effect. If, after the *Titanic* episode, Sarnoff needed further evidence of the value of publicity, here he had it. Realistically, as one industrial historian put it, the creation of RCA was more a "semipatriotic" enterprise; it was all the more impressive that, so far as the public was concerned, the "semi" was effectively concealed.

The war had another lesson for all the participants. It was obviously impossible for radio to advance with various interests separately owning patents vitally necessary in their entirety for fast, reliable communication. Only the lawyers—not the industry—could prosper under such conditions. For this reason, among others, RCA only began its life under GE sponsorship; in the course of the next few years, other companies joined in a quadruple merger. First came the gigantic American Telephone & Telegraph Company. Pressed by the navy, it concluded a loose agreement with RCA, including purchase of preferred stock and a bonus of 500,000 shares of RCA common for the

AT&T patent rights. The next joiner was Westinghouse, which had gained control of the Armstrong and Fessenden patents.

And more: E. E. Bucher, a long-time associate of Sarnoff's and the author of a forty-volume unpublished history of RCA and Sarnoff, writes of a less important entrant, "Odd as it may seem, the fate and welfare of the banana played a considerable part in radio's evolution." As early as 1904 the United Fruit Company, with plantations in Central American countries and, when the natives became obstreperous, the unstinting support of the U.S. Marines, had begun a serious flirtation with "wireless." But in the tropics and subtropics static was even worse than in the temperate latitudes, and United Fruit, with its subsidiary Tropical Radio Telegraph Company, had no easy time of it. After trying various systems, it contracted with American Marconi to install powerful transmitters (50 kilowatts input) at Swan Island in the Caribbean, and in New Orleans. Even this was not enough, and one of the problems inherited by the fledgling RCA was that United Fruit refused to pay in full for these expensive and only intermittently effective installations. This controversy was resolved by United Fruit's throwing $1 million into the kitty in exchange for preferred and common stock.

A less congenial set of partners can hardly be imagined. Within a few years, open warfare broke out between the Radio Group, as it came to be called in litigation, and the Telephone Group. Within RCA itself no employee lay on a bed of roses, least of all Sarnoff. With the title of commercial manager, he was in effect, and soon officially, general manager, provoking resentment in various quarters. Although he was favored by Young and other GE executives, they were not nursemaids, and Sarnoff had to fend for himself—on a larger scale and with different weapons than when he was assaulted by the tough Irish kids in Hell's Kitchen. Gleason L. Archer, who, next to Bucher, is a primary source for early RCA lore, was told by a former company official that in the first years of Sarnoff's service with the company:

> If there were any particularly disagreeable jobs to be done by or for the management, it was almost invariably turned over to David Sarnoff. Tasks regarded as impossible were likewise shouldered upon him. Bores were routed to his office. Even before RCA went into the manufacturing of radio equipment, unwelcome vendors of lumber or other commodities who applied to Westinghouse or General Electric were likely to be sent to Mr. Sarnoff as the one man who could deal

with them, notwithstanding the fact that it was well known to those in authority that Mr. Sarnoff had nothing to do with such matters.

Unfortunately for those who sought to discredit Mr. Sarnoff in early days, the young man actually made good on the difficult or impossible assignments. He made friends with those who were sent on wild-goose errands to his office. In short, the very efforts to unseat the general manager enabled him to demonstrate how necessary he was to the organization, and left him more firmly in the saddle.

Archer adds that despite this pliancy, during his first dozen years at RCA (that is, until he became president) Sarnoff was never free from attack.

As commercial manager Sarnoff received a salary of about $11,000 a year, which a skilled mechanic, or even an assembly-line worker, would scorn today—but the comparison is misleading except insofar as it points up the ravages of inflation over the years. In the second decade of the century, a college graduate could reasonably look forward to a career in which his income as a professional, or a corporate business-man, would top at $40 or $50 a week, or $60 to $70 if he was exception-ally successful. Against this background, Sarnoff was already a conspicu-ous success. When he was elevated to general manager, his salary, according to corporate scuttlebutt, rose to $15,000 a year. On that income, he could, and did, order a Lincoln as a Christmas present for Mrs. Sarnoff and himself and was infuriated when it was not delivered on time. He could not yet consider the later townhouse on the Upper East Side, but he could move from Mount Vernon back to Manhattan. He and Mrs. Sarnoff and the children could live well.

From a corporate angle, though, there was much wrong with the setup. To begin with, RCA was a nearly impotent subsidiary of General Electric and Westinghouse, except insofar as Sarnoff could impress his own logic and foresight on the executives of these formidable compa-nies, who had many pressing problems besides those of a minor subsidi-ary like RCA. This is not to say that Owen D. Young was lacking in vision, but he was not as deeply immersed in radio as Sarnoff had been for many years now. For the time being Sarnoff had to defer to Young and did not resent it, but he had a vision of the future in radio that a corporation lawyer could not encompass.

That vision, in Sarnoff's view, was presently flawed. RCA was still wedded to the marine radio aspect of communications, obvious from the standpoint of safety at sea, and to the international aspect, equally obvious from the Great Power position which the United States was now accepting. What disturbed Sarnoff was RCA's concentration—RCA's, not his own—on transoceanic telegraphy. That was what had preoccupied Young and the other tycoons after World War I—America's need for ownership and control of international communications. The whole emphasis had been—and still was—on transoceanic telegraphy.

Sarnoff did not neglect that aspect of radio. It was important in the never-ending struggle among nations, in which allies turn into enemies and enemies somehow become allies. But where was the "Radio Music Box" in all this? It was to be expected that future statesmen like Young should be preoccupied with international telegraph communications and should have considered their duties largely discharged when they had established a corporation for that purpose (and averted government ownership and operation). It was further to be expected that Sarnoff could not convince such high managerial personages of the greater importance of the domestic aspect—radiotelephony in the form of broadcasting, an art close to the ordinary man's need for information and entertainment. Remembering his own barren youth, that was a need Sarnoff could never overlook.

But he was almost alone in his "Radio Music Box" vision. The majority opinion—if the majority thought of it at all—was that of the radio inspector who had seen no room in the "ether" for entertainment. Even E. W. Rice, president of GE and a highly progressive executive (he had hired Charles Proteus Steinmetz, the hunchbacked mathematical genius who had worked out the indispensable theory of alternating current) was sure, when radio broadcasting made its debut a few years after the founding of RCA, that it was only a passing fad, and that a solidly based corporation like GE, profitably filling basic human needs like refrigeration and other amenities based on electric power, should damned well stay out of such frivolity.

An important development, dictated by the same considerations, was the appointment in January 1923 of Major General James G. Harbord as president of RCA. Owen D. Young personally selected Harbord; a primary factor was Young's conviction that, as a corporation dedicated to American leadership in international communication, RCA should have a president with an outstanding international background. Harbord had been Pershing's chief of staff; later, wishing to lead troops in action, he had commanded the Marine brigade at Cha-

teau-Thierry and the 2nd Division in the Soissons offensive. The fact
that he was only a two-star general (after retirement he received a third
star) gives no idea of his importance. There are now hundreds of
generals with two stars or more in the army and air force, but in World
War I and earlier, generals' stars were not dispensed so liberally. It took
a special act of Congress to make U. S. Grant, commander in chief of
the Union armies, a lieutenant general.

A PIECE
OF THE ACTION

As for almost everybody, including me (in Goldsmith's lab), Sarnoff's "Radio Music Box" was the stuff dreams were made of; at that time we were concerned with overseas communications. By that time the company's marine business was in fair shape, with installations on nearly 600 vessels, but we were only nominally competing with the cable interests. For a weak company like American Marconi, the multimillion-dollar investment in transpacific and transatlantic transmitting and receiving stations, was a heavy burden that showed no signs of paying off.

When RCA took over in the following year, there was some relief, but the situation from both an engineering and a financial standpoint remained unchanged. As engineers we were not proud of the performance, and we were under management pressure to do something about it. The trouble was natural static, generated by lightning. When lightning was nearby, there was nothing to do but ground the receiving antenna and wait for the storm to pass. But the static could be disabling, even when it came from far away. It was especially strong on the long wavelengths—up in the 10–15 kilometer range—which we thought were the only ones that would work for long-distance communication. All sorts of schemes were thought up to eliminate it, but none did much good because the static was electrically identical with the signal. Often transoceanic radiotelegraphy was impossible for hours—even days on end—or everything had to be sent "double"—each word repeated—at very low speeds. This was no way to compete with the cables, even if they charged 25 cents a word while RCA charged only 17 cents.

The static was particularly bad during the summer season and in the afternoons, but from 4 A.M. to perhaps 9 A.M. there might be relative quiet. During that interval, the stations got off all the accumulated traffic they could, but hand-sending and copying in pencil or on the typewriter limited transmission to 25 five-letter words per minute at most. An obvious remedy was to send and receive automatically at high speeds during the good hours. On telegraph land lines, teletypewriters were in use at a standard speed of 60 words per minute, but teletype radio reception was not yet feasible. The best solution seemed to be an ink recorder, consisting of a moving paper tape on which a stylus fed with ink would trace the incoming dots and dashes. The cables had long used a device of this type.

Sarnoff authorized Goldsmith to develop an ink recorder for radio. The Doctor engaged a retired cable engineer to aid in the design and construction of a model. Julius Weinberger worked with the cable engineer. After the model had been tested in the laboratory, I was sent to the RCA receiving station at Belmar, New Jersey, for field tests. The device was installed in a spare room in the station building, situated on a tidewater inlet with a line of 400-foot guyed steel masts running inland on higher ground. The reason for this gargantuan receiving antenna was that the Marconi Company would not recognize the amplifiers that were already available. Therefore their receiving stations had to collect all the signal strength they could with the unaided antenna. Everything else was in keeping—a large hotel for the operators, bungalows for the superintendent and assistant superintendent, and of course land-line connections to New York City. All the buildings were brick: apparently the architects had built for the ages, not taking into account the client's precarious present and even more precarious future.

The ink recorder worked beautifully. We had competition, though. The General Electric Company, with its 60 percent stock interest in RCA, shortly installed at Belmar a photographic recorder developed in the Schenectady research laboratory by an elderly, highly respected scientist-engineer named Charles A. Hoxie. The dots and dashes were impressed on a light-sensitive tape in a dark compartment and developed, fixed and dried in another, after which the tape could be handled externally. Either type of tape could be cut up and distributed among a number of operators for retelegraphing to RCA's overseas communications office in the Wall Street district in New York City.

After both recorders had been in operation for only a few days, I was certain that the ink recorder was simpler and less expensive, and no more vulnerable to disruption by static than the photographic recorder.

I so reported to Goldsmith and Weinberger. The test period, however, was extended to several weeks, during which I stayed at the operators' hotel and ate at the operators' mess.

The showdown came when Sarnoff arrived at Belmar with Goldsmith, in the Doctor's chauffeur-driven limousine, to decide between the Hoxie photographic recorder and ink recorder. The Hoxie device was in charge of a GE research laboratory mechanic, Foster Card, whose skill was equalled only by his aversion to speech. He knew a lot about radio machinery and, later, motion picture equipment, but as far as he was concerned silence was golden. However, the Hoxie recorder was sponsored by an RCA engineer, Richard H. Ranger, who had retained his World War I military title and was addressed as "Captain" by his peers and inferiors. Ranger was as articulate as Card was taciturn.

In the room where the decision was to be made, besides Ranger and myself, was the station superintendent, William H. Barsby, a naturalized Englishman who had had the distinction of having hand-carried to the White House the generally favorable German reply to President Wilson's Fourteen Point offer. Also present was E. T. Dickey, another of Goldsmith's assistants. When Goldsmith and Sarnoff came in, Card happened to be out of the room.

Sarnoff shook hands with me, but not with Ranger—possibly, but not necessarily a tip-off, since he saw Ranger more often than me. At that age—31—Sarnoff was a solidly built man of medium height—what is known in the clothing trade as a "short stout"—but he carried himself well and gave the impression of being taller than he was. He had a broad brownish face with a high-domed forehead, full cheeks and a wide nose and mouth. His hair was brown but his eyes were blue. The steely eyes and the firm set of the mouth gave the face a peculiarly commanding expression.

Without preliminaries, Sarnoff, glowering, began a savage cross-examination of Ranger, firing technical questions about the Hoxie recorder like a prosecutor interrogating a guilty defendant in a felony case. I was standing beside Ranger, looking alternately at him and at Sarnoff as the questions machine-gunned forth.

Ranger kept cool and made the best of a bad case, but he never had a chance. I realized before a minute had passed that Sarnoff knew as much about the characteristics of the two machines as I did. His questions were based on engineering insight and had logical coherence and a crushing cumulative effect. It was an early application of what we now call systems engineering, coupled with managerial ability of a high order and almost terrifying determination.

Ranger's ordeal lasted no more than five minutes. Gesturing toward the ink recorder, Sarnoff said to the Doctor, "Order three of them." Then he turned on his heel. "I've done my day's work," he added, in a tone implying that Ranger, by sponsoring the Hoxie machine, had wasted his own time—not too important—but also Sarnoff's quintessentially valuable time.

Card had returned. In his shirtsleeves, he stood self-effacingly against the wall. Sarnoff paused. "This gentlemen I have not met," he said. Card was hastily introduced. Sarnoff exchanged a few words with him and left the room.

Through a window on my right, I watched Sarnoff. He chewed on his cigar as he started on the uphill walk to the company hotel. He still looked sore. I pondered. The source of his technical information was obvious: Goldsmith had briefed him on the ride down. Still, the display had been remarkable. The cram electrical engineering evening course at Pratt Institute could not account for the way Sarnoff had absorbed Goldsmith's indoctrination and converted it in his own mind into that whipcrack interrogation. That Sarnoff's was no ordinary mind I knew already, but I had not realized how brilliantly and rapidly it could function in the face of conflicting engineering data and recommendations.

What was still not clear was why Sarnoff had been so angry while he was raking Ranger over the coals. It wasn't such a big deal, after all, and his wrath—even his coming down to Belmar—seemed out of proportion to the issue. The total order might amount to ten recorders, at perhaps $1,000 each. Even for the nascent RCA, it hardly merited that much of Sarnoff's time.

I was a late bloomer in such high-level corporate affairs, beyond those directly affecting my income and prospects. It was some time before I found out what had been eating Sarnoff on that occasion. Dr. Goldsmith explained to me that Sarnoff had long planned to make RCA the General Motors of the radio industry. "And he's going to do it, too," the Doctor added.

Obviously that involved long-term, radical changes in the whole setup, but Sarnoff was not daunted. He was not satisfied to remain general manager of an organization that was no more than a sales agency for General Electric and Westinghouse, which did all the designing and manufacturing. Sarnoff's secret goal was complete emancipation, with RCA doing the manufacturing as well as the selling. In the present setup he could intervene occasionally, but only in minor matters, such as the ink recorder getting the decision over General Electric's photographic recorder. But Sarnoff's style called for big decisions, not little ones.

Sarnoff's attention to Card was also significant in the light of later events. At one time I wrongly regarded Sarnoff as one of the least democratic men I ever came across. While he wasn't the most democratic, he was far from the least, I later learned. In every situation, except perhaps when he was overburdened or felt someone was wasting his time, he had manners, manners he exercised with a peculiar dignity that encompassed both the other person and himself. It was a part of his impressiveness. More than fifty years after such a minor incident, I can see him still, the level gaze directed at Card, a modest man who hadn't expected any notice and looked a bit startled. I can still hear the authoritative voice requesting the introduction. It may seem trivial, but it wasn't.

And finally: Hoxie. His photographic telegraph recorder was a failure, but it paved the way for RCA's motion picture recording, developed by General Electric and opposed to the Telephone Group's rival system. Both relied on sound-on-film. Accompanying the picture with sound on discs was inherently clumsy, took up too much space in the projection booth, and involved synchronization difficulties. De Forest found this out early in his experimentation with sound movies and recorded the sound track on the film alongside the picture. On Hoxie's part, it was a typical case of serendipity, a word coined by the eighteenth-century British writer Horace Walpole and adapted in modern times to engineers who don't know where they are going but get there anyway. They might not find what they set out to look for, but they might happen on something just as good, or, as in this case, a lot better.

KDKA

Now that Sarnoff had a new boss who, though so far engrossed in wireless telegraphy, might be more flexible and sympathetic to the "Radio Music Box" notion, he brought it up again—and with an added feature. RCA had taken over from Marconi a monthly magazine, *Wireless Age*, read largely by amateurs. Sarnoff made a proposal to Young incorporating his early "Music Box" memo and adding a circulation idea for the magazine:

> Every purchaser of a "Radio Music Box" would be encouraged to become a subscriber to the *Wireless Age* which would announce in its columns an advance schedule of all lectures, recitals, etc., to be given in various cities of the country. With this arrangement, the owner of the "Radio Music Box" can learn from the columns of the *Wireless Age* what is going on the air at any given time and throw the "Radio Music Box" switch to the point [wavelength] corresponding with the music or lecture desired to be heard.
>
> If this plan worked out, the volume of paid advertising that can be obtained for the *Wireless Age* on the basis of such proposed increased circulation would in itself be a profitable venture.

This quotation from John Tebel's *David Sarnoff; Putting Electrons to Work* contains the idea *TV Guide* exploited with enormous success decades later. It was, of course, unsuitable for a monthly, but Sarnoff was working with what there was at hand—and he had the idea, quite fully developed, in the spring of 1920.

However, he fared little better than in 1916. The GE management did not brush him off entirely; indeed, they generously appropriated $2,000 for construction of a model of the "Radio Music Box." This task was entrusted to E. P. Edwards, assistant manager of the GE lighting department, who some years back, had described radio as not a business, but a *disease.* What Edwards meant was that while radio—wireless telegraphy—was working after a fashion, it was not making money.

He probably had little more confidence in Sarnoff's even more bizarre "Radio Music Box" idea, but what he thought no longer made the slightest difference. At this point, explosive developments forced revolutionary thinking on many who had lapsed into comfortable conservatism. Of that industrial sin Sarnoff had surely never been guilty.

The arrangement within the Radio Group was that General Electric would manufacture 60 percent, Westinghouse 40 percent, of whatever RCA could find a market for. Westinghouse was not as strong as General Electric—hence the 60/40 ratio—but it was faster on its feet. With the end of the war and reversion to "normalcy," Warren G. Harding's 1920 campaign slogan, Frank Conrad, a code amateur before the war, tore the navy seal off his transmitting equipment and went back on the air. His equipment was in a workshop over his garage in Wilkinsburg, Pennsylvania, near the Westinghouse main plant at East Pittsburgh. But there was a difference—in 1920, he had vacuum tubes and could transmit voice and music instead of dots and dashes. And Conrad was no ordinary amateur. His call letters were 8XK, the X denoting an officially recognized experimental station. He also differed from run-of-the-mill amateurs in that he was assistant chief engineer of the Westinghouse Company.

Conrad was a self-educated engineer who had come up from the shop bench in Westinghouse factories. His education was even sparser than Sarnoff's: he had left school in the seventh grade. One of his subordinates, Donald Little, had been more fortunate; he was an amateur of long experience who had studied electrical engineering at the University of Michigan and developed compact Signal Corps transmitters and receivers for Westinghouse manufacture. The Signal Corps stationed Little at East Pittsburgh to watch over the development. Little soon realized Conrad was an outstanding engineer, and they got along well together. After the war Little was employed by Westinghouse, but at first he was not working on radio equipment with Conrad, as he had hoped. Still, the two maintained contact at Conrad's amateur station.

Another principal in the ensuing drama was Harry P. Davis, a vice-president of Westinghouse with long experience in major engineering projects. He had been one of the top people in the electrification of the New Haven Railroad; anyone who could survive *that* could survive anything. He was old now, but his mind was as alert as Sarnoff's; he was a senior official in a big company, who could take the initiative where Sarnoff had to sell his ideas to less imaginative superiors.

Conrad's amateur broadcasting began to attract attention—and not only among amateurs—here was the difference between De Forest in 1916 and Conrad in 1920. Members of the amateur fraternity had long been in the habit of writing postcards to one another, commenting on loudness of signal, tonal quality, etc. In 1920 the mail praised the quality of Conrad's voice and musical reproduction—he was using phonograph records—a kind of primitive hi-fi evaluation. And now came the breakthrough: Horne's department store in Pittsburgh installed a receiving set that picked up Conrad's programs and people gathered around to listen. The store ran an ad in the Pittsburgh *Sun* (September 29, 1920) calling attention to Conrad's transmissions. The ad, in the form of a simulated news item, read:

> Victrola music, played into the air over a wireless telephone, was "picked up" by listeners on the wireless receiving station which was recently installed here for patrons interested in wireless experiments. The concert was heard Thursday night about 10 o'clock, and continued 20 minutes. Two orchestra numbers, a soprano solo—which rang particularly high and clear through the air—and a juvenile "talking piece" constituted the program.
>
> The music was from a Victrola pulled up close to the transmitter of a wireless telephone in the home of Frank Conrad, Penn and Peebles Avenues, Wilkinsburg. Mr. Conrad is a wireless enthusiast and "puts on" the wireless concerts periodically for the entertainment of the many people in this district who have wireless sets.
>
> Amateur Wireless Sets, made by the maker of the Set which is in operation in our store, are on sale here $10.00 and up.

Conrad was not the only one engaged in this kind of experimentation. Many amateurs had served in the Signal Corps or the navy, and some had emerged not only with discharge papers but purloined vacuum tubes. When they resumed transmitting, it was by telephone instead of code. Especially noteworthy was the institutional station of the *Detroit News,* which on August 31, 1920, ran an announcement in a box on page 1 in connection with a primary election:

RADIO OPERATORS! ATTENTION!
Here is the necessary data by use of which you may listen in tonight
and get election returns and hear a concert sent out by the Detroit
News Radiophone:
FOR LISTENING: Use wave length of 200 meters.
FOR CALLING THE NEWS TO REPORT RESULTS: Use
call "8MK."
Transmitting begins 8 O'CLOCK TONIGHT.

The *News* plugged its primary election broadcast heavily the following day and promised that presidential returns in November would also
be broadcast by 8MK:

> The sending of the election returns by the *Detroit News* radiophone
> on Tuesday night was fraught with romance and must go down in
> the history of man's conquest of the elements as a gigantic step in
> his progress. In the four hours that the apparatus, set up in an
> out-of-the-way corner of the *News* building, was hissing and whirring
> its message into space, few realized that a dream and a prediction had
> come true. The news of the world was being given forth through this
> invisible trumpet to the unseen crowds in the unseen marketplace.

Nothing about De Forest, nothing about Sarnoff. But the most
important event happened quietly. H. P. Davis (called "H.P." by
Westinghouse intimates) saw the September 29 Horne ad in the Pittsburgh *Sun.* Conrad reported to Davis, who had known about Conrad's
radio telephoning from his Wilkinsburg garage but had not given it
much thought—until he read the ad. Then, as he said later in an
address before Harvard's Graduate School of Business Administration,
he realized, "Here was an idea of limitless opportunity."
Davis acted. Had he known of Sarnoff's memo to Nally, he might
have acted sooner, but the Horne ad was enough to set him off. He
persuaded Conrad to build a more powerful transmitter at the East
Pittsburgh plant, with a higher antenna. Could Conrad have it ready
for the presidential election? He could. That was the beginning of
KDKA, licensed by the Department of Commerce radio division on
October 27, 1920 to operate on its own wavelength of 360 meters.
There can be endless argument about broadcast pioneering (by those
who never heard of the De Forest Highbridge station), but KDKA is
undoubtedly the most successful and enduring of all the broadcasters
who got on the air in the twenties. More than fifty years later, it

operates with the same call letters in one of the country's primary commercial markets, now, of course on TV as well as radio.

Sarnoff, by that time RCA's general manager de jure as well as de facto, was deeply chagrined, but he refrained from protesting that he had had the idea four years earlier; in his public utterances he had nothing but praise for KDKA and its founders. Plans for mass production of broadcast receivers were now being pushed, but he also wanted to get into the transmitting end as soon as possible. The heavyweight championship prizefight between Jack Dempsey and Georges Carpentier, the French champion, was scheduled for July 2, 1921 at Jersey City. The Lackawanna Railroad had a radio tower and antenna nearby with which it was conducting experiments in communication with moving trains. Sarnoff arranged to borrow a transmitter GE had made for the navy but had not yet delivered. Editor J. Andrew ("Major") White of the *Wireless Age* was a boxing aficionado and could do the announcing. A line was run from the Lackawanna transmitter to the arena. But apparently the line was so faulty that White's voice never reached the listeners. Instead, J. O. Smith, a technical writer for the *Wireless Age* and a good engineer, jotted down White's description and repeated it as nearly as he could, blow-by-blow, into the microphone.

Luckily, Dempsey knocked out Carpentier in the fourth round. The transmitter was operated at more than rated power and, according to *This Thing Called Broadcasting,* by Dr. Goldsmith and Austin Lescaboura, became virtually a "molten mass" right after the knockout. Since there were said to be 300,000 listeners, luck was certainly with Sarnoff that time.

In the inevitable contest between Westinghouse and RCA, though, Sarnoff needed a good deal more than luck. Emboldened by its success in Pittsburgh, Westinghouse established stations in Newark, New Jersey, and Springfield, Massachusetts, with call letters WJZ and WBZ, respectively. The locations were dictated by Westinghouse's having factories at those locations. Newark furnished coverage in the New York metropolitan area which Sarnoff was determined to take for RCA.

He had J. O. Smith set up a station, WDY, at the RCA Aldene factory. That maneuver failed. It was difficult to get performers to come to Aldene, out in the sticks. WJZ had found it necessary to lease a Western Union line from studios it established at the old Waldorf Astoria, to the Newark transmitter. Also, there was interference between WJZ and WDY. Sarnoff gave up WDY and bought into WJZ with a 50 percent investment, including an equal share in the operating costs. His next move was to liquidate the Newark station entirely, a maneuver made less painful for Westinghouse by the fact that the line from the Waldorf to Newark was so noisy that when Newcomb Carleton, the president of Western Union, broadcast over it, his voice was completely drowned out.

These were originally telegraph lines and the only reason they were adapted for telephone service was because of that conflict—much more serious—between the Radio Group and the Telephone Group. However, within New York City, Western Union could furnish lines for outside pickups at theaters, nightclubs, hotels, etc. that were reasonably noise-free; and Sarnoff could argue that a station with transmitter and studios in the same building would not have a noise problem for studio events, which would constitute the bulk of its program material.

Sarnoff prevailed in the corporate infighting, and a wholly owned RCA station was established at Aeolian Hall, a player-piano headquarters on 42nd Street in New York, between Fifth and Sixth Avenues and diagonally opposite the main public library. This station, where Howard Armstrong aroused Sarnoff's ire with his tower climbing, was conveniently located for outside pickups, and the elegant piano store with its show window on the street floor lent an artistic atmosphere. It was a dual station, WJZ, imported from Newark, and WJY. The latter never amounted to much, except to enable RCA publicists to refer to the combination as "Broadcast Central." The New York WJZ, however, like its Newark predecessors, made radio history. It was also the beginning of my personal history in the broadcasting field, and involved more contact with Sarnoff than I had had before.

Prior to 1923, I had been more or less an exile for two years. In 1919–1921 there was a sharp postwar depression, staff had to be cut, and since I was a telegrapher I could serve as an operating engineer at an outlying station where the money was coming in (although not much of it) instead of going out, as in research. While I was thus engaged, the underlying technique of overseas radio changed radically. Instead of housing the operators in places like Chatham on Cape Cod, or Belmar in New Jersey, and retelegraphing to New York City, the dots and dashes were impressed on a line to New York and recorded there. On the East Coast all the receiving was eventually concentrated at Riverhead, Long Island, with a staff of four engineers. Their job was to adjust the receivers and make the stuff as readable as possible for the operating staff at Broad Street.

During my stay at Riverhead, I saw Sarnoff only once, when he and General Harbord, with Guglielmo Marconi in tow, paid us an afternoon visit. The two RCA bosses were showing Signor Marconi how RCA operated in the transoceanic receiving branch of its business. When they alighted from the obligatory limousine (probably hired for the occasion), all three were seen to be carrying canes of the shepherd's crook design. I suspected that Marconi had set this fashion for Sarnoff and Harbord. Harbord still bore traces of his farmland origins. He wore a white cotton glove on his right hand and when he shook hands with me said, "Excuse my glove," as he had been taught as a boy, explaining he was suffering from arthritis. Neither he, nor Sarnoff, risen from the ghettos of Minsk and New York, could have foreseen they would be carrying canes in the company of the Irish-Anglo-Italian aristocrat.

I escaped from Riverhead and from transoceanic telegraphy, because the RCA engineering heads felt I was possibly overqualified for the job and, as usually happens in such cases, in other respects underqualified. I had been doing a good deal of writing, both technical and literary, and my superiors reasoned that I might feel more at home and be more useful to the company in the entertainment end of the business.

NOTES FROM THE
MUSIC BOX

For three years, 1923–1926, WJZ–WJY was of considerable importance in Sarnoff's operations within RCA and particularly in the contest between the Radio and Telephone groups. Against modern broadcast studios and transmitters, the station was like a tugboat compared
with an ocean liner, but it served its purpose. The sixth-floor studios
were connected with the transmitters by cables run up the side of the
building—cables that embarrassed Sarnoff personally a few months
later and nearly proved my undoing. The WJZ studio was about the
size of a modern ranch-house living room, the WJY studio even
smaller. The control room was situated between the two, with a large
window in the partition between, so that the control operator could see
what was going on in the studio and the announcer could see the
control operator's hand signals in emergencies, which were rather fre-
quent. Visitors came in through a small room where the receptionist-
telephone operator sat at her switchboard, then into a waiting room
where a charming and tactful cloakroom attendant, Alvin E. Simmons,
received visitors. He was black, and the only black in the place, whether
employee or visitor.

I started as the chief control operator and shortly ascended to engineer-in-charge. There was a typical piece of corporate unfairness in this
selection. George Bliziotis, the engineer at the Newark WJZ, who had
borne the brunt of breaking in the station, asked for the job at Aeolian
Hall. He should have got it, but he was a Westinghouse man, and I
was RCA. In the case of the program manager, the balance tipped the
other way. J. Andrew White wanted the job, but Sarnoff gave it to
Charles B. Popenoe, who had been station manager at Newark and was
chosen for his experience. Popenoe had been selected originally by
blind luck; he was a mechanical engineer with a degree from some

Texas school, and what he knew about show business and radio programming he learned on the job. White was designated sports announcer.

Besides Popenoe, most of the program staff and some of the operating crew came from Newark. There was Milton Cross: at Newark he had both sung and announced. In New York I never heard him sing —much better, he became the chief air impresario of musical events, especially opera which, at his death fifty years later, he was still explicating for a well-heeled sponsoring corporation. But the chief acquisition from Newark was Thomas H. ("Tommy") Cowan. He had been an employee of Thomas A. Edison in the West Orange Edison plant and could tell us how the renowned inventor, famed for his twenty-hour working days, got his sleep on the job.

Tommy did not have a good announcing voice. It lacked resonance and the sexy quality that made some famous, but he made up for that with wit and personality. He had been a spear carrier at the Met and at the outset knew at least as much about opera as Milton Cross; but Milton had the dignified voice the functionaries at the advertising agencies favored, hence his distinguished career.

Except for Popenoe, Sarnoff had nothing to do with the choice of these station-level functionaries; he was already far above such minor decisions. But he did insist that Popenoe report directly to him, which shows how seriously he took broadcasting—both on the transmitting end, where the money was going out, and the receiving, where it was now coming in through the sale of receivers. Popenoe's job was difficult for one set of reasons, mine for another. By this time AT&T, RCA's former ally, had cut loose and was operating a broadcasting station of its own—WEAF. It was better on the technical end than we were. The late Raymond Guy, who came from Newark and was in charge of my outside squad—the operators who picked up programs around town— sums it up in his reminiscences, recorded many years later at Columbia University's Oral History Research Office: "AT&T did things with a more thorough knowledge of what they were doing. . . . They just knew more about telephony than we did, as you might expect. They had the best telephone engineers in the world. The entire Bell Laboratories were at their disposal."

All things considered, we gave a good account of ourselves in a contest Sarnoff observed from his position of power, in the evenings when he was at home, or at other people's houses and listening there. Aside from the normal pride which engineers take in their profession, this kept us on our toes; but that technical competition with the Telephone Company was an uphill fight, as Ray Guy implied, and I would be the last to deny. Popenoe was in an even more disadvantageous position. WEAF, cautiously at first, began to sell time and develop an income. When WJZ–WJY went on the air on May 15, 1923, neither we nor WEAF were paying the artists. After a while, WEAF was in a position to do so, and we were not, until the National Broadcasting Company was organized in 1926 and WJZ became the key station of the Blue Network, later taken over by the American Broadcasting Company.

In the early days, most of the performers were not *worth* paying—mediocre church choir singers with hopeless aspirations to become concert artists—still, they filled air time. A few were beyond price and broadcast for the novelty of it; in between, there were those who could simply use the publicity. A recurring difficulty with the top performers was that many, accustomed though they were to precisely timed stage entrances and exits, could not understand the same necessity in radio programming, where the audience, though out of sight, was immensely larger. A young Metropolitan diva, as handsome as she was talented and —what was rare in opera at that time, with a figure—was scheduled for a solo program. She arrived at the station a few minutes early while we had a middle-aged female quartet on the air. The star's face darkened. "What!" she exclaimed. "You mean I must wait for those cows in labor!" Tommy Cowan summoned up all his charm, cut the quartet's last number, gave the operatic star a flowery introduction, and escorted her to the microphone. She was all smiles and sang beautifully. Nobody but Tommy could have managed it.

At the WJZ–WJY premiere Sarnoff said on the air that he was ashamed not to be able to pay the performers, but he kept a tight rein on Popenoe in that respect and in everything else. "You're my best spender," he chided him.

One way of holding down expenses was to pay low salaries, and for a time that consideration prolonged the Newark practice of not permitting announcers to use their names on the air. Instead, code letters were used. Cowan, for instance, was ACN, *A* standing for announcer, *C* for Cowan, *N* for Newark, later for New York. Operators still occasionally announced on outside pickups, and their call letters started with *O*. If a name initial had already been preempted, as in the case of the later-famous Norman Brokenshire, another letter was substituted; thus Brokenshire became AON. But the personality came through, especially in Brokenshire's case. He had a gift for badinage and indirect self-advertising, and he began getting fan letters, as many as a hundred a day. Then, at such events as the inauguration of President Coolidge, he did not hide his face from the press photographers, his name appeared in the captions and so, gradually, Popenoe's ukase was frustrated. However, the WEAF practice of glorifying the announcers (Graham McNamee, for instance, with his infectious excitement at prizefights) was not followed at WJZ until shortly before NBC came into being.

While Sarnoff kept Popenoe thoroughly underfoot, he was more accessible to him than to almost anyone else in RCA. He did not see him often, but he talked with him on the telephone nearly every day. Popenoe usually called Sarnoff—if Sarnoff called Popenoe it was a sign of trouble. To staff members who overheard Popenoe's end of these conversations, it was clear Popenoe was even more afraid of Sarnoff than most RCA people by that time were. In Newark he was broadcasting from a Westinghouse electric meter factory, and there was no one with anything approaching Sarnoff's authority and direct supervision any nearer than East Pittsburgh. In New York he was forced to curb the aggressiveness natural to him. He relied on Sarnoff for guidance and was careful not to stick his neck out.

Popenoe towered over Sarnoff physically, but in no other way. They were contrasts in temperament as well. Sarnoff dominated by force of personality and intelligence; Popenoe was only average in understanding and, being unable to assert himself in any other way, was an office martinet. From his private office, the door always open, he would call subordinates in a stentorian voice that annoyed the one summoned and everybody else. It was impossible to imagine Sarnoff operating that way.

I was friendly with Popenoe, though he seemed to me a corporate Babbitt in contrast to Sarnoff's ambition, which was of immensely larger scope and thoroughly healthy. Popenoe seemed always afraid of failure, while Sarnoff, if he had ever been subject to that fear, had got over it long ago. Popenoe was in his mid-thirties and several times remarked to me that it was now or never for him. He was the kind of man who had to make it to a vice-presidency or die. He died.

His death came only a few years later, of pneumonia, after he was kicked upstairs to the post of NBC treasurer. I was sure, though the term had not yet been popularized, that his illness was psychosomatic. Of course, pneumonia was a far more serious disease then; but once it got him down, he lacked the dogged resistance which enabled many to survive.

WJZ could not use telephone circuits for outside pickup, but occasionally Sarnoff pressured Telephone Company executives into furnishing their lines for special events. That obviated one difficulty; another was that for the first few years, radio was held in about the same repute in "society" as the theater had been in Elizabethan England. That persistent snobbery contributed to the worst debacle in WJZ's history. David Lloyd George, the British wartime prime minister, came to the United States in the autumn of 1923, shortly after his fall from power and my ascension to engineer-in-charge at WJZ. One of his principal addresses was scheduled before a distinguished gathering at the Lotos Club on 57th Street in New York City. By adroit maneuvering, Sarnoff took the event away from WEAF, and to make sure there would be no failure, he put the screws on the Telephone Company to furnish wire service from the club to the WJZ control room.

So far so good, but when Raymond Guy started to set up a microphone on the speakers' table, a club functionary declared it was out of the question to put the intrusive instrument before the eminent though disowned statesman. Ray argued vehemently, pointing out that Mr. Sarnoff, a member of the club, had made the arrangements. After much ado they compromised—the microphone would be concealed in a bowl of roses.

None of us had had experience with the acoustic properties of roses, but we were soon enlightened. The vowels came through but the consonants, riding on higher frequencies, were way down. Still, the quality would have got by, had it not been for an error in the original installation of the lines between the control room and the transmitter house. The electricians had put in lead-armored cable in accordance with their interpretation of the fire underwriters' code, and no one had corrected them. The lead gave good mechanical protection, but discriminated against the higher tones. The combination of the two attenuations was fatal.

I usually listened to the station at home and kept in touch with the control room via an order wire furnished by Western Union, but for important occasions I stayed at the station. When Lloyd George began speaking, I was in the control room. He sounded as if he were shouting into a rain barrel. Now and then an intelligible word came through, but only now and then. The Telephone Company's representative called my attention to the fact that the speech coming over the line was understandable, while the monitoring signal we were taking off the air was not. I knew, moreover, that the telephone circuit was "flat"— equalized to transmit all essential frequencies within the speech range. The trouble was entirely ours.

Soon the switchboard was swamped with calls from listeners who had tuned to other stations to check their receiving sets, and wanted to tell us what we already knew only too well. There was nothing we could do. As any high-fidelity fan will understand, with modern equipment much could have been done—we could have boosted the high frequencies, attenuated the lows, and probably got by. But then, today's speaker, whether he is the President of the United States or some two-bit dictator, has the microphones stuck under his nose and would not be without them.

Sarnoff ruled by the baronial charm he had displayed at Belmar after cutting down Ranger and requesting an introduction to Card, but he exercised this quality sparingly. More often he ruled by hurling administrative lightnings, and we knew it was going to be the lightnings this time. A high-level conference was convened at his Woolworth Tower office thirty-six hours after the fatal broadcast, and I was invited.

Dr. Goldsmith's department was responsible for the design of the station, and until the microphone was buried in the roses, none of us had realized how serious the cable losses were. Still, results are what count, and these results would take a lot of explaining. Walking up and down the subway platform, waiting for the train that would take me down to the Woolworth Building, perhaps to my doom (would I still be engineer-in-charge on my way back?) I decided on a battle plan. I would wait out the inevitable recriminations and counter-recriminations, and then make as clear and candid a statement as I could, not concealing the fact that if I had had a sharper ear, I could have detected the cable trouble earlier and taken steps to have it corrected.

Sarnoff was loaded for bear. Sitting at the head of the big conference table, he referred to his mortification at having wrested Lloyd George from the Telephone Company and, on top of that, extorting high-quality lines from them, and then having the job botched by his own technical people. Why?

At first everyone felt obliged to defend the past decisions and actions of his own department. I was silent. Failing to get a clear-cut answer,

Sarnoff's fury rose. At one point he said to the assistant chief engineer, an august personage two levels above me in the hierarchy, "If the engineer-in-charge isn't competent, he shouldn't be the engineer-in-charge."

I was past quaking at that. What was most to be feared was not the loss of the job, not even the setback of a career, but Sarnoff's contempt. Finally there was an opening, and I began to speak. Desperation made me suddenly fluent. I could hardly believe it was myself I heard talking. I looked at Sarnoff and around the table, and back at Sarnoff. It was the only occasion, before or since, on which people have hung on my words. I ended with the assurance that with what we now knew and remedial measures already under way, it could not happen again.

"*That* was a good speech," Sarnoff said, and ended the conference. He knew what he needed to know. He was not vindictive, only efficient. Had there been a recurrence, heads would have rolled, but we had learned our lesson.

Another debacle was on the program end, but in this case no one was at fault, in RCA at least. Queen Marie of Romania was visiting the United States on a mission by now as familiar to the American taxpayer as the rising and setting of the sun—to raise money for her ailing country on behalf of her royal offspring. After delicate negotiations, an agreement was reached that the queen would address the American people over WJZ at 8:30 P.M. the following day. The city was hysterical with expectancy: the visit of the queen mother crowded most other news off the front pages. Within the station, the royal charisma reached even higher intensity. The station was a bower of flowers. All the staff—male and female—wore evening dress. Sarnoff, if I remember, came in white tie and tails. On 42nd Street a detachment of police awaited the arrival of the queen and her entourage.

Her Majesty had been expected a quarter or half hour before she was to go on the air, but there was no sign of her. At 8:15 the staff was getting jumpy and the program manager was on the phone to Her Majesty's hotel. She was told that Her Majesty had departed at 8:00. For WJZ? No one knew.

At 8:30 the studio pianist began playing soothing melodies and continued until 9:00. Sometime in between it became known that Her Majesty was at a banquet of the Iron and Steel Institute at the Commodore Hotel a few blocks away, and had no intention of showing up at WJZ. She had simply not bothered to notify the station. Sarnoff, no doubt chagrined but not showing it, departed. So far as I was concerned, it was a big laugh, but I didn't show that either—at least not while Sarnoff was still around. All it amounted to was that more money was represented by the steel magnates than by RCA.

One evening I spent half an hour with Sarnoff alone in the WJY studio, which was on the air only in the afternoon. He was going on one of his rare vacations, to a nice middle-class resort in the Adirondacks, which would probably not see his like again. The railroad tickets had been picked up for him at Grand Central during the day and I turned them over to him. He said he had been working too hard and was afraid if he did not knock off for a couple of weeks he might get sick and lose more time.

Like everyone else, I marveled at his command of the language. He who at ten had spoken only Yiddish (he still remembered some Hebrew but only because he heard it in the synagogue) now expressed himself in pellucid English sentences, with never the slightest hesitation, as if he were reading from a manuscript. But if you interrupted him with a question or an observation he could not have anticipated, he took off on the altered course with equal fluency.

Waving his hand around the studio, he said, "What do you think of all this? Will it last?"

"I can't imagine anything with the advertising potential of radio proving evanescent," I said. I enlarged on the thought for maybe half a minute while Sarnoff listened intently, although everything I told him must have occurred to him a hundred times before. When I stopped, he asked "What does 'evanescent' mean?"

He could tell from the context, but he wanted to know exactly. He wrote well, too, but his speech was more distinctive than his writing. His sole object in writing was clarity, and that he achieved without fail in dictation and without redrafting.

I had occasional contacts with him through my department, "As the Broadcaster Sees It," in the Doubleday, Page monthly, *Radio Broadcast*, an intelligent slick paper periodical, ably edited first by Arthur Lynch, then by Willis Kingsley Wing, who later became a prominent literary agent, with me as an early—perhaps the first—client. Everything I wrote was censored, first by Dr. Goldsmith as chief broadcast engineer and well versed not only in company policy but in developments of national scope; then by the publicity department, then by the patent department, lest I reveal some technical secret or project an unfavorable image of the corporation. Actually there were few deletions, since by its nature broadcasting was a public activity and I kept my political views out of the column. Sarnoff read it, and now and then wrote me a flattering comment.

Except once. I proposed a system of priorities in the issuance of broadcasting licenses based on the technical quality of transmission and the cultural level of the programs. The piece must have hit a sensitive nerve because it elicited a sharply worded letter from Sarnoff: "I cannot understand," he wrote, "how anyone who makes his living though this industry and, in particular, RCA, can express publicly views at such variance with the interests of the Company."

If he was irritated, so was I. He evidently didn't know that what I wrote had already survived a triple censorship: and I couldn't see then (although I can now) how this scheme could damage the company. I suppose Sarnoff preferred to rely on RCA's political drag and his own lobbying to keep RCA at the top, rather than on some visionary scheme subject to unpredictable interpretations. Anyway, I came right back at him. It is a measure of the relative democracy of the 1925 RCA and the authoritarian giant of later years, and the parallel difference between the early and late Sarnoff, that I wrote my rebuttal without the least hesitation, and Sarnoff did not resent it. Nor did the censorship become more stringent afterward.

While such incidents loom large in the consciousness of the subordinate in a company run by a manager of Sarnoff's herculean personality, events of transcendent importance to the whole radio industry, even to other sectors of big business, were unfolding. It seemed RCA had no sooner been launched than it was coming apart at the seams. If anybody could keep it from foundering, it was David Sarnoff.

12

THE LEGAL LABYRINTH

John Dewey said that ours was not a government of laws, as advertised, but of lawyers. If this is true of government, it is all the more valid in connection with corporate struggles for advantage, in which lawyers advise the directors of their rights and risks and what the courts and the Department of Justice will probably let them get away with. Obviously lawyers and judges are indispensable in both government and business, but the legal tangle that resulted when the Telephone Group and the Radio Group fell out was a sore affliction to Sarnoff. What was most frustrating to his orderly mind was that the longer the quarrel lasted, the more confusing it became. The underlying difficulty was the same as in the Armstrong-De Forest litigation: the Supreme Court justices tried to apply the abstract concepts of the law to highly technical matters in which they had no experience, no competence, and none of the feel of things that engineers acquire by an altogether different kind of training and experience. The result in the Telephone-Radio contest was that the same lawyers who had drawn up the contracts between the parties could not agree—even among themselves—on what the language meant and what the rights of the parties were; so contention led only to further contention. Sarnoff, almost single-handedly, finally cut the Gordian knot.

At the beginning all anyone on the outside knew, was that suddenly the Telephone Company disposed of a block of 200,000 shares of RCA on the New York Stock Exchange and the two Telephone directors resigned from the RCA board. This development made me vaguely uneasy, and not without reason. When RCA was put together, I, as an engineer, experienced a pleasant feeling that most of the patent fights had been resolved and that from now on the industry could proceed constructively. Now I had a contrary feeling of insecurity.

There was never any lack of minor, resolvable conflict among the partners in the RCA combine, but this was a far more serious matter, on the scale of a world war as compared to a "brushfire." The Telephone Group and the Radio Group had exchanged licenses under their respective patents, but at a time when their major concern was with international wireless telegraphy. Now that radio broadcasting had come to the fore, their interests clashed, or, more precisely, it was not clear to the top management of either alliance *what* their interests were, and what rights they were bound to protect in situations quite unforeseeable in the present. There was a great deal that even Sarnoff could not envision in the future, but he knew what he had envisioned in the past—radiotelephony as the technical basis of a new industry vying with the older media for public patronage—and he was determined not to yield any of the rights to which, by way of RCA, he felt entitled.

This was also the attitude of Owen D. Young, but it was not his nature to be precipitate. In business he was the equivalent of Henry Clay, the "Great Compromiser" of pre-Civil War politics; accordingly, he first tried to define the respective rights of the parties in the agreement linking General Electric and the Telephone Company, by suggesting as a conciliator Charles Neave of Fish, Richardson & Neave. Although the firm was now retained by RCA, Fish was a former president of AT&T and Neave had been at different times patent counsel for GE and AT&T. Moreover, he had helped draft the original agreement. Better qualifications for healing the breach could hardly have been imagined, but even in these experienced hands the effort failed.

When General Harbord took office as president of RCA he walked right into this hornet's nest. On January 29, 1923, he wrote to Sarnoff:

> I have been over these papers which pertain to the telephone situation carefully by myself, and have also had some discussion of the situation with Mr. A. G. Davis.
>
> Among these papers are some from you. I take it that you are probably more familiar with the situation than anyone else in our immediate organization. If not too much trouble I should like to have you give me: 1. A succinct statement of the matters at issue with the AT&T Company, rated in their importance to the RCA, showing concisely their contention and our contention in each case. 2. The points on which the Radio Corporation of America can afford to

trade or yield. 3. The concessions most desirable to obtain from the AT&T through trading or yielding under the preceding paragraph. 4. The principal damage now being done to our interest by failure to agree or by non-observance of the contract by the AT&T. 5. Your suggested action.

Sarnoff replied on February 6 and, while everything he said was compressed, the wide-ranging differences between the parties necessitated a lengthy treatment. The topics he discussed were the intent of the existing contract; broadcast transmission; broadcast reception; wire line connections; carrier current ("wired wireless");*the foreign field, etc.

Under each subdivision Sarnoff defined the issues and appended recommendations. His final proposals:

> Endeavor to negotiate and trade with the Telephone Company along the lines indicated in this memorandum. . . . Should negotiations fail, arbitrate the dispute. I believe that despite the present ambiguities of the contract, our position is sufficiently clear and meritorious to justify resting our case on the decision of competent and impartial arbitrators. . . . Should negotiations fail and arbitration be declined, file suit against the Telephone Company for violation of the present contract and, pending court decision, carry on as at present.

This is all ancient history and extensive quotation would be pointless, but even the above fragment shows how clearly Sarnoff's mind worked and how Harbord, with a mind fully as resolute and decisive as Sarnoff's, was already beginning to rely on the younger man for facts, figures, background, and policy guidance.

When the RCA-GE-AT&T cross-licensing agreement was concluded in June 1921, except for Sarnoff, neither the principals nor their lawyers foresaw that broadcasting would become big business as big and as fast as turned out to be the case. In itself this is to no one's discredit, but even making allowances for a universal human failing, much of the thinking and terminology that went into the contract was scarcely worthy of the reputably steel-trap minds of the eminent counsel who drafted the documents. For one thing, they apparently did not realize

---

*Wired wireless was an invention of the Chief Signal Officer, Maj. Gen. George O. Squier—a primitive form of what is now distribution of television pictures and sound by coaxial cable instead of over the air.

they were heading for trouble with the antitrust division of the Department of Justice. The original intent of the patent system was to reward the individual inventor who devised a better mousetrap or, to go beyond that ancient cliché, something no more complex than the steam engine of James Watt (British) and Oliver Evans (American, and strangely neglected in his own country). Actually RCA, with AT&T as a partner, had assembled a pool of nearly 2,000 (later 8,000) patents with the intended, though unstated, objective (in which Sarnoff concurred) of giving the owners something close to a monopoly of an entire industry; one, moreover, invested with the public interest. On the other hand, as the owners saw it, patents were pɪ ˌperty—and this accumulation was legitimate in that it had the potential of ridding the industry of the incubus of litigation.

Third parties had still another view. When the broadcasting boom got under way, thousands of amateurs began assembling receiving sets for friends and relatives, and from such small beginnings several hundred went into the business of manufacturing and selling. Most fell by the wayside, but the survivors were to be reckoned with. Herbert Hoover, then Secretary of Commerce, wrote in *Radio Broadcast* that the boom had been created by "the genius of the American boy." This rather transcended the limits of nonsense traditionally allowed to cabinet members, and certainly was not the way Sarnoff saw it. The patents RCA had contributed to the RCA-Telephone pool, the research leading up to the inside patents, and the money invested in those that had been bought from outside, seemed to him more instrumental in creating the boom than the genius of interlopers—whether boys or men. And, in fact, among these latecomers there were some businessmen not quite as hardheaded and forehanded as Sarnoff himself, but pretty close.

The prophet scorned can be forgiven for a certain rancor. Because the Marconi management had been so shortsighted and General Electric not overeager, RCA did not get into the business of marketing receiving sets until 1922. Its sales in that year were $11 million. On that the factory was entitled to show a profit, followed by profit margin for RCA, then the distributor, then the retailer—$11 million out of a total industrywide business in sets and parts of $60 million! Sarnoff wanted more, if not all, of the $49 million escaping RCA. He was even more exercised when, in 1923, RCA's sales were only $22.5 million out of $136 million. True, $22.5 million was a bonanza compared to RCA's wireless telegraph business, but Sarnoff was not a man to be satisfied with a mere 16.5 percent share of the total business of the industry, especially when he felt he had the law on his side. He was, to be sure, willing to grant licenses to a limited number of competitors, but on terms that at first were grossly exorbitant. Sarnoff could argue that RCA should rightfully strive to recover its investment as soon as possible, but that was one of his mistakes, a mistake whose consequences would prove serious.

The Telephone Company's position was different. It already had a safe, profitable business, with the largest capitalization of any American corporation. It was not manufacturing broadcast receivers, but under its interpretation of the contract it might engage in such manufacture through its subsidiary, Western Electric. Sarnoff was well aware of this sword of Damocles. RCA, though growing, was still small compared with the AT&T colossus. Given the ambiguity of the contract, the Telephone interests *could* claim the same right to manufacture broadcast receivers for the mass audience that the Radio Group claimed, and was exercising. At the beginning of 1924 RCA sales were running at the rate of $50 million a year. Total industry sales were $358 million, and still on the rise. In the currency of the 1920s, that market was no small prize—General Electric's gross income was about $270 million a year.

Sarnoff's memo to Harbord had brought the RCA-Telephone hostilities into sharp focus and a letter Harbord wrote to Young a week later contained a paragraph indicating that he was more than a little exercised:

> The present state of affairs is that the Telephone Company is each day getting more aggressive and is consolidating its position in violation of our rights as I see them to such an extent that every day of delay will make it more difficult for them to accept any compromise which we suggest. The need for expedition is therefore apparent.

Much of the argument between the officials and lawyers of the contending parties centered on the meaning of "amateur." Since about 1906 wireless amateurs had been a special caste of young men (indeed, many were boys) who assembled their own transmitters and receivers for telegraphic code communication among themselves and for listening to commercial and naval stations. By 1921 they numbered thousands. Some, holding commercial operator's licenses and highly proficient in radio technology, were scarcely distinguishable from professional radio operators and engineers. Obviously this was not the audience Sarnoff had in mind in his 1916 memo when he proposed to make radio a "household utility," which in fact it had now become. But equally obviously the broadcast listeners, "BCLs" as they were called in the newspaper radio sections who were now crowding the counters of radio stores four-deep, were amateurs only in the dictionary sense of one who pursues an art without intent to profit by it commercially. By this time many were wiring up their own receivers and sitting up nights to hear distant stations ("Dx" in the jargon of the boom) but whether they bought factory-built sets or assembled their own, their sole objective was plucking music or speech out of the air or, among the more advanced, hearing and identifying distant stations. "I heard Denver last night," one commuter might say to another, who had got only as far as Chicago but the following night hoped to make it to Salt Lake City.

The mischief that neglect of Sarnoff's prescience had brought about was now fully apparent. If his "radio music box" idea had been implemented during the five years between 1916 and the onset of the radio boom, there could have been no mistaking the intent and meaning of the 1921 agreement between the Radio and Telephone groups. At the very least, the contract would have taken a less ambiguous form. But as the situation developed in the absence of recognition of Sarnoff's vision, the contract gave RCA only the right to sell to "amateurs." Nothing in the wording referred to broadcast listeners, since "broadcasting" had not yet been assimilated into radio usage. Thus the RCA lawyers were driven to the farfetched argument that as soon as a broadcast listener touched the knob of a broadcast receiver he became ipso facto an amateur, even though he usually hadn't the faintest idea of what turning the knob did inside the set—only that it brought in music.

Aside from the legal aspects, the rivalry between WJZ and WEAF was not a pointless contest. On our end it was important to Sarnoff—while we were competing with the Telephone Company on the program and engineering end, he was competing on the corporate level and WJZ was one of his tools or, more accurately, one of his weapons. It was vital to him that WJZ should put on a good show, so that even if our technology was not quite on a par with the Telephone Company's, it would be close enough so that they would realize they had formidable competition. Above all, it was vital for RCA to have a licensed broadcasting station in the largest American city, with what amounted to a federal franchise on the air.

By 1924 or 1925 it was becoming obvious, however, that Sarnoff had scored only a Pyrrhic victory in taking WJZ away from Westinghouse and moving it to midtown Manhattan. With our 500-watt transmitter on the Aeolian Hall roof, we thundered in on receivers within a radius of a fraction of a mile, drowning out WEAF and lesser stations—but we laid down a barely audible signal, or none at all, in sections of upper Manhattan and the Bronx. The studios obviously had to be in the central city, but the transmitter belonged out in the suburbs, with much higher power than a half-kilowatt (500 watts). By that time KDKA was operating outside Pittsburgh with a power of 50,000 watts. On Goldsmith's recommendation, Sarnoff decided to equip WJZ with a transmitter of equal size, to be built by Westinghouse, since they had acquired the know-how through KDKA.

The location chosen was Bound Brook, New Jersey, some 33 miles southwest of the existing Manhattan transmitter location. So, while the legal contest with the Telephone Group was still going on, Sarnoff was not neglecting the technical problems of broadcast transmission. At the same time other groups of engineers in General Electric and Westinghouse, with collaboration from engineers in RCA, were designing improved broadcast receivers. The contest was joined on two or more fronts, between ostensible allies as well as actual enemies.

While the powerful Bound Brook transmitter was being built, I happened to be descending in one of the Woolworth Building elevators when it stopped at a lower floor and Sarnoff and Weagant got on. We nodded and Sarnoff asked me how Bound Brook was coming along. Then; "What will be the total cost?"

I gave him a figure. "What about the wire connection to the studio?" he asked.

"We have a special Western Union line," I said. "It's noise-free and equalized between fifty and five thousand cycles now, and we can improve on that."

"When do you think the transmitter can get on the air?" he asked as the elevator reached the lobby floor.

I gave him an approximate date and we said goodnight. Only then I realized that in half a minute he had got all the information on the project he needed.

When we did start transmitting from Bound Brook, we had a problem similar to the one on 42nd Street transferred, however, to a different location. This time we had a solution. When we were on 42nd Street, between Times Square and Grand Central, our signal was overpowering north and south of 42nd Street on the East Side, one of the city's most elite neighborhoods. The people who lived there were the wrong ones to annoy, and sometimes we annoyed them. One evening WEAF was broadcasting a prizefight, which meant they had practically the entire audience, while we were offering "square" competition —a concert of classical music. I was at the station when a call came in from a Westinghouse vice-president. He lived on Park Avenue in the 40s or 50s and practically ordered me to take WJZ off the air so that he and his guests could listen to McNamee broadcasting the fight. I said I was sorry, but the concert was a scheduled event and, after all, some people actually liked classical music.

That argument didn't work. The Westinghouse man became so abusive that I finally hung up on him and typed out a memo to Sarnoff describing the incident. Sarnoff sent a copy to the Westinghouse vice-president so he could get "a good laugh at himself." I doubted the memo had that effect, but Sarnoff wasn't sorry to put a Westinghouse VP in his place. By that time the only superiors he recognized were Young and Harbord.

As this incident shows, the operating department at WJZ functioned on the borderline between engineering and show business. It was also a microcosm of America in the twenties, with Prohibition the law of the land and more drinking than ever before. There was no drinking on the job among the operators, except possibly when the outside gang, picking up orchestras at hotels and nightclubs, might be offered a snifter. Since it never showed on the air, it was of no concern to me. Once an operator landed a right to the jaw of his teammate just before going on the air, but neither had had a drink. I fired the one who had struck the blow.

The WJZ operating staff comprised about twenty-five men, whose careers in later life ranged all the way from Ray Guy—he rose to the presidency of the Institute of Radio Engineers, the highest honor that could befall an electronics engineer—down to the fate of George W. Rogers, who committed a series of murders and died in the New Jersey State Penitentiary. Though he got into trouble at WJZ, I never had any personal difficulty with him and never suspected that he might be dangerous.

Rogers worked in the penthouse which housed the transmitters at

Aeolian Hall—a burly young man with an odd baby-faced expression. The trouble started with a break-in and the theft of two 50-watt tubes, worth about $300 in all. The New York Police Department detective who investigated was quite sure it was an inside job. I did not take the burglary too seriously because in a way RCA had brought it on itself. Well-heeled amateurs wanted to buy such tubes, and the only reason RCA did not make them available was because of some legal technicality connected with the litigation between it and the Telephone Company. The inevitable consequence was a black market.

At first there was no evidence connecting Rogers with the burglary, but John S. Harley, the RCA security chief, uncovered a criminal record Rogers had accumulated since the age of twelve—theft, assault, sodomy. He was an orphan and in the reform schools to which he was committed he was reported to be a "petty thief, untruthful, a moral pervert, etc." Furthermore, Harley found some connection between Rogers and fences who had sold stolen tubes to amateurs.

This conclusive bit of evidence was obtained by what may have been the first bugging operation—certainly the only one I was ever involved in. The idea was Harley's. Could I, he asked, install a WJZ microphone in the kneehole of his desk, wired to an amplifier and telephone receivers in another room. He would question a pair of suspects (brought in by NYPD detectives with whom RCA had close relations) then excuse himself and listen to their conversation when they thought they were alone together. I made the installation myself, sometime in 1924. So far as I know, it never became known outside of Harley's department.

Harley insisted that Rogers be discharged and my superiors agreed. There seemed to be nothing else to do, but it left a bad taste. Most if not all of Rogers's criminal record was juvenile, and in a way he had rehabilitated himself. As he grew up he showed a talent for chemistry and electrical work and finally qualified as a radio operator. After he was discharged at WJZ he was still well regarded by J. B. Duffy, the superintendent in charge of hiring at the Radio Marine Corporation of America. I had many contacts with Duffy and considered him a good judge of character. So was Harley, but he was a cop, whose business it was to think the worst of people.

After some dubious business ventures, Rogers resumed his career as a marine radio operator. And here the real drama begins. Rogers was the chief operator on the Ward Line cruise ship *Morro Castle* when she burned off Asbury Park in September 1934 with a loss of 134 lives. In *Fire at Sea, the Story of the Morro Castle* (1959) Thomas Gallagher adduces circumstantial evidence tending to show that Rogers was an arsonist and set the ship on fire so that he could pose as a hero of the disaster, the man who sent out the SOS after an unconscionable delay on the bridge and with the radio room almost in flames. A vaudeville agent put him onstage in that role, but Rogers was not a success as an actor.

He retired from the sea and in 1936 joined the police department of Bayonne, New Jersey, in charge of the radio repair room, with the rank of patrolman. In 1938 he tried to kill his superior, Lieutenant Vincent Doyle, by planting a bomb on him. The motive was to get Doyle's job. Though Doyle was severely injured, including the loss of all the fingers of his left hand, he survived. The bombing was definitely pinned on Rogers. The judge called it "a crime of a diabolical nature" and sentenced Rogers to from twelve to twenty years in state prison.

In 1942 Rogers received a conditional parole to enter military service, but neither the army, which at that time included the air force, nor the navy wanted any part of him. He served as radio operator on a freighter. He might have continued as a radio operator after the war, but he was an ingenious young man. He became friendly with William Hummel, a retired printer in Bayonne who set him up in business with a capital of slightly more than $7,500. After a time, Hummel and his spinster daughter wanted to move to Florida, and they needed the money Hummel had lent Rogers. Previously Hummel had believed in Rogers's innocence; now, eighty-three years old, he was afraid of him, not without reason. Shortly afterward, Hummel and his daughter were found bludgeoned to death. The murders were traced to Rogers and a jury convicted him, on strong circumstantial evidence. He was given two concurrent life sentences and sent back to the state penitentiary, where he was interviewed by Thomas Gallagher in connection with *Fire at Sea*. He professed deep religious feelings and avowed his innocence. He died of a stroke in prison in January 1958.

I did not know of his later record but at the time of the *Morro Castle* disaster, I read the newspaper accounts, studied the photographs of Rogers, and concluded that he was probably a psychopathic criminal. I moralized about the enormous range of character among human beings and in particular the contrast between a man like Sarnoff and one like Rogers. Was it all preordained? The two had never met: they lived in separate worlds. Could the early death of his parents have been a factor in Rogers's apparently compulsive behavior? There was a single outstanding difference in their early, probably formative lives. Sarnoff was poorer than Rogers as a child, but he had a good family life; he was loved. It is not implausible that in Rogers, deprived of affection, ambition took a warped, solipsistic turn.

With 50,000 watts at Bound Brook, we were the only station the people over a large part of northern New Jersey and New York across the line could hear. We had to engage a radio service company to install wave traps which, when switched into the antenna circuit, eliminated WJZ. It cost us a few dollars per complainant, but it was obviously necessary. On the other hand, we now had an enormous audience spread over a considerable territory in the northeastern section of the country. As receivers became more selective, what remained of the problem solved itself.

THE GESTATION
OF NBC

One of the great compensations of early broadcasting for RCA was that all of us—engineers and others—were constantly aware we were working for an authentic genius in our field. Except when we really botched things up, as in the Lloyd George disaster, in the engineering department we were not afraid of him—admiration was the predominant emotion. W. A. Swanberg, in *Luce and His Empire,* quotes one of Luce's employees who told Swanberg that no matter how many years you worked for Luce, whenever he sent for you, your palms started to sweat. There was a lot of that in RCA later, but it was good to be young and working for Sarnoff when he was young himself. You never doubted he knew what he was doing, and he transmitted to everybody in the company some of his aggressiveness and clarity of mind. Without consciously teaching, he taught. However you felt about him in later years, you remembered him with the same gratitude as the best instructors you had from elementary school on through college—no small tribute to a man who never got beyond elementary school himself.

As early as 1922, NBC was taking shape in his mind. While the Westinghouse WJZ was still broadcasting from Newark, he wrote to E. W. Rice of GE:

> First, it seems to me that in seeking a solution to the broadcasting problem, we must recognize that the answer must be along national rather than local lines, for the problem is distinctly a national one.
>
> Secondly, I think that the principal elements of broadcasting service are entertainment, information, and education, with emphasis on the first feature—entertainment, although not underestimating the importance of the other two elements. Expressed in other words,

and considered from its broadest aspect, this means that broadcasting represents a job of entertaining, informing, and educating the nation and should, therefore, be distinctly regarded as a public service.

And further:

That this kind of job calls for specialists in the respective fields and that it requires expert knowledge of the public's taste and the manner in which to cater to the public's taste. . . . That manufacturing companies or communication companies are not at present organized and equipped to do this kind of job in a consistent and successful way is to my mind also clear.

If the foregoing premises be correct, it would seem that the two fundamental problems calling for a solution are—1. Who is to pay for broadcasting? 2. Who is to do the broadcasting job?

I think that at the time he wrote this Sarnoff was not indulging in the standard phony idealism of business—a reasonable inference from the fact that he was then considering philanthropy as the answer to the first question. As a whole, the letter clearly foreshadows the broadcasting networks and their contribution to American culture—two faces of the same coin, equally imperfect and their imperfections not to be laid at the door of any one individual.

Some three years after Sarnoff addressed his key questions to Rice, WEAF was cautiously embarking on the answer to the first—and *their* answer was not philanthropic. Using the terms deliberately and on legal advice, it was venturing into "toll broadcasting" by means of "radiotelephony." The Telephone concept was that AT&T and its subsidiaries would make radio telephone facilities available for subscribers who would use them for a metered period of time and pay accordingly, as in conventional long-distance telephony. There wasn't much of an analogy between a point-to-point phone call over a wire line and radio broadcasting; nevertheless, ambiguous though the contract was in other respects, WEAF apparently had the right to broadcast for hire and RCA did not.

The first WEAF income-producing program was by a spokesman for a Jackson Heights housing corporation engaged in promoting the sale of cooperative apartments, where New Yorkers could live a "healthful, unconfined life." The fee was $50 for ten minutes in the late afternoon. This epoch-making event took place at the end of August 1922 and the same sponsor bought several more afternoon talks at $50 and an evening talk at $100. In September, Tidewater Oil and American Express bought evening time, but total revenues for the first two months of toll operation amounted to only $550—compare that to $80,000 for a one-minute commercial on the NBC TV network for World Series day games, $130,000 for night games. Superbowl minutes are priced at $214,000 and the tab for one minute on the movie "The Godfather," broadcast by NBC in two installments, was reportedly $225,000.

Toll broadcasting might have moved faster had it not been for the ban on "direct" advertising AT&T felt obliged to impose. Prices and even product descriptions were sternly barred. About the only benefit for the toll payer, or sponsor, was getting his name on the air. There was already a flourishing Madison Avenue and plenty of potential sponsors who would have patronized the station if it had permitted the huckstering which in time became acceptable to the stations and networks and the majority of listeners, but AT&T moved cautiously. The policy-making officials were Ivy League types who frowned on anything that might be considered offensive.

By present-day standards, they were a prissy lot. In *Commercial Advertising Pioneer—the WEAF Experiment, 1922–1926,* William Peck Banning, formerly an assistant vice-president of AT&T, tells how the first sponsored program on behalf of a toothpaste was held up for several weeks while a radio time salesman and the manager of the station argued fiercely about the propriety of mentioning on the air so delicate a matter as the care of teeth. William Peck Banning contrasts this "squeamishness," and "today's frank references to intimately personal subjects," and suggests that the restraint imposed on WEAF in 1922 would enlist the support of 1946 listeners. He underestimated the tolerance of the American public—even in 1946. Toothpaste intimately personal, indeed! What would he have thought of remedies for the "pain and discomfort of hemorrhoids," graphically described on the air by female vendors in the 1970s?

Late in 1923, having exhausted themselves in futile and time-consuming negotiations, the top officials of the Radio and Telephone groups decided on the course Sarnoff had recommended in February of that year: arbitration. The arbitrator was to be Roland W. Boyden, a Boston lawyer, and his decision was to be binding. As matters turned out, it was not, but in order to make more sense than negotiation, arbitration had to be solemnly declared to be binding. But in January 1924, as preliminary statements were being submitted to Judge Boyden, further complications emerged.

The Federal Trade Commission intervened with an action of its own. It charged all the litigants—AT&T, RCA, GE, Westinghouse, United Fruit and its subsidiaries—with conspiring to restrain competition and create a monopoly in the manufacture, purchase, and sale in interstate commerce of radio devices. The charges took in not only broadcasting but also transoceanic communications. In short, while the parties were fighting among themselves, the government, no longer blinded by "quasi-patriotism," was accusing them of a joint conspiracy to do what no doubt they would have liked to do but had not succeeded in doing in such a fluid field as broadcasting. Here was no case of saints and sinners: the government's intervention was due largely to the lobbying of radio manufacturers whose version of free enterprise was to pay as little as possible for patent rights covering inventions without which they would not have been in business.

I attended several of the arbitration hearings but was not called on to testify since I had been stationed at Chatham and Riverhead while broadcasting was in the incubation stage. My interest was in the hearings as a dramatic spectacle. At one of the sessions I wrote irreverent sketches of the officiating lawyers; one in particular, Frederick P. Fish of Fish, Richardson & Neave, could hardly have been taken for anything but a lawyer of the old school, hence a preradio lawyer. "An old duck. A caricature. If you saw him on the stage you would say he was overdrawn. Wore a black frock coat with baggy striped trousers. The coat was ludicrously loose. Badly tied bow tie. Paunch hanging low. Fat, testy face. While one talks to him, an expression of despair suffuses his face; he turns away with a soundless groan."

The arbitrator I described as "a good-looking, judicial, middle-aged lawyer, courteous and phlegmatic." With these and other dramatis personae, the arbitration dragged on. Judge Boyden's wife died toward the close, and there was further delay. Finally came the decision. It proved that about old Mr. Fish I could not have been more mistaken: it was unsafe to judge lawyers of his school by their looks. The arbitrator found for RCA in almost every particular. RCA was even given rights to collect tolls for broadcasting.

It was a stunning defeat for AT&T. But the giant was still carrying a club. The binding arbitration came unbound. The Telephone Company submitted a succinct opinion by John W. Davis, who had been defeated by a landslide in the 1924 election after Al Smith and William Gibbs McAdoo, the favorite of the anti-Catholic Ku Klux Klan, had killed each other off in the prolonged Democratic convention. But his view was not to be taken lightly—he was one of the country's leading lawyers, an authority on antitrust statutes, and a former U.S. Solicitor General. He contended that if the arbitrator's ruling on the cross-licensing agreement of 1921 was valid, its provisions had been illegal in the first place, since there had been a conspiracy in restraint of trade. Since AT&T had sold its shares in RCA soon after the agreement went into effect and had withdrawn from the RCA board, its hands now were clean; but those of RCA were not. In effect, in order to unbind the binding arbitration, AT&T was lining up with the government against RCA.

The arbitration had been a well-kept secret. All the hearings had been held in the offices of the contending attorneys, and not much had leaked out. In a legal sense, there was nothing to prevent AT&T from raising the curtain on this private litigation, disavowing the arbitrator, and taking the matter into court, or forcing the Radio Group to do so, on the plausible grounds Mr. Davis contrived. AT&T might not gain anything for itself by such a move, but it could cut the RCA patent structure to pieces.

That, however, is not the way big business proceeds—or it would not be big business. There were cogent reasons for AT&T not upsetting the applecart, and for RCA not taking full advantage of the arbitrator's ruling. For one thing, AT&T might also be putting its own patent structure in jeopardy; and actually, if its differences with RCA could be adjusted, the patent pool and its cross-licensing arrangements might be of benefit to both groups. Their quarrel had reached a point where they were playing into the hands of their common enemies; those pirate manufacturers who were averse to paying for license rights, whether for broadcast receivers manufactured by RCA or transmitters manufac-tured by Western Electric. Another deterrent was that a big public utility is always unpopular among its customers—and AT&T was the biggest, and perhaps had the most to lose in the public-relations phase of a knock-down-drag-out fight. Looking at the situation coolly, there was what the elder Morgan called "community of interest" between the contending parties, and consequently no sense in going to extremes.

Sarnoff now came forward with a constructive way out: a solution which he had been meditating since his 1922 letter to Rice. Both AT&T and RCA had been starting to link up broadcasting networks, the former on a large scale, the latter more modestly, since the Radio Group was ill equipped with high-quality long-distance connections.

Sarnoff proposed gathering all stations of these growing networks, which had every prospect of spreading nationwide, into a single broadcasting company which by all indications could be self-supporting, perhaps even highly profitable. The Telephone Company would share in the revenue by hooking up the stations with its high-quality land lines or by microwave radio linkages.

A dominant figure in the Telephone Group at that time was Walter S. Gifford, AT&T vice-president—later president—and on his retirement U.S. ambassador to Britain. Through Edgar H. Felix, the perspicacious WEAF publicity man who knew Sarnoff, Gifford ascertained that Sarnoff was amenable to negotiations. Sarnoff was deputized by Young and the other GE and Westinghouse executives to act for the Radio Group; the Telephone executives chose Edgar S. Bloom, an AT&T vice-president. In less than two weeks these two realists reached substantial agreement, with the approval of their respective superiors. The lawyers and some of the other big shots may have asked themselves—they certainly should have—why didn't we let Sarnoff and his opposite number loose to make a deal along these lines originally, instead of wasting all this time and money fighting each other?

When the pieces were put together, it seemed easy. The new company would buy WEAF. How much was the station worth? Sarnoff and Bloom agreed on a fair value of the physical facilities: $200,000. For goodwill—and WEAF's clear channel, kindly supplied by the government at no charge—the Telephone Company had an asking price of over $2 million. In light of later developments, it was low, but it was bargained down to $800,000: a round million for the whole shebang. Sarnoff covered RCA and himself: if AT&T decided to resume broadcasting, the $800,000 would be refunded. Arrangements were made for the air time of AT&T's Washington station to be taken over by RCA's WRC.

AT&T never did resume broadcasting; there was no reason for it to get into that maelstrom again. Simultaneously, it got rid of a formidable number of interests who wanted to construct their own transmitting stations and were at loggerheads with AT&T on their right to do so or, what made much more sense, to buy Western Electric transmitters. As for future revenue, with a beginning chain of fifteen stations and a reasonable charge for wire facilities, in the first year AT&T would take in $800,000 and this rental would rise into the millions as the chain grew. AT&T would be getting a nice income from facilities it already had or could readily add to, and it would be operating without risk in its own field.

By this time, Sarnoff had quietly abandoned his softheaded notion that broadcasting might be supported by philanthropists. Everybody now knew the only way of making the new company viable was to sell time for advertising—and not to keep too tight a rein on the advertisers at that.

Earlier, Sarnoff had been influenced by Herbert Hoover, who declared that turning the public's airwaves over to the advertising agencies was "unthinkable." It proved to be thinkable after all and, besides, Hoover had not put up the money for RCA or NBC. However, it was unwise to be blunt about such conflicts between the virtuous and the practical; and shortly after NBC was incorporated, it recruited an advisory council to consider this and other delicate ethical questions. The members included John W. Davis; William Green, head of the American Federation of Labor; Charles Evans Hughes, former secretary of state and future chief justice of the United States; Dwight W. Morrow, a partner in J. P. Morgan and Company, later to be father-in-law of Charles A. Lindbergh; Julius Rosenwald, the Sears Roebuck magnate and philanthropist; Elihu Root, secretary of war and secretary of state under President McKinley; and other eminences, including, though only briefly, radical educator Robert M. Hutchins.

This collection of celebrities—somewhat held in check, when necessary, by General Harbord; Guy E. Tripp, Westinghouse chairman of the board; and Owen D. Young, by that time General Electric's chairman—had no apparent influence on the conduct of NBC's business. They met a few times, talked, and were heard of no more. Some years later Robert W. Sarnoff, by that time a high executive of NBC and heir apparent at RCA, confessed to a congressional committee he had never even *heard* of the NBC Advisory Council.

If anything was needed to ensure that NBC would pursue the almighty dollar, unimpeded by advisory councils or preachments, it was the election of officers for the company. Merlin H. Aylesworth came to the presidency from the National Electric Light Association, the propaganda arm of the privately owned utilities. While he was director of NELA he pictured public power as a Communist threat to the nation, smuggled private utility propaganda into children's textbooks, put compliant professors and teachers on the NELA payroll, and by every conceivable means undermined public power projects and delayed the advent of the Tennessee Valley Authority. (So did Herbert Hoover, but he was more scrupulous in his methods.) Aylesworth left the NELA in such a public-relations shambles that its name had to be changed to the Edison Electric Institute.

By the business standards of the time, nevertheless, Aylesworth vindicated Young's confidence in him and Sarnoff's acquiescence in the appointment. He did a good job at NBC and was shabbily treated when the company grew fat and prosperous. Personally he was one of the most likable men I came across in business—casual, energetic, astute, and witty.

The vice-president was George F. McClelland, who had been a time salesman at WEAF. He came there from a job as secretary of the Association of National Advertisers—that, more than special success in selling, raised him a notch or two above the other time salesmen. Popenoe, as noted, lost out. The show business bug had bitten him and, now that he was no longer connected with the glamorous side of broadcasting—McClelland dominated programming—he was jealous and unhappy. But at least he died a natural death—McClelland finally shot himself.

NBC wound up with two networks, the senior "Red," with WEAF as the key station; and the "Blue," headed by WJZ. The names came from the colors of the crayons Dr. Goldsmith used in designating the stations and connecting lines on maps of the United States. For a time there was also an unconnected NBC "Orange" network on the West Coast, but soon this was hooked up with "Red" and "Blue," and the two systems were truly nationwide.

In 1927, despite the grim lesson of human experience, the days of wine and roses seemed long. The expanding NBC moved from 195 Broadway and Aeolian Hall to new quarters at 711 Fifth Avenue, in a building that bore its name. It was across 55th Street from the St. Regis and diagonally across from the Gotham, two of New York's most elegant hotels. NBC occupied a major part of the floor space of the 711 building, which was one of the first in the city to be centrally air-conditioned. The studios and control facilities were the last word in technology; yet within six years the company had to move to even grander facilities in Radio City.

THE CONQUEST OF HOLLYWOOD

No form of communication was safe from the innovative drive of electronics. The same vacuum tubes, microphones, loudspeakers that were used in broadcast transmission and reception could be used to bring sound to silent pictures and vast acoustic improvement to the phonograph. The only ones who failed to see the handwriting on the wall were the movie and phonograph magnates.

The Telephone and Radio groups were more alert. Even while making peace in broadcasting, they were preparing for war in the movies through a Western Electric subsidiary, Electrical Research Products, Inc. (ERPI) and RCA Photophone. The movie magnates could have switched to sound through their own efforts, by enticing engineers away from Western Electric, RCA, and allied companies and establishing their own research departments. But this would have called for imaginative top management—and there were no Sarnoffs among them. An equally insurmountable handicap was that silent pictures, with a weekly attendance of 60 million in more than 20,000 U.S. theaters, were making money, and lots of it. Why experiment?

Not by accident, the first converts to sound were the brothers Warner. Sam, the oldest, was the most daring, but he died before the culmination of his efforts. The brothers had started out with a traveling movie show, not even a storefront nickelodeon. Later they got into production. When sound became practicable, it is said they were overextended; if so, that was one reason for their willingness to take a chance on a new medium, while big companies like Paramount and Metro-Goldwyn-Mayer showed no interest. Not until 1926, when Warner Brothers produced *The Jazz Singer* at a cost of $100,000 and grossed millions on it, and when a bad sound picture was more successful at the box office than a good silent picture, did they change their minds.

There were two basic ways of adding sound to picture: mechanical and electronic. The former was obvious: synchronize a phonograph feeding a loud speaker with the picture film. Or one could record sound on film and run the picture and sound films synchronously; later room was made on the picture film for a sound "track," so that only a single film was necessary. There were two methods of recording on film: ERPI used variable density, loudness of reproduction depending on shades of gray between black and transparent; Photophone used variable areas of blackness. Either could produce good sound.

As usual, De Forest was involved and, as usual, financially unsuccessful. He started with the synchronized phonograph, as did Western Electric; although with much superior sound, as one would expect. In 1925 De Forest switched to a system of sound-on-film which he called "Phonofilm," but he did not succeed in selling it to the movie producers. The early Warner Brothers sound was taken off Western Electric discs. Photophone, starting with sound developed by General Electric from Hoxie's wireless telegraph recorder, was committed to sound-on-film from the beginning.

Again, as in broadcasting, Sarnoff took an undeserved shellacking at the start. The major producers all signed up with ERPI, and Sarnoff had to establish his own movie producing and theater company to get a foothold in the field—something that took time and entailed a temporary partnership with the predatory Joseph P. Kennedy. Photophone played the same role as WJZ in broadcasting, except that it was all on a larger scale, including the difficulties and failures—and expenses. Among other differences was the fact that Sarnoff was now a top figure as president of Photophone. Elmer E. Bucher was executive vice-president; Dr. Goldsmith, vice-president in charge of engineering. As chief engineer, I reported to Dr. Goldsmith.

From an engineering standpoint—and every other standpoint, for that matter—Photophone was an example of what a technology-based corporation should not be like. It took full-page ads in leading newspapers proclaiming its advent and great intentions; but since the big producers were already sewed up by ERPI, only also-rans could be influenced by these come-ons. Not only that, but the company was inadequately supervised, in that Sarnoff could not devote any such proportion of his time to it as he had to Popenoe at WJZ a few years before. Moreover, it was as weak within as in the external circumstances of its operations. Bucher was a brash, verbally brilliant former editor of *Wireless Age* and a former sales manager of RCA with a record of antagonizing almost every interest he dealt with, whether outside the company or within. In his favor was boundless energy and managerial drive, both too often misapplied. He had known Sarnoff since 1913 and was one of the small group—outside of fellow wireless operators—who were privileged to call him "Dave," or at least "David." Sarnoff wanted to give Bucher a chance to prove himself as an executive—in a situation where there was little to be lost.

The idea was sound in itself, but, like many good ideas, it didn't work out, even within the company. I knew Dr. Goldsmith as a strong-minded but cooperative engineer-administrator, free from malice and the need to dominate. On the record, I was the same, if in a smaller way: I had never had any serious fights in Marconi, RCA, or NBC. In Photophone, Bucher and Goldsmith were in an interminable wrangle and of course, since I was Goldsmith's man, I, too, was forever in Bucher's bad graces. It seemed that the mailed fist—and no velvet glove either—was his only way of running a company.

Yet this was not the worst of the situation. Photophone did have contractual arrangements with the minor Hollywood studios and, when Joe Kennedy went into action, a new major producer was in the making, and theater chains, both in the United States and abroad, had to have sound or go out of business. But the deal Sarnoff had had to make with the dominating companies in the Radio setup was the same as for manufacture of radio receivers—Westinghouse manufacturing 40 percent, General Electric 60 percent. This division was to be supervised and coordinated by RCA Photophone's engineering department by banging on tables, hypnosis, or whatever means of persuasion could be brought to bear.

None worked. I spent half my time on the road, traveling between New York, Schenectady, and East Pittsburgh (by train—there were no airlines yet, much less company planes) trying to bring order out of chaos, but it just wasn't a workable setup. We were not only fighting ERPI, but Westinghouse was fighting General Electric and vice versa. Since I had no authority over either (nor did Goldsmith, or Bucher) nothing ever really got settled. Sometimes the Doctor would go with me on these trips and impose agreement in principle, but it didn't show up in the equipment that emerged months later, often not only misdesigned but defective in manufacture. It was one of those situations

that only Sarnoff could resolve—necessarily by going outside the immediate setup—but the time for that was not yet.

For example, Westinghouse favored the simpler technique of introducing sound in theaters—mounting a sound "head" between the
picture projector and the pedestal on which the machine rested. General Electric chose to build a picture and sound projector from the
bottom up—the P–2—with improvements such as a forced oil feed for
lubrication of moving parts. Grotesque faults developed, such as oil
squirting out of the machine onto the film—not just on the factory test
floor but when it was projecting a picture in a theater. When that was
corrected, something else went wrong.

I went up to a movie house in the Bronx where a specially favored
P–2 had been installed. Everything seemed to be running fine. The
projectionist said there had been no breakdown that day. I sat in the
audience to appraise the sound quality. It was satisfactory. I was just
about to leave when suddenly the screen went dark and stayed dark.
The audience began to yell. I ran up to the projection room. The
theater manager was right behind me. "Throw the goddamn thing
out!" he shrieked. When he found out I was the chief engineer of
Photophone, I thought he was going to throw a punch at me.

We finally junked the P–2. It was a million-dollar loss, but I don't
believe Sarnoff ever heard about it. If he did, he took no action—just
added it to his mental file for future use against General Electric.

One thing could be said for Photophone—it was educational for engineers, who could learn what distinguished a successful organization
from one bound to fail. This came at high expense for RCA, apart from
the wear and tear on the personnel. However, we were also learning
something about movie production, which was to pay off later. Bucher
succeeded in selling Sarnoff on the idea that Photophone must have
a studio of its own. A stable on East 28th Street off Lexington Avenue,
which had been used for auctioning riding horses, was converted into
"Gramercy Studios," the name being derived from nearby Gramercy
Park. It had a rotunda a block long and three stories high and, after
acoustic treatment, two-reelers were made there with Photophone recording equipment. Bucher soon fancied himself a movie magnate and
was constantly trying to get Sarnoff to finance "shorts" producers who
came to him with ideas. Sarnoff wouldn't give him a cent. Bucher
would call him up at half-past five or six—maybe he thought Sarnoff
might be tired and acquiescent by then—but all these conversations

ran the same way. Bucher would outline his project. After a brief silence on our end, Bucher would interject, "But, David . . ." which was as far as he ever got. Finally he would hang up disconsolately.

Rallying, he would telephone Dr. Goldsmith at his home. The Doctor came in early and left relatively early; Bucher came in late and stayed late. Bucher made a practice of calling Goldsmith during the dinner hour. "Doctor, this thing is all botched up!" he would exclaim, and demand Goldsmith's presence without delay. He had as much chance of getting it as he had of getting production money from Sarnoff.

In a different way, ERPI's invasion of the picture business was equally bizarre. Its victory over Photophone entailed circumstances so implausible that, if a writer incorporated them in a novel about big business, the critics would tear him to pieces. As early as 1922, Western Electric had developed a photographic sound recorder and to stimulate interest in such a device for educational purposes a prominent telephone engineer, E. B. Craft, gave a demonstration at Yale University. Further independent laboratory demonstrations by Western Electric and General Electric followed. In the period 1923–1926, the voices of the noted stage actress Maude Adams, movie actress Mabel Boardman, General Pershing, and General Harbord were recorded. In 1924 Western Electric demonstrated its sound-on-disc system to leading motion picture people, who showed scant interest in it.

Western Electric and its associates in the Telephone Group were not threadbare pioneers like De Forest. Given a modicum of confidence and foresight, they could have afforded to sit back and wait. What actually happened was that an alert promoter named Walter Rich was sufficiently impressed to conjecture that the Western Electric recording system might at least displace the piano, pipe organ, or pit orchestra which invariably accompanied silent-film showings. By contract dated May 27, 1925, Rich secured from Western Electric *exclusive* exploitation rights to their system for a trial period of nine months, during which Western Electric would endeavor to further improve technical performance and Rich would try to sign up customers.

Within a month, Rich concluded an agreement with Warner Brothers, the latter securing a 50 percent interest in Rich's exclusive contract. In April 1926, Rich and Warner Brothers organized the Vitaphone Corporation which, in Bucher's words, "was to become licensor to the industry for the Western Electric system." *Don Juan,* starring

John Barrymore, premiered in New York with a synchronized musical score on August 6, 1926. *The Jazz Singer* followed. With Warner Brothers all-talking *Lights of New York* (1928), the die was cast. The heads of the major studios *had* to reconsider.

Presenting a rare united front, the studio heads concluded a standstill agreement among themselves and sent to New York Roy J. Pomeroy, a Paramount expert on process photography, and two other representatives to survey the situation. An adaptable technician, Pomeroy was by this time well versed in the intricacies of sound. His committee decided in favor of ERPI, and they were right. ERPI was ready, RCA was not; or, perhaps more accurately, ERPI was less unready than General Electric.

J. E. Otterson, commercial manager of Western Electric, on his promotion to the presidency of ERPI, saw that farming out exclusive rights to Vitaphone had been a regrettable error. After the formation of ERPI, he persuaded Vitaphone to restore its commercial talking-picture rights to ERPI, retaining for itself only a nonexclusive license. Rich was reportedly reimbursed with $1 million for his interest in Vitaphone.

The rivalry between the Radio and Telephone groups redounded in motion pictures to the disadvantage of both. General Electric's C. W. Stone, who had been delegated as special assistant to Sarnoff to get RCA Photophone under way, had contemplated securing from the major studios an agreement under which Photophone would participate in the income from each licensed picture; so when a studio struck it rich, Photophone and RCA would benefit proportionately. But Otterson, eager to sign up the majors, acquiesced in their proposal to pay a royalty fee of $1,000 per negative reel. If the picture was eight reels long, the most ERPI could realize was $8,000 on a picture whose negative cost might be a million or more and which might gross tens of millions. Of course, if a picture lost money, ERPI or RCA would still get its royalty of a few thousand dollars, but that was no bonanza in an industry which flourished on bonanzas.

Next to Warner Brothers, William Fox of Twentieth Century-Fox was the most enterprising of the movie moguls in the realm of sound. RCA Photophone was not incorporated until March 1928, but more than a year earlier General Electric had provided sound, on separate film, for the Paramount picture *Wings*, released in 1927. In the meantime, William Fox had acquired rights in a system developed by Theodore

W. Case, a former associate of De Forest's. Fox wanted to combine the Case system with General Electric's system and reached an agreement in principle with Owen D. Young while Sarnoff was in Europe. When he returned, Sarnoff advised against concluding the agreement. He argued that the Case system added nothing of consequence to what GE already had and which Sarnoff was in line to acquire through Photophone against the opposition of some highly placed GE executives, who wanted to keep RCA in the subordinate position of a mere sales agency. As had become usual by that time, Sarnoff prevailed, with RCA buying into Photophone with a 60 percent interest.

Fox tried to persuade Sarnoff to change his mind at a private lunch in the New York Fox Films headquarters on Tenth Avenue. He wanted to deal with Sarnoff on a personal basis, rather than as a representative of RCA. This account is plausible in that Fox was later proved to have bribed a federal judge who was sent to jail, but Fox escaped prison on grounds of ill health.

A thoroughly one-sided and misleading account of Fox's troubles with ERPI is provided in *Upton Sinclair Presents William Fox.* Upton Sinclair was an admirable political figure, but Fox pulled the wool over his eyes. Sarnoff was more than a match for Fox and would have been more than a match for the other film magnates if, at the crucial time, he had not been encumbered with General Electric and Westinghouse as his associates and AT&T as his opposition. But he still held a trump card.

Standing at the Grand Central Oyster Bar one afternoon in October 1928, Sarnoff and Joseph P. Kennedy jointly created Radio-Keith-Orpheum, an $80-million holding company with RKO Studios as its film-producing subsidiary, and several hundred theaters in need of sound—Photophone sound, naturally, after the bugs had been taken out of it. Sarnoff and Kennedy had been conferring all morning and they needed some light nourishment to complete the job of organization.

The sequence of events preceding the nativity of RKO and the accompanying strategy were alike characteristic of Sarnoff. Gramercy Studios—no more than a rental stage and a showcase for Photophone recording, made some brilliant shorts and one of the directors, Mark Sandrich, became a leading musical comedy director in Hollywood. Yet Sarnoff never gave Bucher any rein as a producer, and apparently Bucher never had an encompassing idea of what Sarnoff was up to in the movie field. As a producer, Bucher would have been small time; like the rest of us in Photophone, he was only learning, and Sarnoff was not wasting his time on neophytes. He was planning to force his way into the ranks of the major Hollywood studios. Kennedy had already made profitable progress in that direction; consequently he was a fit ally.

They met through Louis E. Kirstein, the department store magnate (Filene's in Boston, Bloomingdale's in New York). Kirstein was also helpful in the negotiations that followed; for a time he served as a director of RKO, but movies were not one of his primary interests. He was a useful intermediary when one was required: Kennedy and Sarnoff came from disparate backgrounds and were different personality types, while Sarnoff and Kirstein had both experienced poverty in early life and acquired power, wealth, and culture despite lack of formal education—or perhaps in some ways because of that very deficiency. In the usual pattern in the next generation, this was reversed; all the Sarnoff and Kirstein sons earned degrees at Harvard and Kirstein père received an honorary degree there, but he was not a collector of commencement baubles like Sarnoff. Another disparity was in politics. Kirstein was a friend of Franklin D. Roosevelt, hence to the left of Sarnoff, and still farther to the left of Kennedy.

Kennedy was not a movie producer himself; he used producers and directors as Sarnoff used engineers. The ultimate criterion at the decision-and-risk-taking level Sarnoff had now reached was accumulation of capital. Capital was power to control the future, insofar as the future *could* be controlled; for an entrepreneur like Sarnoff, it was a primary consideration. By that measure Kennedy had shown his mettle; consequently Sarnoff needed him.

Not that money, and more money, and still more was Sarnoff's personal objective. If it had been, he could have hooked up with William Fox, and it is possible that in consequence of such a partnership, the development of talking movies might have taken another turn and Fox would not have found it necessary to pass a bundle of cash, folded into a newspaper, to a federal judge in a building lobby.

Or Sarnoff could have gone into the clothing trades. For a few weeks, in one of the periods of frustration with radio amid the Gentiles, he considered that—but not for long. Radio was where he belonged, and in radio he remained. Just the same, in order to become a potent factor in the movies Sarnoff, the creative man in the role of director of technology, at that point needed Kennedy, the supersuccessful money man.

In *The Founding Father, the Story of Joseph P. Kennedy,* Richard J. Whalen quotes Kennedy in 1926: "Look at that bunch of pants pressers in Hollywood making themselves millionaires. I could take the whole business away from them." That was stretching Kennedy ebullience rather far, but in that year Kennedy gained control of Film Booking Office, a misnamed $7-million Hollywood film-producing company owned by British interests caught in a credit squeeze. FBO made mostly low-budget Westerns and melodramas—"second features"—at the rate of fifty a year, rising later to seventy-five. On the basis of his investment, Kennedy could make money on pictures aimed at this artistically humble box-office target. All he was interested in was the balance sheet.

FBO also had a modest roster of stars—Richard Talmadge and Evelyn Brent, and a trio of big box-office boot-and-saddle attractions: Tom Mix, Bob Custer, Fred Thomson, and his equally famous horse Silver King. The gridiron hero Red Grange was also under contract for a time. Thomson's income was of the same order of magnitude as Mary Pickford's, whose take was $10,000 a week plus half the profits of her pictures. Adolph Zukor groaned, "I don't have to diet, Mary dear. Every time you come to my office, I lose ten pounds." But he paid.

Kennedy was equally shrewd. He did not mind paying his star attractions big salaries, but when it came to the lower echelons, he was an accomplished cost-cutter. He added Pathé, like FBO in between the majors and the minors, to his string, and Keith-Albee-Orpheum, a vaudeville theater chain which was being ruined by radio and talkies. Kennedy noted that ordinary accountants, who in most industries earned between $5,000 and $10,000 a year, rated as much as $20,000 in the movie studios. They were riding piggyback on the star actors and directors, and Kennedy couldn't see why these and similar functionaries should be allowed such largess. He changed most of that, with the result that Pathé's weekly overhead dropped from $110,000 to $80,000 —a tidy saving, part of which accrued to Kennedy.

He often acquired companies at a fraction of book value, using other people's money as well as his own. The FBO takeover was managed by a syndicate consisting of Kennedy; Frederick H. Prince, the railroad financier; Guy Currier, a Boston lawyer whom President Taft once considered appointing to the Supreme Court; and Kirstein. The Sarnoff-Kennedy introduction by Kirstein resulted in RCA's investing

$500,000 in FBO, for a start. Later Sarnoff acquired an option for control of FBO.

To get control of Keith-Albee-Orpheum, Kennedy and a Wall Street syndicate paid $4,200,000 for 200,000 shares. Albee remained as president for a few months with Kennedy as chairman, until Kennedy told him, "You're all washed up," and summarily ousted him. The stock which Albee had sold at $21 a share went up to $50, presumably in anticipation of the formation of Radio-Keith-Orpheum.

While engaged in the operations leading up to the entrance of RCA into the picture business, Kennedy was not starving himself. He drew down $2,000 a week from FBO, another $2,000 from KAO, and still another $2,000 from Pathé. At $6,000 a week he was making far more in salaries than Sarnoff; consequently, by the biblical rule that to him that hath shall be given, he felt he was deserving of still more. This was arranged through stock options, enabling Kennedy to speculate with little or no risk. A momentary quivering, like a minor California earthquake, would send the market down; then it would rise again.

Kennedy got out near the top in 1929. According to the perhaps apocryphal story, a bootblack who did not know who he was, while shining his shoes, accurately forecast how certain stocks would perform that day. Kennedy mulled this over and decided that either something was wrong with himself, who was unable to predict the market as precisely as the shoeshine boy, or something was wrong with the market. He acted on the latter hypothesis and sold his holdings, with great benefit to his further enrichment through liquor, the Merchandise Mart in Chicago, and other successful ventures. From his movie experience alone, he may have realized as much as $5 million; and when the stock market crashed, he allied himself with the bears and is reported to have made another fortune in short selling.

SARNOFF AND KENNEDY

The business and personal relationship between Kennedy and Sarnoff, the influence of their respective forebears, the circumstances under which they grew up, their political views and actions, and the immense disparity in the fortunes they accumulated are all conducive to an understanding of David Sarnoff's life and character. The two were roughly of an age—Kennedy was the senior by three years. Academically Kennedy got off to an incomparably better start: Boston Latin School and Harvard. A few years after graduation, he was ensconced in a Boston office with "Joseph P. Kennedy, Banker," emblazoned on the door. When, later, he invaded the movies, Marcus Loew exclaimed in wonder, "But he's not a furrier!" Nor a junk dealer, like Louis B. Mayer. Only Jesse Lasky came from show business: vaudeville.

While we are on that well-worn topic, let me try to dissipate the notion that the early Jewish movie magnates were a bunch of clowns. They were shrewd and resourceful, and Lasky, for one, was a cultivated man. He had only a secondary-school education, but he made the most of it, as Sarnoff did with only primary school. Mayer was the one who came closest to the stereotype, but he was not merely a junk dealer who had made it in the movies and commanded the largest income of any American during the Depression years. He was no Sarnoff, but anyone who thought he was a fool made a serious and usually costly error. As for Sam Goldwyn, anyone who reads Garson Kanin, who knew him intimately, must acknowledge that his malapropisms, when not concocted by press agents, made at least as much sense as the correct forms.

In this milieu—in any milieu—Kennedy was perfectly at home. He could even capitalize on the fact that he had *not* been a furrier. His Harvard degree enabled him to organize a series of lectures at the university on the movie industry, with some of the studio heads and their New York counterparts as the speakers. Marcus Loew expressed his gratification at speaking at Harvard—an honor he had never expected to come his way.

If there was a bit of patronization implicit in this project of Kennedy's, it was something that could never have been inflicted on Sarnoff. Kennedy and Sarnoff were both proud to the point of vainglory: they were saved only in that their pride impelled them to formidable achievements. Sarnoff came to Hollywood only once or twice during my eight-year tenure there. He addressed a glittering motion picture audience, and I gathered that he impressed Hollywood more than Hollywood him.

In one respect—not unimportant—Sarnoff and Kennedy were alike: both began as outsiders, one poor, one well-off, and however they may have scorned the mediocrities among the insiders, they were galled by the necessity of forcing people to accept them who were so obviously their inferiors in everything else. But there are numerous ways of being outside—Sarnoff's was abysmal, while Kennedy's father, a saloon-keeper, was also a political power in Irish Boston, a ward boss and state senator. Young Kennedy married the daughter of "Honey Fitz"— Mayor John F. Fitzgerald. The sense in which Joseph P. Kennedy was an outsider is illustrated by an anecdote of Richard Whalen's:

> "You have plenty of Irish depositors," Mayor Fitzgerald remarked to a Boston bank president, apparently a New England WASP type. "Why don't you have some Irishmen on your board of directors?" "Well," the banker replied, "a couple of the tellers are Irish." "Yes," rejoined the Mayor. "And I suppose the charwomen are, too."

In some circles Sarnoff remained an outsider all his life and it will not surprise anyone who knows the stratifications of U.S. Jewish society to learn that the scornful insiders included Jews. Stephen Birmingham relates in *Our Crowd* that when in 1950 Robert W. Sarnoff, David's eldest son, married Felicia Warburg, one member of the "crowd" felt called on to explain that the bridegroom was the son of "that Russian radio man," Brigadier General David Sarnoff, chairman of the board of RCA.

Kennedy was more a family man than Sarnoff, not only in number of offspring, but Kennedy seems to have found more time to devote to his nine children than Sarnoff to his three. Both, however, seem to have been acutely worried, at times, about the future welfare of their families; and the nature of that worry, and the way in which each expressed it, reveals something of the psychology of the rich and powerful in times of stress. In connection with this probably intermittent concern of Sarnoff's, I am indebted to my friend, William H. Offenhauser Jr., for a chance revelation.

Sarnoff had put in an appearance late one afternoon in the thirties for a filmed interview at a small studio Photophone retained on the top floor of 411 Fifth Avenue after the big studio on 28th Street had been liquidated. Offenhauser was one of the engineers in charge of the operation and after the filming he accompanied Sarnoff down in the elevator with another engineer, Bob Fitzgerald, who had been a wireless operator with Sarnoff in the early years. Sarnoff had put in a full day at the office, he had been sweating under the hot lights, and he was and looked tired.

"Dave," Fitzgerald said to the president of RCA, "why do you keep plugging away day and night, now that you've made it?"

"Bob," Sarnoff said, "do you remember how I used to take your watch when you had a date with a girl?"

"Sure I remember," Fitzgerald said.

"I had real poverty staring me in the face in those days," Sarnoff said. "I took your watch because I needed the money. I resolved then"— he looked at Fitzgerald earnestly—"that none of my children would ever know the devastation of such poverty."

His income was $100,000 a year (in Depression dollars!) and he was living accordingly. His sons were headed for Phillips Andover, one of the top prep schools in the country, and for Ivy League universities, where they were satisfied with a "gentleman's C." With all the uncertainties of life, the chance that those three boys would have to undergo anything remotely resembling their father's early hardships was infinitesimal.

But Kennedy, with no history of early poverty, was subject to similar anxieties. Whalen quotes him: "I am not ashamed to record that in those days [during the Depression] I felt and said I would be willing to part with half of what I had if I could be sure of keeping, under law and order, the other half. Then it seemed that I should be able to hold nothing for the protection of my family."

He was willing to submit to a 50 percent capital levy if he could keep the rest of his fortune intact! Whalen, an authentic conservative, comes down on Kennedy for this admission. A part of what he says bears on the contrast between Sarnoff and Kennedy in the buildup of RKO and its subsequent decline, and in a broader sense on the nature of capitalist enterprise:

> [Kennedy's] view of the economy was superficial and self-centered. He was a capitalist, yet one who stood apart from the *system* of finance, production, and distribution (Whalen's emphasis). He had no business, in the ordinary sense, and wanted none. He was adept at manipulating the externals—the price of a stock, the structure of a corporation, yet he had no deep understanding of the inner mechanism of the market economy, the interplay of individual decisions and actions that circulated goods and wealth through society . . ."

Because Kennedy made a lot of money out of his movie activities and the formation of RKO, some observers have concluded that Kennedy played a more important role than Sarnoff in the changeover from silent pictures to sound. Actually—Whalen's comment goes to the heart of the matter—Kennedy manipulated the externals, while Sarnoff succeeded in making a place for RCA Photophone in the movie industry. Sarnoff knew, too, how far Kennedy could be trusted—not very far. When Kennedy made a bid for the presidency of Photophone, Sarnoff promptly countermanded it. That camel was not going to get his head into the RCA tent.

The difference between Sarnoff and Kennedy as businessmen is nowhere more clearly contrasted than in their complementary roles in converting from silent pictures to sound. So far as Kennedy was concerned, we would still be gazing at silent pictures. He resembled the movie pioneers in that respect: they built up a highly profitable industry but one with long intervals of boredom between pictures that said something vital about life, or were comical in an adult fashion. They took D. W. Griffith's innovations and cashed in on them. At a critical juncture, when the industry was in confusion in the transition to sound, Kennedy saw his chance and muscled in. He was ahead of Sarnoff, who had more irons in the fire, more difficulties to surmount and, what with General Electric and Westinghouse still on his flanks, a financial situation so cumbersome that a lesser man would have thrown up the job long before. But Sarnoff neither gave up nor did he ever lose sight of the almost illimitable possibilities of electronics in every sector of communications; in this instance, in adding sound to motion pictures and thereby subordinating to television, with its less sophisticated audience (convinced, moreover, that they were getting their entertainment *free*) the ordinary run of motion pictures.

Five out of six were bound to be ordinary or worse, if only because there wasn't enough writing and directing talent available to make a better showing. That time might come, but it did not need to be reckoned with in the thirties and forties—or even in the seventies. But while Kennedy's eye was always on the money, Sarnoff's was always on innovation. He repeatedly risked financial tribulation, if not bankruptcy, in creative endeavor. About the result there could be argument, but not about the all-powerful urge which preceded the innovation. And that is why the Princeton David Sarnoff Library has been erected to Sarnoff's memory, while Kennedy, though not a nonentity by any means, is good only for books taking him apart.

To these must be added the political successes of Robert F. Kennedy and Edward M. Kennedy, and Joseph P. Kennedy's early support of Franklin D. Roosevelt and his curbing of the more flagrant predatory practices of Wall Street in his service as the first chairman of the Securities and Exchange Commission. But on the minus side, again, were his pro-Nazi attitudes when Roosevelt appointed him ambassador to Britain; these made him so obnoxious that on a visit of Kennedy to Hyde Park he ordered Mrs. Roosevelt to "get that man out of here immediately," although this entailed driving Kennedy around aimlessly for more than an hour until she could leave him at the Poughkeepsie New York Central station to catch a train to New York City.

Sarnoff, in contrast, became an understudy in an international drama. He was called on to play the lead in accordance with the timeworn formula, and did it with success more astonishing than anything that ever happened in the theater. This came about when President Coolidge appointed Owen D. Young to head a commission to revise the Dawes Plan of 1924 for payment of German reparations to the Allies of World War I. Charles G. Dawes (vice-president, 1925–1929) shared the Nobel Peace Prize for concocting a totally unworkable scheme, the product of a persistent postwar delusion—that the Germans could be made to pay for the hideous destruction of the war, since, according to the Treaty of Versailles, they had been the aggressors and, officially, the losers.

The flaw in this argument and the diplomacy based on it was that Field Marshal Paul von Hindenburg had seen to it that the Allied forces had never set foot on German soil, thus fostering the legend that the Wehrmacht had been forced to surrender only because it had been stabbed in the back by Jews, Communists, and other traitors. The German armies were pulled back more or less intact, including antileftist effectives eager to prevent the spread of Bolshevism, which would have been as unwelcome to the semivictorious Allies as to the Junkers, industrialists, and embryonic fascists.

On the other hand, there had to be some pretense of curbing German militarism, or what would have been the sense of four years of bloody fighting? The compromise took the form of the Weimar Republic, which was neither potent enough to survive nor impotent enough to collapse prematurely, before Nazism had organized itself sufficiently to take care of the "Jewish question" and the Communist peril in convenient juxtaposition, and when the French had lost their nerve to such a degree that they did not resist Hitler's 1936 invasion of the Rhineland, while there was still a chance to stop him without a general war.

The delegation Young headed consisted of J. P. Morgan (the son— the elder Morgan had died in 1913); Thomas Lamont, a Morgan partner; Thomas W. Perkins, a leading Boston lawyer; and other prominent Americans, joined later by representatives of Allied nations. The United States had waived German reparations (uncollectible in any case, but as a political necessity Washington still pretended to believe that it could collect from its allies. "They hired the money, didn't they?" as Coolidge put it in his usual oversimplified manner, and with the politician's usual tender solicitude for the oppressed taxpayer.)

By that time Young was sufficiently impressed with Sarnoff's skill in negotiation to take him along. He had seen Sarnoff resolve seemingly insurmountable differences between contesting corporations. International diplomacy was a field in which Sarnoff had no experience, but Young knew that he learned quickly.

The delegation sailed early in February 1929 on the *Aquitania*. Young had a scheme for a new settlement, but it was no more than a basis of discussion. Sarnoff studied the situation on the way over. He had reason to be proud. In contrast to the stinking steerage passage to the United States when he was a boy, here he was a plenipotentiary —if only as yet a secondary one—traveling in luxury with the wealthy and powerful.

The delegation knew with whom they would have to negotiate—Dr.

Hjalmar Schacht, the financier who had made Germany "the most successful fraudulent bankrupt in the history of the world." The American delegation had no one to match him. Schacht dominated the conference. Morgan's yacht was waiting, and he was eager to get on to his annual grouse shooting in Scotland. Young was ill much of the time. Finally, with the consent of the other plenipotentiaries, Young asked Sarnoff to undertake the negotiations. It was Sarnoff and Schacht, like Sarnoff and Bloom at the end of the Telephone-Radio conflict; but there was no constructive solution this time.

Sarnoff and Schacht dined at the best restaurants and became friendly. Among other personal bonds that developed outside of their business discussions, Schacht asked Sarnoff if he spoke Hebrew. Sarnoff acknowledged that he only understood it, whereupon Schacht launched into the opening passages of Genesis in perfect Hebrew—at least perfect enough for Sarnoff. Schacht had taken his doctorate with Hebrew studies at a German University—which did not prevent him from cooperating with Hitler in the murder of six million Jews.

The Sarnoff-Schacht agreement, officially known as the Young Plan, was described by Young in a tribute to Sarnoff, quoted by David Lawrence in an article in the June 14, 1930 *Saturday Evening Post*:

> He was our principal point of contact with Dr. Schacht . . . and he did an extraordinary piece of work in negotiating for us with the Germans. Dr. Schacht had confidence in Sarnoff and believed in him. They worked well together. . . . there came a time when only one man could save the situation, and that arose toward the end with Sarnoff and the German delegation.

In a letter to Sarnoff, Young wrote that "Dr. Schacht has taken the occasion to tell me personally of his gratitude for the assistance you have given to him and to the entire German group." Considering Schacht's character and the fact that the German delegation consisted mostly of incipient Nazis, one might deduce that Sarnoff was taken in by Schacht, who narrowly escaped conviction at the Nuremberg trial after World War II. He was one of the most wily and unscrupulous of German politicians, and it would have been no disgrace to be bested by him. But actually Sarnoff's task was to reach an agreement on almost any terms. If the conference did not end in a battle royal among the delegates, it could be accounted a success of sorts. Even if it had been a triumph of creative statesmanship, with Hitler's ascension to power a few years later and Schacht as his money manager, it would have gone into the wastebasket anyway.

Morgan had promised Sarnoff he would give him anything he asked for if he succeeded in concluding an agreement. Sarnoff asked for a white meerschaum pipe like the one Morgan smoked. These pipes were handmade by a London craftsman who had previously fabricated them for the elder Morgan. An aide was immediately dispatched to London by chartered plane, and Sarnoff received his meerschaum within a few days. (It later came into the possession of Dr. Nathan A. Perilman, senior rabbi of Temple Emanu-El.)

When Sarnoff returned home he was elected to the presidency of RCA, effective January 3, 1930. Two months later Franklin D. Roosevelt was inaugurated. Joseph P. Kennedy would not have been eligible for either office. The principal reason was that people trusted Sarnoff while, as *Fortune* said in September 1937 Kennedy was "fated always to be living down distrust." This widespread feeling about him was voiced by the banker Floyd Odlum, interviewed by Robert A. Wright in *The New York Times,* on January 28, 1973. Odlum related how, before taking over Paramount Pictures, he hired Kennedy as a consultant on the acquisition. But, the story goes on, Mr. Odlum became convinced that "Mr. Kennedy was working in that capacity to take over the company for himself and dismissed him.

" 'Would he like to be remembered as the man who fired Joe Kennedy?'

" 'Yes, I would,' Mr. Odlum replied without a trace of a smile."

THE GREAT RADIO BOOM —AND BUST

RCA common was the bellwether of the frenzied stock market boom of the twenties. Sarnoff has been pictured as a kind of corporate virgin, sternly dedicated to the advancement of radio technology and living on his salary. This is part of the legend that has been built up around his name, partly by Sarnoff himself and partly through the tendency of biographers to make supermen of their subjects, or simply to follow the crowd. The truth is that a man in Sarnoff's position could make money on the side by conniving at rigging the market, and Sarnoff did, as anyone else might with his opportunities.

As a relatively innocuous example: if one had the good opinion of J. P. Morgan, or might be potentially useful to the Morgan firm, his name was likely to be found on the "preferred lists" described by Ferdinand Pecora in *Wall Street Under Oath* and in Congressional reports. Pecora was the lawyer who conducted the hearings before the U.S. Senate Banking and Currency Committee, 1933–1934, so he had all the facts at his command. Pecora says the publication of the preferred lists

> stirred the nation, and opened the eyes of millions of citizens to the hidden ways of Wall Street. In each case, stock was offered by J. P. Morgan & Co. to the individuals on these lists at cost, or practically at cost. In each case, the offer was made with full and irrefutable knowledge that there was, or would shortly be, a public market for the stock at a much higher figure. In effect, it was the offer of a gift of very substantial dimensions.

Almost 500 persons were on one or another of these preferred lists, including those of Drexel & Co., the Morgan affiliate in Philadelphia.

They were primarily, Pecora writes, "men who were exceedingly eminent and powerful in finance, business, industry, politics or public life." Sarnoff was one of the favored ones, and he was in good company, e.g.:

Ex-President Calvin Coolidge

General John J. Pershing

Colonel Charles A. Lindbergh

Charles Francis Adams, Secretary of the Navy under President Hoover

Newton D. Baker, Secretary of War under President Wilson

Sen. William Gibbs McAdoo, ex-Secretary of the Treasury and a member of the investigating committee

William Woodin, current Secretary of the Treasury

Bernard M. Baruch

Owen D. Young

Myron C. Taylor of U.S. Steel

Walter Gifford of AT&T

Albert H. Wiggin of Chase National Bank

Most of the nation's important bankers were beneficiaries of the Morgan firm. Wiggin, as one of the biggest, got 10,000 shares of Alleghany Corporation at twenty/thirty-five. If he sold immediately his gratuity was $150,000. "I assumed it was a favor," he testified, "and I was very glad to get it."

An even bigger banker, or one for some reason more favored, might get 20,000 shares at the same 20/35 ratio and stand to gain $300,000. Of course if this was in February 1929 and he kept the stock through part of October, he might end up with little gain; if he held on longer he might lose, like the poor jerk who held 50 shares on margin. But that wasn't Morgan's responsibility, and most of these beneficiaries knew when to sell, or were tipped off by kindly friends.

The opportunities in RCA stock were fabulous until near the end of the decade. In *Only Yesterday*, Frederick Lewis Allen quotes an "astute banker" who early in 1928 told an investor, "Stocks look dangerously high to me." The banker was right, but he was premature by about twenty months. Astuteness is sometimes the worst guide to short-term profit.

In the early twenties Radio had sold for around $10 a share. Early in March 1928 it had ascended to $94, still without paying a dividend —Sarnoff was plowing earnings back into research. The banker's astuteness was not the only kind; another type was exemplified by John J. Raskob, chairman of the finance committee of General Motors. With other big bull operators he knew his public—one that could not resist the appeal of a surging market. He also knew Sarnoff.

In March 1928 Radio was leapfrogging at the rate of about 20 points a day—again we must realize that this was in hard gold-backed dollars. It was by no means alone, but it exhibited a special madness. It might jump 20 points at the opening above the closing of the night before. Michael J. Meehan, the specialist in Radio, was frequently the center of what looked to one observer like a street fight.

In June there was a setback. Radio had climbed well over the 200 mark but on June 12 it lost over 23 points. Some halfway sober speculators thought the bull market had collapsed, but they were only forgoing profits. Many stock market analysts had expressed doubt that 5 million shares would ever be traded in a single day, but in November the volume approached 7 million. By that time Radio was trading at 400, and the peak was still some way off. There was, however, a premonitory symptom: on December 7 Radio opened at 361, could not advance, and fell to 296. But, after the shock waves had subsided, the market began another advance that led on into 1929.

The election of Herbert Hoover in 1928 resulted in the "Hoover bull market." Of course, in all these upward surges, the market was rigged by the big fellows, using public euphoria and greed as motive power. Then as now, a lot of people used the stock exchanges as "gambling casinos," in Lord Keynes's phrase. For all they knew about Radio stock, they might as well have been playing the horses. Except that this race was fixed—but fixing a "securities" race was not illegal then.

In September 1929 the upward push flagged. Radio had been split 5 to 1, and it dropped from its high at 114–3/4 to 82 1/2. There had been bad breaks earlier in the year, but small operators had been indoctrinated with the notion that when the market dropped sharply and disaster seemed imminent, *that* was the time to buy. Many speculators still held to that article of faith, for brokers' loans—an index of margin buyers—rose to a new high of nearly $7 billion.

Little alarm was shown when, during the first weeks of October 1929, the market failed to respond vigorously to the usual stimuli. Disaster lay just ahead for hundreds of thousands of small holders of stock and even for a few medium-large ones, but trading went on as usual, and the public certainly was not apprehensive.

The way Sarnoff was involved in the chicanery of the great bull market is illustrated by a typical pool operating in March 1929. A pool was a recognized technique by which big operators extracted short-term gains from the mass of small holders and gullible speculators who were enticed into the market to be fleeced. When Radio reached 500 and was split 5 for 1, it seemed a propitious time for a pool operation in the new stock, "as issued." The pool operated through M. J. Meehan & Co. and W. W. Hutton & Co.

Some details of this particular operation, as disclosed in the 73rd Congress U.S. Senate Banking and Currency Committee Hearings on stock-market practices, were as follows:

Participant	Number of Shares	Deposit	Profit
John J. Raskob	50,000	$1,000,000	$291,710.80
Charles M. Schwab	10,000	200,000	58,342.15
Mrs. Ed Wiesel	10,000	154,000	58,342.15
Mrs. D. Sarnoff	10,000	None	58,342.15

During the seven days that the pool operated at full volume (March 12–20, 1929) it drove the price up from 79 to a high of 109 1/4 on March 16, then began unloading and the stock fell back to 87 1/4 on March 23. The lambs who bought at 100 and above were duly shorn. Overall, the pool managers bought 1,493,400 shares at a cost of $141,-424,328.52. They sold exactly the same number of shares for $146,-987,527, leaving a gross profit of $5,563,198.48. (These were "wash" sales—a churning about of stock to rig the market, requiring only a moderate amount of capital to achieve the desired result.) Management fees and other payments accounted for $639,119.80, leaving net proceeds of $4,924,078.68 to be divided pro rata among the pool participants and bystanders like Mrs. D. Sarnoff, who was identified by a witness in 1932 as "the wife of the head of the Radio Corporation of America."

At the time of this particular pool operation, Sarnoff was not yet president of RCA; he had been appointed executive vice-president, effective January 1, 1929. While the pool was in operation he was in Europe which, aside from considerations of decorum, may account for his interest being in Mrs. Sarnoff's name; however, it was common practice for pool participants to trade in their wives' names. (Mrs. Ed

Wiesel was the wife of a broker's representative; why her deposit was less than Schwab's for the same profit I do not know, unless it was inconvenient for Wiesel to come up with more, while Schwab, a millionaire steel magnate, could easily spare $200,000.)

That Sarnoff was a freeloader in this particular arrangement is obvious. It is possible that if Mrs. Sarnoff signed the syndicate agreement, she would have been legally liable for any loss that might have resulted, but that a pool operating with the resources and know-how of practiced manipulators like Meehan and Raskob could result in a loss was a remote possibility, if possible at all.

The pleasant events of March 1929 were in contrast to the collapse of the stock market in the last eight days of October. On Wednesday, October 23, in Allen's words, there was "a perfect Niagara of liquidation," with volume over 6 million shares, the ticker 104 minutes late, and a loss of over 18 points for *The New York Times* average of 50 leading railroad and industrial stocks. But worse was to come—everybody in Wall Street realized that an enormous number of calls for more margin must be going out to insecurely margined traders.

The next day, October 24, went down in history as "Black Thursday." Prices were moderately steady at the opening, but selling orders cascaded on a fearful scale during the first hour. Allen believed the major cause of the debacle was forced selling: "the dumping on the market of hundreds of thousands of shares held in the names of miserable traders whose margins were exhausted or about to be exhausted. The gigantic edifice of prices was honeycombed with speculative credit and was now breaking under its own weight."

Panic followed. The bottom was dropping out of the market. Radio had opened at 68–3/4; soon it was selling at 44 1/2, or rather *had been* selling at that level. The ticker was an hour and a half late; the customer who went into a broker's branch office at 1:00 P.M. was getting information of what had been happening at 11:30 A.M. Nobody who was not on the exchange floor knew the full dimensions of the disaster, and things were happening so fast that even the floor brokers were bewildered.

A bankers' supporting pool organized under Morgan auspices averted utter chaos, but on Monday, October 28, further waves of selling overswept the market. Tuesday was even worse—Black Thursday was supplanted by Black Tuesday. Everyone was trying to sell, and in the absence of buying orders, the market became demoralized. The governors of the exchange considered closing it, but decided to remain open. Banks, brokerage houses, and corporations teetered on the edge of insolvency.

Amid the chaos, there were instances of gallantry. Allen cites the story of one banker who authorized taking over loan after loan by his bank until a white-faced subordinate came in and told him the bank was insolvent. "I daresay," said the banker, and continued trying to avert general insolvency at his own risk.

After weeks of gyrations, the 1929 bottom was reached on November 13. A list of blue-chip stocks in two columns, showing the high price on September 3, 1929, and the low on November 13, 1929, showed an average decline to about 50 percent of the earlier value. The best performers were AT&T (197/304 = 65 percent) and New York Central—railroads were still prime investments in those years—with 160/256 = 63 percent. The worst performers were Electric Bond & Share, the General Electric utility holding company (50/187 = 27 percent)—and Radio (28/101 = 28 percent).

The legality and the morality of the Radio pool, and others like it, are two different things. This was brought out in an exchange between Senator Carter Glass, a member of the investigating committee, and William A. Gray, counsel to the committee. Senator Glass's views carried special weight because of his twenty-six years as a Senate member, several years' service as a secretary of the treasury, and his role in the formation of the Federal Reserve System. Referring to the capacity of pools to send stocks "skyrocketing or to send them to the depths," Senator Glass inquired:

> Right there let me ask you: do you call transactions of that kind investments? . . .
>
> Mr. Gray: No, I would call it manipulation of the market, because here you have the picture of M. J. Meehan & Co. organizing this Radio pool, and M. J. Meehan & Co. being specialists in Radio and handling the stock on the floor . . .
>
> Senator Glass: Wasn't it just as much gambling as in the case of a man who might sit at a card table with an extra card up his sleeve?
>
> Mr. Gray: Yes, and a little more so, because . . . the fellow sitting at the card table had at least a chance to get a few of the cards, but they couldn't do it here.

> Senator Glass (summarizing): People who organize syndicates are at liberty individually to buy stocks that they think are going to advance, that they think should advance, but why organize a syndicate if it is not to combine the resources of various members of the syndicate in order to affect the market fictitiously?

The operation from which Sarnoff benefited was crooked, and under present laws the principals could go to jail. Even in 1932 Meehan was scared enough—or sufficiently embarrassed by the publicity—so that he sailed for Europe, reportedly on the advice of three doctors, on the night before the day he was to testify before the Senate committee. But such manipulations were not illegal at the time, and were reported ex post facto in the financial sections of the newspapers in the form of simulated conjectures that a pool had been operating in this or that stock and was now believed to have terminated its operations. So, while one may deplore Sarnoff, who had been poor himself, taking part in a scheme to deprive people of their meager savings (even though these people had been greedy and foolish enough to play the market), what he did was in no way actionable. I do not believe that Sarnoff ever knowingly did anything illegal in his life. Within those limits, as this incident shows, he might cut corners, or connive at others doing so for their and his benefit; which is to say that his morality was that of his time and associates.

One question remains: what services did Sarnoff perform that would induce the syndicate to bestow on him a gratuity of $58,000 without requiring him to put up any money of his own? I do not have the answer to that, but it could could have been no more than a tacit agreement to pass on to Meehan impending developments in the radio field which could be used as bait for the next run-up of RCA stock. Or not even anything positive. It might have been no more than a tacit understanding that Sarnoff would advise the pool operators when *not* to spring the trap, in that developments might be impending that could make the pool unprofitable, or even boomerang on its sponsors.

THE PHONOGRAPH
MERGERS

The phonograph industry, while also recalcitrant, was an easier setup for radio technology than the movies. Thomas A. Edison had invented the primeval phonograph, but he came nowhere near "perfecting" it —the purposely imprecise term patent lawyers still use to denote improving an invention with the means at hand. Even with cumulative improvements, nearly fifty years after the original invention the sound produced by the average phonograph from the average record was so badly distorted that one wondered by what mysterious talent the Victor Talking Machine Company's famous dog managed to recognize "His Master's Voice."

In orchestral recording, to achieve even this acoustic simulacrum required resort to all kinds of makeshifts—like seating the violin section of the typical small recording orchestra close to the sound-collecting horn, with megaphones mounted on the instruments, while the cellist perched on an elevated platform behind them. This had been going on for decades with no substantial change and, as is normally the case in slow-moving or static technologies, it was regarded as a hard-won and final, though limited, method. It could not be used to record a regulation symphony orchestra, but it worked well enough on superlative operatic voices like Caruso's to satisfy the public, especially the majority who had never heard Caruso on stage. All it amounted to was that Caruso's voice was so splendid, had such emotional effect, that even with much of its acoustic richness lost what remained was enough to stir the listener.

Happily, there are always those in technology who are not content to let well enough alone. Along came a Bell Labs scientist, J. P. Maxfield, a bold and original thinker in electronics and acoustics. At first he applied his knowledge conservatively, taking the mechanical phonograph apart and finding the major causes of distortion. Then he greatly improved the sound which came out of the horn. Maxfield's work showed the difference between the empiricist—even an empiricist of genius like Edison—and the scientist, who doesn't need to be a genius.

From that achievement—one the phonograph magnates could not fail to recognize as a significant improvement—Maxfield and other Bell Laboratories people went on to electronic recording and reproduction, with further improvement, this time on a revolutionary scale. In 1925, while WJZ was still grappling with WEAF on the radio end, Western Electric recording equipment had been installed in the Victor record- ing studios on 43rd Street, right across from Aeolian Hall, and one of the pickup points for Victor-WJZ programs, which were among the best on the air. The orchestra was arranged the way the conductor wanted it, and he could conduct in his accustomed style. The clumsy pickup horn had been replaced by microphones. There was no longer any worry about getting sufficient acoustic energy to cut the original record—vacuum tube amplification took care of that.

All technological advance comes at a cost, economic and human. A pathetic side effect of these advances—the latest of the protean ap- plications of radio technology—was the subdued presence in the con- trol room of two middle-aged men who for many years had been the Victor recording experts. They were learning about electronic record- ing from a Telephone Company engineer half their age who had come with the equipment and knew how to operate it. The older men's expertise in nonelectronic recording had been superannuated.

By this time Sarnoff was in the picture. He was no predator. He did not conceive of radio ruining the phonograph industry, though for the present it certainly posed a problem for its owners. As Sarnoff saw it, the answer was to merge the phonograph and radio industries. Such a merger made sense; unquestionably the two industries complemented each other functionally and in what they offered in entertainment and artistry.

But their immediate, predominantly financial interests clashed. The phonograph reaction was predictable: it was no more than a replay of Edison's naïve, near-senile denigration of radio. The initial Victor reaction was one of derision. There must have been private forebod- ings; but the public emphasis was on howls and squeals in reception, overproduction of receivers, radio receiver companies going into liqui- dation, and other besetting ailments of a young industry. All had some foundation in fact, yet not one was relevant to the underlying realities.

The cardinal fact was that radio was cutting into phonograph profits. Radio entertainment was not on a par with the better phonograph offerings, let alone the best; but it was effortless on the part of the listeners (automatic record changers were not yet available) and apparently cost-free. Of course the cost of the advertising came out of the radio listeners' pockets, but not in the form of cash.

Outwardly, the phonograph people were oblivious to the rapid pace of electronic research and development and the consequent certainty that the faults of radio broadcasting were essentially diseases of infancy. They seemed to sense no difference between their own static technology and the dynamic character of radio invention. The Victor Talking Machine management did secure licenses under the Western Electric recording and reproducing patents; that much was inescapable. The question to which they seemed unable to address themselves was how to compete with radio in distribution and sales.

Victor began having trouble with its trade channels. Lacking a workable policy, the company stalled. In addition to incomplete development of the radio art and overproduction, it cited uncertainties of "a volunteer and unregulated broadcasting service." On June 14, 1924 the Victor sales manager told the distributors and retailers: "We now beg to advise that we will not undertake quantity production and distribution of Victor Radio Units during this calendar year."

Both the wording—"beg to advise"—and the policy were archaic.

Clearly, however, something had to be done to quiet the outcries from the field. Victor invited their outlets to view a display at its Camden, New Jersey, manufacturing plant of radio receiving sets and data concerning their characteristic. Victor, however, would not be responsible for performance of receivers installed in Victor cabinets in radio-phonograph combinations. In effect, Victor was passing the buck to its distributors and dealers.

Sarnoff watched the gyrations and knew he had only to bide his time. Victor's earnings declined dramatically from nearly $17.5 million in 1923 to about $1.3 million in 1924 and showed a deficit of $141,000 in 1925. Deficits, especially when circumstances appear to presage their indefinite continuance, impel businessmen to parley with the organizations that are causing the decline in earnings—in this case, RCA. Negotiations in April 1925 led to an RCA-Victor agreement, cautiously entered into on both sides, for combining radio receivers and electronic phonographs with a single audio amplifier and loud speaker serving the combination. Victor was even warier than RCA, in that RCA was in the position of securing an additional outlet for its products, while Victor could only conjecture about public acceptance of these rather costly combinations.

Victor's earnings recovered, however, approaching $7.5 million in 1926 and exceeding $6.6 million in 1927. But it was only a temporary solution. By the time 1928 rolled around (the stock market playing a part), it was evident that either Victor would have to choose between embarking on the risky business of manufacturing its own receivers, which meant meeting the strenuous competition of some twenty-five leading radio manufacturers in addition to its protem ally RCA, or it had to sell out to a radio manufacturer in a position to further the development of both radio and phonograph. In 1928 the Victor interests sensibly resumed negotiations with RCA—meaning Sarnoff—to this end.

In engineering the RCA Victor merger (the hyphen was dropped after the merger was consummated), Sarnoff had a second objective in mind. Victor's Camden plant could be adapted to every variety of electronic production. RCA could never hope to free itself from its dependence on GE and Westinghouse until it had a manufacturing plant of its own. In his negotiations with the Victor management, that necessity was never out of Sarnoff's mind. While he had the advice, and needed the consent (and loans) of the GE and Westinghouse officials and directors for concluding the deal, his ulterior motive did not coincide with theirs.

The RCA-Victor discussions dragged on for years and Sarnoff's participation was interrupted by his negotiation with Schacht that resulted in the Young Plan. In the meantime, the RCA-Victor deal was concluded, with both Young and Sarnoff out of touch, by Harbord, Gerald Swope of General Electric, Andrew Robertson of Westinghouse, and the usual attendant corps of lawyers. When Sarnoff returned—by this time he was a board member as well as executive vice-president of RCA, and known to be slated for the presidency—he was not at all satisfied with the terms. RCA was obligated for no less than $150 million, and the Camden plant was to be operated by a newly created subsidiary in which GE and Westinghouse had the same 60/40 manufacturing ratio as before. Sarnoff was not only prepared to argue against ratification of the contract by the RCA board, but was prepared to resign if he lost.

He won. He had got into the habit of winning; and his masters in GE and Westinghouse, as well as in RCA itself, were becoming masters in name only. The contract was discarded and the parties agreed on a new organization plan with 50 percent RCA ownership in the Camden plant, 30 percent allocated to GE, and 20 percent to Westinghouse. The RCA Victor Company was incorporated on December 26, 1929, and at a special meeting of the RCA board Sarnoff was elected president. He was not quite thirty-nine. Considering where he began, it was a phenomenal rise.

When Photophone became impossible, I was offered a job by H. P. Davis at Camden: simultaneously Sarnoff sent word to me through Goldsmith that I would somehow be taken care of. The solution was to consecrate me director of recording at RKO Studios in Hollywood. When I arrived there, I was taken around by Sammis, whom I remembered from his confrontation with Sarnoff at the IRE meeting. Somewhere along the line they had patched up their differences, and Sammis had been put in charge of the Photophone plant in Hollywood. Sarnoff did not bear grudges.

I found Camden instructive to visit on my trips east. For a year or two after the amalgamation, the factory was murder; with former GE, Westinghouse, and RCA engineers competing for power at the upper levels and for jobs and survival at the lower. While the elite of RCA and the electrical companies were struggling with the problems of great organizations, in the early 1930s a jobless engineer could find himself selling apples on a street corner.

On the other hand, some of the engineers who passed unscathed through the Camden ordeal, by merit and not by cutting others' throats, came out the stronger for it. The outstanding case was that of Elmer W. Engstrom, with whom I had worked when we were both young engineers. He rose to the post of director of the RCA Research Laboratory later established at Princeton, then to senior executive vice-president of RCA, and finally was appointed to the presidency when Sarnoff vacated it for the chairmanship of the board.

I carried some of the glamour of Hollywood with me on these visits to Camden. At RKO my salary was double what I had been getting at Photophone. I had a one-year contract, and if the studio took up the option, I would get another hefty jump in salary. Some of my friends at RCA were dubious. RCA had a pension plan that I was losing. I had no concern about that—if I could last in the movies, the part of my income that I could save would be my pension. The pessimists also said the movie magnates were monsters who would cut my throat. I found them no different from their opposite numbers in Eastern corporations; the movies were a more volatile industry—that was all.

At Camden I was envied by some of the successful engineers; the unsuccessful ones were no longer there. I was making more than the top engineers there, and for the moment had more job security. Moreover, even after the crash, which occurred almost simultaneously with my arrival in Hollywood, RKO Studios remained a beacon of hope amid the tragedy. On the north side of the lot, perhaps symbolically adjacent to the Hollywood Cemetery, great sound stages were being erected. The walls of the older stages had already been treated with sound-absorbing material, and films were in production. Everybody said that RKO, affiliated with RCA and the electric companies and their bankers and, not least, David Sarnoff—would become the biggest studio in Hollywood, eclipsing its neighbor Paramount; Warner Brothers and Universal out in the San Fernando Valley; Twentieth Century-Fox in Westwood; even Metro-Goldwyn-Mayer in Culver City. Everybody thought the Big Five would become the Big Six, an opinion shared at Camden, where they didn't really know but assumed that since everybody said so, everybody must be right.

Everybody proved to be wrong. But for the moment Hollywood, partly insulated from the Depression, was the place to be. Sarnoff wrote me a note—"Dear Carl"—the end of which read:

> I am glad to know that you are in the RKO Studios and congratulate you on pioneering again in a new field. Yours is a colorful career.
> With all good wishes for your continued success.
>
> Sincerely yours,
> David Sarnoff

His signature was always perfectly legible, seemingly unhurried, straightforward like his mind. But trouble lay ahead even for him.

DAVID SARNOFF'S SECRET RECIPE FOR LEMONADE

Two months after Sarnoff became President of RCA, Franklin D. Roosevelt was inaugurated as President of the United States. It was scarcely a propitious time to be president of anything, except perhaps a chain of pawnshops. Immediately after the inauguration, all the banks in the country closed their doors in what became known as the bank "holiday," although there was nothing at all jolly about it. This was probably the nadir of the Depression, out of which the country emerged only partially as a result of the preparations for World War II, and fully only after Pearl Harbor.

In 1933 Elmer Davis wrote of "the searchings of the heart to which people are driven by hard times." I am sure Sarnoff searched his heart in those years of widespread frustration and anguish, but he did not spend too much time on such introspection—he was too busy keeping the Radio Corporation from going under. Not only that, but during the Depression he found the means to make the company stronger than ever before. To no one were the lines in Henry V more applicable: "Gloucester, 'tis true that we are in great danger/The greater therefore should our courage be."

Yet amid the common danger, and apart from the long-continued sickness of the stock market, almost every individual, almost every organization (except such economic principalities as General Motors) had troubles peculiar to themselves. Sarnoff's antedated the Depression and culminated during it. In 1924, while Calvin Coolidge, surely no radical—"the business of America is business"—was President, the Department of Justice had started an antitrust proceeding against RCA. It was a mild menace, unaccompanied by the fustian of Theodore Roosevelt's brand of trust-busting ("malefactors of great wealth, etc.") and by 1928 it was settled—or seemed to be settled—in the normal way, by a consent decree, the accused corporation admitting nothing but promising not to do it again. Sarnoff came to terms with the "independents"—a term used also in the earlier fight between the Motion Picture Patents Company and the rebellious moviemakers of 1908, and in other conflicts in which "independent" exerted a magical public relations influence.

To some extent, Sarnoff brought this earlier trouble on himself. His initial asking price for an RCA license to manufacture broadcast receivers *was* exorbitant. In October 1925 he recommended to a committee of the RCA board of directors that royalties should be on a sliding scale of 15 percent on the first $10 million of the licensee's business; 20 percent on the next $10 million; and 25 percent thereafter! Obviously he was trying to offset the advantage the independents had by making their own, while RCA was compelled to purchase similar merchandise from the electric companies, which exacted a profit over factory cost, thus leaving less profit margin for RCA. But this was clearly an illegitimate application of the licensing power. It was none of the independents' concern that RCA was hobbled in this way. It must have been clear to Sarnoff, too. While upholding these extortionate and unenforceable royalty rates, Sarnoff was reminding the RCA directors of the handicaps under which the 1925 RCA labored, and preparing the way for his future war of independence—ultimately the only way in which RCA could function efficiently and compete with the independents while exacting a reasonable royalty to compensate for its patent rights.

In the interim, principally by negotiation between Sarnoff and Eugene McDonald of Zenith, a leading independent, the royalty rate was reduced to 7 1/2 percent. Another concession was that Howard Armstrong's superheterodyne—then and now the preferred circuit for broadcast and most other types of reception—which Sarnoff had originally intended to reserve for RCA and did succeed in excluding from the licensing agreements of 1927, was opened to the licensees in 1930. In that year the licensing provisions were broadened in other respects and eventually royalties were reduced to 5 percent of manufacturers' billing prices.

Further, in the 1929 to 1931 period, RCA allowed deductions for cabinets. Until then Sarnoff had insisted that the royalty should be calculated on the total cost of the receiver, including the cabinet, which, especially in the console types, was prized by many customers largely for its presumed elegance as an article of furniture. The cabinet accounted for a substantial part of the cost, but involved no RCA patent rights and never should have been subject to royalty payments.

These reforms and further reductions in the royalty rates came too late. On May 31, 1930, five months after Sarnoff assumed the presidency, an unexpected blow fell. On the previous evening, the story goes, he was on his way to a dinner party at the New York apartment of Frank Altschul, a prominent investment banker and an RCA board member. In the lobby of Altschul's apartment house, a federal marshal intercepted Sarnoff and served him with a copy of a complaint which the government had filed in federal court that afternoon. If Sarnoff was not altogether satisfied with the new relationship between RCA and the electric companies, the Department of Justice was even less satisfied. With the Great Depression under way, it chose to bring an antitrust action against RCA, GE, Westinghouse, AT&T, and their various subsidiaries. The patent pool was alleged to be illegal, and so, the government held, was the GE and Westinghouse ownership of RCA stock. The government wanted GE and Westinghouse to compete with RCA and with each other.

Ironically, the dinner party was in honor of Sarnoff's rise to the presidency. He had no time to study the paper which had been served on him, and the festivities went on as if nothing had happened. It was only later in the evening that Sarnoff broke the news to a select few. The next morning the suit made headlines in the financial sections. RCA stock took another dive.

When the matter was analyzed, however, the two principal aims of the government were clearly distinguishable. The disruption of the patent pool Sarnoff certainly did not want, but the other chief complaint, the government's demand for competition between RCA and the electric companies, could well have been written by him. Given time to get under way, he was confident he could compete; nothing could please him more than a board of directors acquiescent to his will instead of one that controlled him or, at the least, with which he had to share control.

The General Electric and Westinghouse incubi still sat on Sarnoff's chest. By this time he had persuaded them to surrender their stock holdings in RCA Victor; National Broadcasting; Photophone; the tube manufacturing subsidiary, RCA Radiotron; and other subsidiaries, together with all physical assets, and, further, their rights to manufacture receivers, transmitters and other equipment for sale by RCA—all in exchange for 6,500,000 newly issued shares of RCA common of dubious value. But the GE and Westinghouse directors still sat on the RCA board, and their companies still had majority stock ownership. Functionally the situation was greatly improved, but Sarnoff's aim of complete independence was far from achieved. Nor, at a time of such stress and uncertainty in the entire economy, did it seem a likely prospect—until the government moved against an RCA still dominated by its progenitors.

All the members of the Radio Group, Sarnoff realized, would have to be prepared to yield to some of the government's demands. In the matter of possible guilt in restraint of trade, RCA was vulnerable under policies in which Sarnoff had acquiesced, if not initiated. Some of the independents claimed that it was impossible for them to continue to compete while paying tribute even in the amount of 7 1/2 percent, and their testimony before congressional investigating committees had been a factor in spurring the Department of Justice to action.

One manufacturer, Grigsby-Grunow, producing sets under the Majestic trademark, testified that they had been unable to obtain an RCA license: they had been rejected because RCA had imposed a limit of twenty-five licensees. Finally they obtained a license by buying out a licensee that was on the verge of collapse. B. J. Grigsby testified that during the next two years he had paid RCA over $5 million in royalties and he was not sure for what. He asserted that he had been denied specific information on what patents were covered under the license agreement and whether or not they were valid. All he was buying, he maintained, was immunity from suit.

This immunity was necessary because dealers and jobbers, receiving letters from Fish, Richardson & Neave alleging infringement of patents, would handle only radios manufactured under RCA license. Equally serious was the refusal of bankers to lend to unlicensed companies. The bankers were in no position to judge the validity of the patents involved. All they knew was that an RCA suit might force the company out of business and jeopardize the loans. If the company did obtain a license, the stiff royalty involved might likewise result in default. As long as business was good, nobody balked at that risk. With the business downturn in the Depression, the licensees were in trouble either way.

Another grievance which led to the antitrust action was RCA's stipulation that only RCA tubes be used in the licensees' sets. In this, as in the 7 1/2 percent royalty requirement, RCA had overreached itself. Other weaknesses were emerging in the RCA position, such as questions regarding the validity of some RCA-controlled patents. In particular, the original tube patents (Fleming and De Forest) had run out, and had been succeeded by patents of GE's Irving Langmuir and AT&T's H. P. Arnold. There was no question that these two distinguished scientist-engineers had greatly improved vacuum tube technology by better evacuation in mass manufacture and other improvements, so that their tubes gave uniform performance while De Forest's tubes contained residual gas after vacuum pumping, resulting in each tube being more or less sui generis and erratic in performance. But in May 1931 the Supreme Court ruled that these were refinements, not inventions; consequently, the Langmuir-Arnold patents were invalid.

Another RCA-GE-Westinghouse problem, and a very serious one, was that under the 1927 Radio Act, the Federal Radio Commission was required to refuse broadcasting licenses to applicants guilty of monopolistic practices. In 1931, when the NBC licenses came up for renewal, the Federal Radio Commission decided 3–2 that because RCA had been guilty only of monopolistic practices involving equipment, but not communications, the licenses could be renewed. What with this narrow escape, atop a barrage of triple-damage civil suits, adverse court decisions, injunctions, the antitrust action (brought under President Hoover's administration; what would Franklin D. Roosevelt's policies be like?) prudence required that RCA should give ground, such as further lowering of royalty terms.

Another weakness in the RCA position was that, as in the twenties, the Telephone Company was disposed to make a separate peace with the government. It was in any case a secondary defendant, since it had disposed of its RCA stock long ago. In the expectation of inducing the attorney general to discontinue suit against it, the Telephone Company elected to exercise its right to cancel its cross-licensing agreement by giving the required three years' notice as of December 18, 1931.

In this whole royalty-license imbroglio, RCA has been pictured by its image-makers not precisely as an angel of light, but a virtuous corporation wronged by the actions of a government at whose behest it had patriotically established itself. This was nonsense, and so were many of the charges leveled against RCA by its competitors who, we may be sure, would have behaved exactly like RCA—or worse, if they had been in its position. RCA licensees were as anxious as the RCA management to maintain a "healthy industry" immune from "cutthroat competition." Once they got a license and were making money, they wanted other applicants kept out, much as newly arrived suburbanites have usually been the staunchest defenders of "the character of the neighborhood."

As for Sarnoff, we must view him in this context as an apostle of competition and free enterprise, especially when he was top dog as against the competition. But he was no diehard. As in the earlier contests with the Telephone Company, his basic instincts were those of a moderator. Besides, his principal interest was in unifying RCA and securing his own independence in managing it. He did not know how far he could go and he was unusually emotional about the issue. The account occurs somewhere in Bucher's forty-one unpublished volumes, but I have taken it from Gleason L. Archer, *Big Business and Radio*, 1939:

> Elmer E. Bucher tells the story of a dramatic taxicab ride, during which David Sarnoff made the fateful decision to fight for complete unification. It happened in the late summer of 1929, after a banquet —at one o'clock in the morning. The two men had discussed the situation—Sarnoff growing more agitated as he talked.
>
> "We have reached the point," he said, as though reasoning with himself, "when I think we can have either participation or unification. Which shall it be?"—flinging his derby hat on the floor of the taxicab in sheer weariness of soul.
>
> "Why ask me?" replied Bucher. "Your mind has always been set on complete unification."
>
> "Yes—yes—I know—complete unification—but can we get it?"
>
> "Why not?"
>
> Mr. Sarnoff picked up his hat—dusty and crumpled—and clapped it on his head.
>
> "Well, boy! Unification it is!"

After two years of complex negotiations within the Radio Group and between members of the group and the Department of Justice— negotiations in which Sarnoff played a crucial role and was greatly aided by Owen D. Young—agreement was reached all around. The government's suit never came to trial. On November 21, 1932, two weeks after Roosevelt's election, another consent decree was signed.

Under the decree Sarnoff got everything he wanted in intergroup relationships. The electrical companies gave up their seats on the RCA board and agreed to distribute their RCA shares among their own stockholders, thus obviating the danger to RCA of large blocks of stock overhanging the market. They agreed further to defer competing with

RCA for a period of two and a half years, giving time for the dust to settle and for RCA to get its manufacturing facilities in order.

Yet RCA was by no means out of the woods in the early thirties. The agreements consequent on the arrangement with the government added $18 million to its debts and, among other curtailments, eventually forced the sale of RKO. And profits were way down, had in fact disappeared. Archer tabulates a net profit of nearly $16 million in 1929, which was reduced to about $5.5 million in 1930, then to slightly over $750,000 in 1931; in 1932 the net *loss* was well over $1 million. In 1933 RCA got back into the sadly depleted ranks of profitable corporations and stayed there, though in no spectacular fashion. In 1937 it paid a dividend, which it has maintained ever since, though, if Sarnoff realized his ambition to establish an electronic General Motors, financially he never came near the performance of that colossus.

That an antitrust action should agitate the officials and directors of a large corporation may seem strange, even under the troubled conditions of 1930. For a corporation to have an antitrust suit brought against it is tantamount to an accolade of success. To the same effect, experience antedating the turn of the century shows that antitrust is one of the least effective functions of American government. After all the nineteenth-century populism, the breakup of Standard Oil and a succession of forced dissolutions, after Franklin D. Roosevelt's reputed —and much exaggerated—hostility to business (the speech about driving the money changers out of the temple was no more than necessary presidential rhetoric in one of the gravest crises in American history) —after all this and much more along the same lines, presently about half of American manufacturing business is in the hands of some 200 corporations, including RCA. The rise of conglomerates—again including RCA—has increased the concentration of wealth that is generally viewed (except by those who benefit by it for the time being) as a dubious feature of the American economy. So what is so frightening about an antitrust action, whether against RCA and its partners in 1930 or against ITT, IBM, or AT&T, fifty years later?

Still, it does disturb business leaders. For one thing, it is bad publicity, not only as regards the general public—that could be borne with equanimity—but it scares stockholders and possible buyers of the stock, and in the case of utility companies, may embolden the regulatory commissions. For another, it involves legal expenses and takes up the time of directors and officials of the accused company. And then, they cannot be sure they—or some of their subordinates—have not actually been guilty of restraint of trade, or worse, and the government, having a strong case, may be able to dispose the courts to severe punitive measures.

It can happen, and in the 1950s it did. The electric power equipment price-fixing conspiracy of those years is not to be compared with anything RCA, General Electric, and Westinghouse were accused of in the 1930s, but the outcome in the later case was enough to scare the most avaricious executive—$2 million in corporate fines, seven otherwise respectable executives, including two GE vice-presidents, fined *and* sent to jail, and another twenty-four fined and receiving suspended sentences. The judge said it would be naïve to suppose that those responsible for the conduct of the corporation were unaware of what was going on; and the resulting lawsuits by aggrieved utilities against GE required calling a former president back to active duty to negotiate settlements.

There are also psychological reasons for the disturbance that antitrust action may cause its accused corporations. The men who run large companies have a built-in antipathy to any interference with their uninhibited power to pursue their normal objectives of unlimited growth of the organizations with which they identify themselves. Sarnoff had his share of that temperamental aversion, but he was prudent in his pursuit of an RCA untrammeled by the parental authority and constraint to which he had had to submit in the earlier years. He neglected no opportunity to enhance his power, but he proceeded cautiously.

Regardless of immediate effects on the balance sheet, the outcome of the antitrust suit and the revision of RCA-GE-Westinghouse relations was regarded in the industry as still another personal triumph for Sarnoff. He summed it up without false modesty, to which he was never addicted: "The Department of Justice handed me a lemon and I made lemonade out of it." The crack neglected a great deal, but it was substantially true. With Sarnoff in undisputed control, RCA was now complete and whole, and launched on a steeply rising curve in electronic leadership for the next three decades.

TELEVISION:
EARLY BEGINNINGS

Sarnoff was ridiculed—though not to his face—for an alleged forecast in 1926 that television was "right around the corner," but the statement was not as absurd as it later sounded. Serious TV research was under way and the technical difficulties were beginning to be surmounted. H. E. Ives of AT&T's research laboratories was working on TV by wire and in 1927 sent a well-publicized picture of Herbert Hoover, then secretary of commerce, from Washington to New York. Sarnoff understandably had a healthy respect for the Telephone Company's research potential; he kept in touch with everything going on in video as well as audio transmission, so he knew about Ives's work. Out in California young Philo Farnsworth was working on an electronic TV system, and in New Jersey Allen B. Dumont was building picture tubes and other components. John L. Baird was busy in England, C. F. Jenkins in the United States, with mechanical systems. Invention is a precarious business even when carried on by teams of experts in well-heeled corporations. It is even more hazardous when carried on independently, as we have seen in De Forest's case, but there is always the possibility that success will come from an unexpected quarter.

I remember a twenty-minute telephone conversation early one morning with Howard Armstrong before I left for work at WJZ; he questioned me closely about the stage of progress of TV and moving picture transmission generally. He was not working in this field himself, but he wanted to know what effects it might have on improvements in audio broadcasting, which was important to him both from an engineering and a financial standpoint. It is a reasonable conclusion that even if Sarnoff was premature in his estimate of when TV might become a public utility, it was rather evidence of his assiduity in keeping up with current technology and not letting any pending development catch him unaware.

Better authenticated than the "around the corner" remark is a lecture he gave at the Harvard Business School during the 1927–1928 semester on the opportunities for business graduates in science, or, more accurately, technology. He pointed to the spread of radio telegraphic technique to radiotelephony, thence to mass communication in broadcasting; he ended with a reference to future prospects in television. It was a reasonable extrapolation, as later events proved. Had it not been for World War II, in all probability TV would have got under way in 1939. It was said in praise of the elder Morgan that almost alone among financiers, he thought a decade ahead in railroad building and the like. Should not the same tribute be accorded to Sarnoff, who had a much broader perspective, embracing both engineering and financial aspects? *Fortune* has answered the question by coupling Sarnoff with Morgan in its call for a "Business Hall of Fame."

Technically, TV already had a history while Guglielmo Marconi was still in knee pants. In 1884, Paul Nipkow, a German, invented the scanning wheel, a rapidly rotating disc with holes spaced spirally inward from the circumference. The key word here is *scanning.* Reading is a slow, longitudinal form of scanning: the eye starts on a page at the upper left, traverses a line of print all the way to the right, and returns to the left for the next line. The initial problem for scanning and transmitting a picture was to cause a dot of light to fly sequentially over the picture, line by line from top to bottom: this a Nipkow disc could do. The next problem was to change the light into electrical energy, send these impulses over a telegraph line, and then reverse the process at the receiving end with a similar disc revolving in exact synchronism with the transmitting disc.

Nipkow's invention never came into commercial use, but he clearly delineated for later inventors the fixed and invariant nature of the problem of picture transmission. A picture—any picture, still or moving—cannot be transmitted and received *en bloc.* This inescapable fact was one of the obstacles Sarnoff encountered in his promotion of TV —since the picture must be broken down into its elements at the transmitter, and reassembled at the receiver, the industry must agree on standards which, once adopted, all must follow. Scanning resolves the picture into optical-electrical elements for transmission and reconstitutes these elements at the receiver. It does not matter whether the televised object is the *Pietà* or a commercial for a purported remedy for athlete's foot—it must be dissected with this technique and put together again, if it is to be seen at a distance.

The systemic requirements of dissection and reassembly were thus solved well before the turn of the century, but there were no buyers. Mass distribution in the form of broadcasting was still more than three decades in the future, and, because the early systems were mechanical, the art was beset by severe technical difficulties. One was keeping the transmitting and receiving discs in synchronism. Another was that the number of scanning lines was so limited that only a crude picture resulted even when synchronism was achieved: the fewer the number of lines, the less detail could be reproduced. And, for discs of reasonable size, the picture was so small that only one person could view it, in peep-show fashion.

In short, in the way of commercial TV nothing was possible—even for a promoter of Sarnoff's caliber—until after electronic technology had reached the broadcasting stage and after it had conquered the movies and superseded the mechanical phonograph. Once that point was reached, TV became not only possible, but inevitable. Sarnoff and the extraordinary corps of engineers available to him never considered a mechanical system as a commercial proposition. To their way of thinking, a practicable system had to be wholly electronic, with no moving parts. If it could not be done that way, so far as they were concerned, it had better not be done at all.

Yet, as an illustration of the persistence of error even in well-informed quarters (error originating in or reinforced by commercial considerations) after electronic black-and-white TV had been in use for years and RCA was striving to develop an all-electronic color system, Columbia Broadcasting countered with a mechanical color system, incompatible with black-and-white, which, even harder to believe, was approved by the Federal Communications Commission until, with further development of the RCA system, the commission had to reverse itself. The commission's about-face followed an all-industry decision, in which CBS concurred.

All this, and much else, brought Sarnoff no end of headaches before his usual good sense and determination prevailed. Even so, he would have been frustrated in the absence of first-rate engineering advice and support which, where grave risks are unavoidable, is more essential to innovative management than the best legal counsel.

Sarnoff's chief consultant and doer in TV was Vladimir K. Zworykin, whose career should once more remind us never to underrate either Russians or Hungarians as scientific and technological prodigies—or Germans, for that matter. The receiving tube for electronic TV was the familiar nineteenth-century cathode-ray tube, originally developed as a measuring device to study the shapes of electric waves. When the new field of television opened up, the shapes of young women became a staple of electronic show business. The German inventor of the cathode-ray tube, Carl F. Braun, shared the Nobel prize with Marconi in 1909, but he died in 1918; he never saw the *Playboy*-type contours on what developed into the kinescope, or picture tube.

The possible usefulness of the Braun cathode-ray tube in TV reception was conceived independently around 1911 by a well-known British scientist, A. Campbell Swinton, and Boris Rosing, a professor at the University at St. Petersburg. One of Rosing's brightest students was Zworykin, who emigrated to the United States late in 1919. He worked intermittently as a research assistant at Westinghouse and in 1923 applied for a patent on an electronic pickup tube which he called the iconoscope and which became the progenitor of the modern television camera. He did not get much backing at Westinghouse, thus furnishing one more illustration of the blindness that corporate strength and prosperity seem to engender, like cataracts in the eyes of the old. Westinghouse exploited audio broadcasting vigorously and forged ahead of RCA, although Sarnoff had had the "Radio Music Box" idea several years earlier. Westinghouse could have done the same with TV: it had Zworykin. But it didn't have Sarnoff, and this time he was not hampered by a myopic board of directors.

In 1929 Zworykin outlined his ideas to Sarnoff, who was impressed. The story is that Sarnoff asked how much it would cost to develop a TV system and Zworykin pulled an estimate out of the air: $100,000. The figure was absurdly low, but Zworykin had his foot in the door. The development of TV to entertainment quality cost RCA $10,-000,000, and $50,000,000 before a dollar of profit resulted from the investment. Even $10,000,000 was a considerable strain on RCA's financial resources, especially as the bottom fell out of the stock market just at the point when Zworykin joined RCA; and most of the initial investment had to be made during the Depression.

It turned out to be money well spent—but it took a Sarnoff to spend it. In the later 1930s NBC was experimenting with television in one of its Radio City studios and an antenna on the Empire State Tower, with receivers in the homes of RCA officials in various locations in the metropolitan area. Dr. Goldsmith had one at his apartment on Madison Avenue, and I saw the programs on trips to New York. The picture quality was quite acceptable. However, in yearly bulletins through the Academy of Motion Picture Arts & Sciences, I informed the studio heads that commercial television was not around the corner—not yet.

And in fact it wasn't, although at the opening of the New York World's Fair in April 1939, after seven years of TV development, Sarnoff made a feint at it. Standing before an iconoscopic camera at the dedication of the RCA building, be announced the beginning of regular television service by NBC, adding:

> Now we add radio sight to sound. It is with a feeling of humbleness that I come to the moment of announcing the birth in this country of a new art so important in its implications that it is bound to affect all society. It is an art which shines like a torch in a troubled world. It is a creative force which we must learn to utilize for the benefit of all mankind.

It was a typical mishmash of verbal idealism and hard-nosed commercialism; still, the commerical part of it might have been valid had it not been for the clouds of war overhanging the scene. As it was, a few hundred receivers, providing nine-inch direct-viewing pictures, and some twelve-inch reflecting types, were given away or sold at high prices—over $600, equivalent to over $1,500 in 1975 currency—and a few hours of programming per week were broadcast for officials of RCA and advertising agencies and a small free-spending clientele. The number of lines was 441, which gave passable definition, although it was later upgraded to the present lineage of 525.

It is perhaps fortunate that the war blocked mass exploitation at this juncture. Sarnoff was understandably eager to be first on the air with TV, as he deserved to be, but the enterprise was immature in several respects. As yet, industry agreement on standards was lacking. Then, there was the service problem, seemingly insoluble with the techniques and personnel available. In the air corps in World War II, I had some experience with radar. It was immediately clear that the complexities of radar reflected only partially the complexities to be expected of television receivers in the hands of the public. When a receiver went out of order, would there be servicemen qualified to repair it? After all the trouble we had had with the relatively simple design and servicing of sound-and-picture equipment in motion picture theaters, where the projectionists were at least qualified on the picture end and had a vocational interest in learning enough about sound to cope with routine difficulties, what could be expected from servicemen with insufficient experience to diagnose and correct TV receiver ailments with the efficiency expected, say, of an oil-burner serviceman?

However, if Sarnoff had been in too much of a hurry, the war had given him a period of surcease. Air corps radar servicemen in World War II were mainly lieutenants, and their skills warranted the grade. It was a reasonable expectation that the radar technicians released by the air corps at the end of the war would be a considerable help in getting television under way with only an acceptable amount of equipment trouble.

SARNOFF AND RCA IN WORLD WAR II

World War I furthered Sarnoff's career in that it gave him additional experience in management of corporate-governmental relations, although on a limited scale, since American Marconi was a small corporation. By the time the Japanese attacked Pearl Harbor, American Marconi had long been absorbed into RCA, a powerful corporation with widespread interests, although still far from the multibillion-dollar giant it later became. Sarnoff was recognized as one of America's leading industrialists, and RCA and he were more closely identified than any other company and its top executive—even more closely than Alfred P. Sloan and General Motors. Another difference between Sarnoff's situation in the two wars was that as a colonel in the Signal Corps Reserve, he was eligible for active duty in the second although, at fifty, he was not obligated to serve. The navy, which had spurned him in World War I because he was Jewish, would have been glad to have him aboard this time around, but General Harbord had seen to it that he belonged to the army.

Following Franklin D. Roosevelt's lead, Sarnoff, did not wait for the Japanese attack to prepare for war. Everyone knew it was coming. When it came, on that momentous Sunday, December 7, 1941, RCA was already fully converted for war production. The telegram Sarnoff fired off to Roosevelt later that afternoon—"All our facilities and personnel are ready and at your instant service. We await your commands" —was a statement of fact as well as a ceremonial assurance.

The commands were not long in coming. Actually, Sarnoff's principal contribution was in his civilian capacity as head of RCA. His direct military contribution amounted to less than a year in uniform: seven months in Europe, the rest in Washington. His several tours of duty in Washington in the Signal Corps were for service as a consultant and troubleshooter. As in any war, there was plenty of internal trouble and confusion in the supporting echelons. Except for a few high administrative officers, such as General George C. Marshall and, for the air corps, General H. H. Arnold, the services had no one to equal Sarnoff as a fast problem-solver.

Rank was of no importance. Colonel Sarnoff might be dealing with a brigadier or major general, or with a group of generals, but they all knew he was the boss at RCA, where any one of them might be lucky to rise to a vice-presidency. Even the chief signal officer was overwhelmed with problems, not of his own making, but he was responsible for the mistakes or shortcomings of his subordinates. Both he and they were glad to have Sarnoff come down and help out with ideas for organization and reorganization when it would help the war effort or, as in one case, when he served as president of a special board of officers charged with investigating allegations of deficiencies in Signal Corps procurement or operations. As soon as he got through with these chores, Sarnoff would revert to civilian status and busy himself with deficiencies in RCA which, though generally in better shape than the services, was falling short of wartime demands in some quarters. It is in the nature of war that few men and organizations can fully measure up to the requirements imposed on them.

RCA was charged not only with supplying the insatiable needs of the American armed forces, which at the peak of the war effort had over 12 million men and women in uniform, but also met heavy demands abroad under the lend-lease program. It is impossible to describe within reasonable space what the total research and production effort of the various RCA divisions entailed; and even to attempt to do so would require a similar description of the correlated activities of General Electric, Westinghouse, Western Electric, Bell Telephone Labs, Massachusetts Institute of Technology and several other organizations as important as RCA. The whole gigantic task was carried out under the direction of the Office of Scientific Research and Development, headed by Vannevar Bush. A number of officials of other companies than RCA, in uniform or as civilian aides, made contributions on the same scale as Sarnoff's.

Sarnoff's service in Europe is of special interest, however. It was in the European theater that he earned his star as a brigadier general, which he treasured for the rest of his life. It was more important to him, as a foreign-born citizen, than it might have been to native-born Americans, at least one of whom returned to civilian life as a major general and did not use his military title thereafter. Traditionally, however, a military title carries special prestige and deservedly so, at least until the hapless Indochinese venture severely damaged the services' claims to moral standing. Nor should it matter whether the man in uniform is sent into combat, sits at a safe stateside desk, or performs his duty as a planner and organizer in a theater of war. He will be used in whatever capacity his superiors decide he can best serve.

In combat, the saying is that a soldier should march toward the sound of the guns. That maxim, through no fault of his, Sarnoff never had a chance to follow—and neither did Eisenhower. In World War I Eisenhower was commander of a tank-training center near Gettysburg, Pennsylvania. By the time the United States was at war again, he was too valuable as an administrator to be used for anything less than U.S. commander of the European Theater of Operations. Sarnoff likewise was best fitted as a communications administrator on Eisenhower's staff. Harbord said that Sarnoff would have made a first-rate battlefield strategist, and Harbord was in a position to know; but the nearest Sarnoff came to that was when, in field uniform and with the regulation .45 automatic on his hip, he was driven to liberated Paris in a jeep. The pistol was just symbolic.

Sarnoff's job in Europe consisted of the kind of large-scale organizing and troubleshooting he had done in the States and, in particular, preparing for printed and electronic press coverage of the D-Day landings and subsequent progress of the Allied invasion of the Continent. This, on top of military communications, was an enormous undertaking. Eisenhower asked Washington to send him the best communications expert in the country to manage it. Not only that, but the man had to be a diplomat, adept at handling people of Allied nations not necessarily amenable to U.S. direction. If Eisenhower had not been acquainted with Sarnoff before, he soon found out that Sarnoff was the logical choice.

Washington notified Sarnoff and cut his orders. He arrived in London by air on March 20, 1944. London was half bombed-out and in a grim mood after nearly five years of war. The communications situation was grim, too. There were two major things wrong with the way Sarnoff had been commandeered. First, the idea that he would be needed for only sixty days was short by five months. Second, he should have been called in months earlier. D-Day, as it turned out, was June

6, giving him only a little over two months to get things in shape—he had to have the system tested and functioning late in May. Fortunately, prior U.S. experience in North Africa provided a certain amount of guidance.

He was quartered at the Claridge and provided with office space at the Ministry of Information. Early on his second day in London he was taken in to see General Eisenhower by the chief of staff, General W. Bedell Smith, who after the war became a director of RCA and, like Eisenhower, a friend of Sarnoff's. Eisenhower was businesslike and cordial in his usual style. He outlined for Sarnoff the three things he wanted most. One was an American station for broadcast communication with the troops in all European and Mediterranean theaters, in place of the British Broadcasting Company's service. Second, Sarnoff was to inspect and improve the military communications for the invasion and the subsequent operations in France and Germany. Third, press communications for the invasion and the subsequent fighting must be adequate.

A large order but, with full authority from Eisenhower, (and shortly afterward from Churchill, too) not impossible. Nevertheless, it was probably the biggest job Sarnoff had ever tackled, and certainly the most urgent.

To give an idea of the magnitude of only one part of the problem: the existing westbound transatlantic news capacity was 130,000 words a day. The expected D-Day requirement was estimated at 500,000 words. It was a pretty good estimate—on D-Day, beginning at 7:32 Greenwich Mean Time (2:32 A.M. Eastern Standard Time) the system carried 570,000 words. To achieve that capacity, Sarnoff had to pool facilities under centralized management, borrow Signal Corps channels, erect new transmitters, acquire circuits from the sometimes reluctant British Post Office, and push through other measures of similar magnitude. On May 25 the system underwent a test and performed satisfactorily; on D-Day it did even better.

For a close-up account of Sarnoff's wartime activities I am indebted to Ray Guy (who died in July 1975) and Lieutenant Colonel AUS (Ret.) Walter R. ("Brownie") Brown. Both were among the "Goldcoasters" —retired RCA employees residing in Florida. Their stories have been lightly edited and cut for space.

The first, from Ray's newsletter, sarcastically titled *QRN* (an international abbreviation for static interference) tells of Walter's conversion from civilian to military status and how he came to be Sarnoff's aide in Europe:

> Walter for many years had been NBC's expert in remote broadcasting. . . . So comes the war. Walter immediately applied for a commission as Lieutenant jr. grade. He was turned down because he was missing a few back teeth. . . . He then tried the coast guard, which wanted him badly for Eastern Long Island as a lieutenant sr. grade. Then the army discovered it had a desperate need for Walter, teeth or no teeth. "What in hell did the navy expect you to do?" the recruiter commented. "Bite the Germans to death?"
>
> Walter was commissioned captain, AUS. He was told later that if he had applied just a modicum of resistance he could have got major. Anyway, here he is, just interviewed, no papers, no commission in writing, no uniform. The poor guy didn't even know how to salute properly. And he gets a telephone command to be in London tomorrow morning. He gets four shots, bingo, 1, 2, 3, 4. And then—bingo—receives a handful of papers, commission, orders, transportation, and scrounges up a uniform. And—bingo—he finds himself, via London, in Algiers.
>
> Walt went all through North Africa. When General Eisenhower was made Supreme Commander, David Sarnoff was assigned as a special consultant. . . . And get this! Colonel Sarnoff was, for the time being, technically *under* Walter. They shared abutting desks and were roommates off and on.

Prodded by Ray, Brownie sat down at his typewriter, giving an account not only of his wartime service with Sarnoff but starting with an early incident which shows how understanding Sarnoff could be when broadcasting mishaps occurred, even those involving him personally. Brownie wrote:

> Carl, it is a very long time since we met. In fact it dates back to the days of WJZ and WJY on 42nd Street.
>
> Carl, I admired General Sarnoff very much and have read a great deal about him.
>
> My first encounter with Mr. Sarnoff dates back to the days of Radio Manufacturers Radio Shows at the old Madison Square Garden on 23rd Street. Somewhere in the late twenties or early thirties, NBC built and operated the so-called Crystal Studios at the show, and all the famous radio shows originated there for a week. At the

opening ceremonies, Mr. Sarnoff was the principal speaker, his subject, the advances and progress of radio broadcasting. He spoke from
one of the 711 [Fifth Avenue] studios and the program encountered
a mix-up. Another studio [at the old Winter Garden Theater] was
rehearsing the Jimmy Melton show, and somehow the rehearsal was
superimposed right over Mr. Sarnoff's speech—instruments tuning,
Jimmy warming up—"Mee Mee Mee Mee" and the usual studio
chatter.

At Madison Square Garden all hell broke loose. O. B. [Hanson] the
NBC manager of engineering, and George McElrath [NBC operating engineer] were with me at the Garden studio. . . . With earphones
we went across the Telephone Company lines feeding 711 and O.B.
said, "Brownie, we are clear. It is not coming from here." In a short
time it was determined that a parallel patch [a connection combining
the Madison Square and Winter Garden outputs] had been made at
711 by mistake. The patch was untied but the mischief had been
done and Mitch [the supervisor at 711] was in deep trouble.

When Sarnoff heard of the mix-up, he demanded an "immediate
explanation." He certainly had a right to one. Here he was, the progenitor of broadcasting and president of RCA, talking of the progress of
broadcasting and apparently unable to go on the air over his own
network without interference. Back to Brownie:

Mr. Sarnoff was sailing on the *Europa* at 2:00 A.M. from Pier 36
in Brooklyn and requested that O. B. himself tell him what had
happened. O. B., George, Ed Cullen [another NBC engineer], and
I flagged a taxi at 1:00 A.M. to Brooklyn.

We met Mr. Sarnoff on the dock and explained what had happened in detail. . . . He was very gracious . . . thanked us for the long
taxi ride and all that trouble. He explained he had to have a story for
the reporters.

Other contacts with him were routine, such as during the NBC
Symphony Series (Toscanini directing) and other broadcasts. He was
always courteous and pleasant.

During World War II I had close association with Colonel Sarnoff.
By that time I was a major in the Signal Corps in North Africa,
assigned to the Public Relations and Psychological Warfare Division,
responsible for press and broadcasting of war correspondents and
rehabilitation of captured stations. When General Ike was made
Supreme Commander, I was transferred to London as technical

officer for Allied press and radio in the European theater. I had heard that Colonel Sarnoff was in London by that time to supervise and coordinate the enormous task of all press and radio communications for the Allies.

When I arrived in London, Colonel Sarnoff was one of the first I reported to, together with Colonel Phillips of public relations (as a civilian he had been with *Newsweek*) and General Davis, head of the division. Colonel Sarnoff was overjoyed that one of his RCA "Family Circle" was to assist him. Actually at this stage—this is a laugh—I was in direct charge; he was a "special advisor," or "consultant."

I was given a desk back to back with his. We spent long hours working on plans for the release of news of D-Day, which we knew would involve the greatest flow of news wordage ever experienced. He was quartered at the Claridge and I also had to spend many hours working with him in his room, and sometimes even to bunk down for a few winks.

As D-Day approached, he said one afternoon, "Brownie, let's take a ride around London." I was surprised but rounded up Colonel Phillips and the three of us drove around for a while. During the ride, Colonel Sarnoff said, "Brownie, I want you to draw up the plan of communications for D-Day." I was floored. After some discussion I said I thought the only safe and secure way was to originate all communications from one central location, the PRD HQ at the University of London, known by the British as MOI (Ministry of Information). This had to be coordinated with all the various communications of all the Allies. I remembered my experience in Algiers at the time of the Italian capitulation. A code word was assigned— when we broadcast this word from Algiers, it would be the signal for the War Department in Washington to release the news. As usual, a foul-up occurred in Washington and they released the news to the press before it happened.

In the D-Day situation, all agreed on a generally similar plan, though of much larger scope. The code word was BIGOT and it was even above Top Secret, as we had to have the exact time of day and location of the initial assault. We were worried and kept to ourselves. . . . Among the multiplicity of circuits we had a two-way voice channel to WAR; from there it fed all the networks, likewise on a two-way basis. We could call any net at any time from the mike in London and carry on restricted two-way voice. This was a most secret circuit and no one was allowed to be identified, directly or indirectly. One day Colonel Sarnoff was talking to Washington and NBC; he forgot and said, "This is Colonel Sarnoff." The security people instantly cut the circuit. They respected no one, and Colonel Sarnoff was reported and chewed out. He never went on that circuit again.

In the semifinal arrangements we encountered opposition from Colonel Bill Paley of Psychological Warfare [Chairman William S. Paley of CBS]. He objected strongly because the arrangements did not fit in with his plans for broadcasting to the enemy. But he came around shortly and agreed that the central plan was the only one that would be secure and work on a worldwide basis.

D-Day came and the system worked splendidly. It was the largest hookup of communications ever put together, comprising radio telegraph and telephone, cable and voice broadcasting. It used U.S. and British military, BBC, and every other conceivable facility under our control. We covered all of Europe, the Middle East, India, the U.S.A., Canada and, via the Voice of America, all Latin American countries. Colonel Sarnoff directed all this prodigious flow of wordage, acting as a world traffic director, equalizing channels and avoiding delays and pile-up at any point. Only a communications expert could appreciate the job he did.

We operated together in London through the Normandy campaign, planning and executing movement of press communications in all sectors. We made a few flights to Normandy and toured the fronts in his special DC–3. He had close contact with General Eisenhower and General Bedell Smith and consulted with them many times on press matters.

With the fall of Paris we set up HQ in the Scribe Hotel and moved most of our communications there. The Germans had blown up all communications facilities, completely cutting off the area. Colonel Sarnoff came over and brought order out of chaos. He had a friend of long standing there—Emile Giradeau, president of Radio France. I remember the first meeting. We sat on boxes in the Paris office and talked. Colonel Sarnoff instructed me to assist in reestablishing the facilities and consulted General Eisenhower on this matter, since it was very touchy politically—some of the French Resistance regarded M. Giradeau as a partial collaborator. We had Radio France back on the air in record time.

Colonel Sarnoff had moved from the Carrillon Hotel to the Majestic, near the Signal Corps HQ. Late one night he called me from his room and asked me to come over immediately. I found him in regular uniform—not battle dress—with a big smile on his face.

"What can I do for you, colonel?" I asked.

His smile widened and he handed me a leather box. "Open this and do me a favor," he said.

The case contained a Legion of Merit medal. Standing at attention, Colonel Sarnoff said, "General Ike just awarded me this, but I wouldn't let him pin it on me. I wanted one of my RCA family to do that. You are the senior RCA member here. Will you please pin the medal on me?"

He beamed. So that was how I took the place of General Eisenhower just that one time during the war.

We continued planning and operating in Paris and roomed together at times until things began to revert to normal. After Rome was liberated, Colonel Sarnoff made an inspection trip to Algiers and Italy. When he returned, he had an interesting story to tell me. While he was in Rome he found out that his old and dear friend, Signora Marconi, was living in a village between Rome and Anzio, sick and poverty-stricken. He visited her and made arrangements with the U.S. Army and Military Government people to have her taken care of and restored to her rightful position.

Colonel Sarnoff made several trips from Paris to London; from the last one he did not return. He said he was leaving for the States and returning to RCA. I stayed on for several months and advised him how things were going. I received an especially long letter from him informing me that his appointment as a brigadier general had been confirmed by Congress. So at last, though with fewer stars, he was in the same class as his old boss, Lieutenant General James G. Harbord.

There is one incident I have omitted. While we were in London, Colonel Joe Berhalter, NBC Station Relations, gave a dinner for Colonel Sarnoff. It was at the Claridge, but we ate army chow. After dinner Colonel Sarnoff took off his tie and jacket, lit a cigar, and put his feet up. "You do the same," he said, to the fifteen or twenty men present. "Ask me any questions you like about the future of our RCA family."

I asked the $64 question: "Will we have color TV after the war?"

"I'm glad you asked that, Brownie," he said. "That is one of the first and most important things RCA will do. We're going all out developing color, local and network. Color TV has the highest priority for RCA."

When Sarnoff talked like that, it meant something. RCA was still a long way from commercializing black-and-white, and here he was determined to invest untold millions in color. He succeeded in both, but a side effect of the color effort was one of the factors which resulted, years later and after David Sarnoff's death, in the Edsel-like RCA debacle in computers.

Brownie got his silver leaf, returned to the States, and paid a single visit to Sarnoff at his Radio City office:

> He welcomed me like a long-lost son. But afterwards I made a vow never to use his influence in the company to my advantage and to keep our relations as personal wartime friends. I have kept that vow. Whenever I met him, in the corridors or offices or anywhere, he would greet me as a friend and I would do the same. We had a few chats but they were limited. My only regret is that I could not visit him in his last illness.
>
> I hope this will be of some value to you, Carl, and you can condense it to fit your project. It is something of a personal tribute to a truly great man and special friend—one deserving of the highest honors in radio and electronics history.

TV HEADACHES

Although obviously the money was in television broadcasting, Sarnoff never neglected the specialized applications, as in teaching, security surveillance of various kinds (apprehending shoplifters, burglars, bank robbers, trespassers, etc.) and, especially, military applications. He envisioned military uses long before television existed as a practical system. In an address before the Army War College on January 31, 1927, he said:

> Perhaps it would be too fantastic to consider the part that may be played by direct television in the war of the future, but it is not too early to consider the direction which laboratories should take in its application to military uses. It is conceivable that a radio-television transmitter installed in an aeroplane might be useful in transmitting a direct image of the enemy's terrain, thus enabling greater accuracy in gunfire.

Early in World War II Sarnoff sent a memo to RCA engineers calling attention to "the potentialities of television-directed weapons" and suggesting that the demands of the armed services might turn out to be beyond RCA's productive capacity in this line. There was in fact some experimentation with robot or "slave" aircraft equipped with television cameras sending back to other aircraft, out of range of enemy antiaircraft fire, pictures of targets which could then be bombed by remote control; but these systems never played a significant part in actual World War II operations. A quarter of a century later, in the bombing of North Vietnamese cities, use was made by the USAF of so-called "smart" bombs guided by laser beams and television images and supposedly of high accuracy, but how much of this was air force press agentry and how much had a sound technological basis it is impossible to say at this time.

The resolution Sarnoff had expressed to Walter Brown he carried out with his usual pertinacity—against the opposition of much of the radio industry, which resisted innovation in much the same way that the movie industry resisted the introduction of sound. We can discern in this connection two separate, though interacting, aspects of Sarnoff's genius for innovation. On one he could rely absolutely—his own drive in the sense of V. S. Pritchett's generalized definition of genius as "a greed for more." The other was not under his control, but in practice it was almost equally reliable: the determination of competitors to resist innovation, to stick with a good thing. They were as greedy as Sarnoff for "more," but it was more profit, using current facilities and investment, with a minimum of risk. Of course this left the field to Sarnoff and made him all the more determined to follow through on his ideas.

The crowning irony was that some of the radio receiver manufacturers who owed their affluence to Sarnoff's "Radio Music Box" now attacked him as a disturber of the peace, bent on ruining *their* industry with his project for adding sight to sound. Of course, since RCA had as large a stake in radio broadcasting as any of them, and larger than most, Sarnoff was taking the same short-term risk. At one time—I am not sure when but it was most likely after television was over the hump —Sarnoff believed TV broadcasting would entirely supplant radio broadcasting, except for small portable receivers and the like. It was one of his few mistaken prognostications; nevertheless he was willing to stake his reputation and even his job—a $50 million loss could have been disabling for RCA—because he was sure that in the long run TV would prove more popular and more profitable than sound alone.

But his critics and traducers were in a position to hamstring him; for a while, at least. Television, as we have seen, requires industrywide standardization; and nothing is easier to obstruct, whether in TV or any other intricate technology. So the World's Fair demonstration amounted to hardly more than a bid for the radio industry to share Sarnoff's foresight and cooperate with RCA in promoting television.

Several of RCA's powerful competitors—Dumont, Zenith, Philco— had each proposed its own standards or declared that it was too early to set standards. On the transmitting and program end, CBS demurred at the expense of TV broadcasting and was joined by many network stations, whose owners likewise preferred a sure thing to Sarnoff's adventurism, as they saw it. Another complication was Armstrong's frequency-modulation system. Having finally lost the legal decision on the regenerative audion to De Forest through the technological ineptitude of the Supreme Court, Armstrong plunged into the culminating venture of his life: frequency modulation. That, too, involved patent complications, but of less severity than in the regenerative case. Armstrong did not invent frequency modulation; all he did was to make it into a superior system of radio broadcasting and point-to-point communication, against the advice of theoreticians who proved mathematically that it would never amount to anything.

Frequency modulation by the Armstrong method practically eliminates static. Anyone can check this by listening to a nearby AM station when there is local lightning and listening to an FM station of approximately the same strength. The obliterating crashes of AM static are reduced to brief pops and are not heard at all when the lightning is not nearby. However, in 1940, this and other points of superiority were not enough to put FM over: AM survived and it is still flourishing in coexistence with FM. Questions of frequency allocation were involved (today an FM broadcasting channel is said to be worth about $2 million) and, at bottom, a lethal conflict between Sarnoff, bent on promoting TV, and Armstrong, who was still committed to the improvement of radio broadcasting, and heading toward what we now call high fidelity. Thus the seeds of irreconcilable contention, culminating in tragedy, were sown.

The war was approaching, yet the contestants in these conflicts ignored it almost entirely; some because they were interested only in today's profits, some because, like Sarnoff, they knew the war would come and go, and with peace the TV conflict would be renewed. Sarnoff assumed he had FCC authorization for a further test of the system he had demonstrated at the World's Fair, but now on a scale sufficiently large to demonstrate commercial feasibility. He ordered the factory to produce 25,000 sets for sale in the New York metropolitan area served by RCA's Empire State transmitter. Regular programming was to begin on September 1, 1940. To make sure there would be no misunderstanding, Sarnoff met James Lawrence Fly, the FCC chairman, in New York in advance of that date and showed him the proof of a full-page ad announcing the plans. Fly read the ad and offered no objection, and the ad appeared in New York City newspapers on March 20. According to Sarnoff's account, Fly then branded the RCA plan as "monopolistic" and pictured himself as the champion of the "little fellows."

Apparently what happened was that, as usual, when the FCC contemplated a move, pressures were brought to bear by powerful companies and individuals in the industry—hardly "little fellows"—at any rate, the FCC rescinded its permission to proceed with the 25,000-set test.

Sarnoff was furious but publicly he kept his temper. He and Fly were the principal witnesses in hearings by the Senate Committee on Interstate Commerce. Sarnoff predicted that TV broadcasting would be a billion-dollar industry, employing half a million people. (He was right, though on a basis far removed from Herbert Hoover's—and Sarnoff's own—concept of radio broadcasting as a public service, undefiled by advertising.) Fly argued that it was premature to launch TV at this time. The controversy raged in the printed and electronic media. Sarnoff got the better press: *The New York Times*, for instance, termed the FCC action "absurd and unsound."

President Roosevelt, who had appointed Fly to the FCC, tried to make peace. He had only a superficial view of the controversy and told Sarnoff he would pay for a luncheon meeting between him and Fly at which they could compose their differences. Sarnoff replied with hauteur not often employed in addressing the President of the United States: "Mr. President, this problem is not in the stomach but in the head. . . . No useful purpose would be served by a goodwill lunch."

Various technical changes were made and incorporated in the present system, but the 1940 controversy was overwhelmed by the preparations for war. On May 27 Roosevelt declared a state of national emergency; TV receiver manufacturing and programming received its quietus before it could get under way.

After V-J Day, the sophisticated technologies and expanded manufacturing facilities of RCA were largely turned back to civilian uses, reaching especially for the television market. The first TV network was opened in 1946 via a coaxial cable (later the mainstay of cable television —the future rival, one may hope, of over-the-air) from upstate New York to Washington. The East Coast was joined to the West Coast by coaxial cable and microwave in 1951. Eventually the NBC TV network spread to all 48 mainland states and comprised well over 200 affiliated stations.

For reception, in 1946 RCA Victor marketed a set with a ten-inch picture tube at a price of $375. Elmer Engstrom describes it as television's "Model T." The comparison is apt: even at that price the 630TS became a people's set. I knew of residents in the outskirts of metropolitan suburbs who shared so little in the local affluence that they lacked indoor plumbing, but they bought the 630TS as soon as it became available. The combination of an outhouse and a $375 TV receiver, bought on easy terms, of course, is revealing. As Dr. Goldsmith used to say, entertainment is a serious thing.

A black-and-white receiver of the 630TS size currently retails at $80. But at $375 there was plenty of profit margin, and in 1946 other manufacturers jumped on the bandwagon. By the end of 1947, 175,000 TV receivers were in use. From then on the growth was exponential: 1948, almost one million; 1949, almost 3 million; 1950, 7 million. About half of this bonanza accrued to RCA. Sarnoff soon had his $50 million back, and then some.

MANAGERIAL STYLE

There were top business executives with Sarnoff's combination of force and foresight before his arrival on the American scene. Whether in the future others will arise to emulate him, who can say? It depends not only on personalities, but on the unpredictable course of events in what seems to bode a troubled time, perhaps worse than any the Republic has experienced since the Civil War. One can be sure of one thing, however: whoever aspires to excel Sarnoff in industrial prescience and perseverance will have his work cut out for him. In his time, and in these qualities, Sarnoff was pretty much in a class by himself.

Not everyone loved him as Rabbi Mandelbaum (Dr. Bernard Mandelbaum, then president of the Jewish Theological Seminary) did, who shared only Sarnoff's last fifteen years, never worked for him directly, and could have had only a secondhand view of what went on in a corporation like RCA. A more encompassing summation appeared after Sarnoff's death in the January 1972 *IEEE Spectrum*, a highly professional monthly published by the Institute of Electrical and Electronics Engineers. *Spectrum* ran a portrait of Sarnoff on its cover and featured an obituary piece aptly titled, "Sarnoff, Controversial Pioneer." The author was Alex McKenzie, a senior editor who may not have had much personal contact with his subject but did have access to those surviving members of the institute who knew Sarnoff well. The subcaption of the piece ran: "Ambition, foresight, and endless hard work drove David Sarnoff to high achievements for himself, his associates, and the electronics industry." Then came a carefully balanced lead paragraph:

> Some say his relentless drive left a wake of uneasiness and fear among his employees and colleagues alike. But for every detractor

there are many who remember David Sarnoff as a tough but fair-minded boss, an autocrat whose decisions were right far more often than wrong. Through his singleness of purpose, Sarnoff helped build the electronics industry.

This seems to me a fair evaluation overall, except that, appearing in a semitechnical publication, it could not go into Sarnoff's destructive activities outside of electronics. Confining ourselves for the present to the electronics sector, there is no denying McKenzie's assertion that Sarnoff's was "the binding force that somehow made things work. His visions, sometimes inconsequential, occasionally wrong, were the material for great expansion and growth that, in turn, created additional engineering opportunities in RCA and elsewhere. He had a keen instinct for survival that required the practical approach to engineering accomplishment."

"Sarnoff was always the hard-headed businessman," McKenzie writes. So would McKenzie be, and so would any of us, if at nine years of age we had sold papers on the Lower East Side in a desperate effort to save a family from disintegrating. But then McKenzie adds something which helps to distinguish the Sarnoff reality, truthfully told, from the spurious press agentry which only served to cheapen him.

Sarnoff, McKenzie says, was at first reluctant to approve the large expenditures for establishing the RCA Laboratories at Princeton. With good reason, no doubt, from a financial viewpoint, but the laboratories have been touted as a great Sarnoff creative idea. Actually, Sarnoff was led into these expenditures by Otto S. Schairer, RCA's chief patent attorney: "Dr. Schairer recalls that Sarnoff was later generous in supporting and promoting expansion and development of the laboratories into the outstanding industrial research organization known today as the David Sarnoff Research Center."

This is typical. Sarnoff had brilliant ideas of his own, but no one—be he president of a corporation or of the United States—has a brain fruitful enough and so free from distraction and error that he can run the enterprise all by himself. That is why we have a legislative as well as an executive branch in the federal government and in the states, and why corporation executives have staffs or advisors and harken more or less to the views of boards of directors. Sarnoff would occasionally throw out an idea at a conference which was politely torn to pieces by the others present, whereupon he would usually agree and waste no more time on it. Or he might convert it into something more practical. When somebody else had a good idea, once Sarnoff was convinced he threw his weight behind it, as when Schairer proposed to consolidate the scattered RCA research efforts into the productive central establishment at Princeton.

At the same time Sarnoff was dangerous; at the office one had to be wary with him. At Princeton he was more relaxed and in his later years he seems to have been quite popular there among all classes of employees. Much earlier, for a while he had an assistant at the Radio City headquarters, Pat Rafferty, a handsome man-about-town who had been General Harbord's aide. He was fine company, equally at home with debutantes and nightclub hostesses, and knowing all the right places. Putting some papers before Sarnoff late one afternoon, Rafferty innocently ventured a remark about an RCA executive who, in point of fact, was giving more trouble than he was worth. Looking over his shoulder, Sarnoff said, "When I want your advice, Rafferty, I'll ask for it."

Rafferty had been in combat in World War I. Discharged as a major, in World War II (but that was long after this rebuke) he served as a colonel. He had the temperament, then, of a professional soldier, one who did not scare easily. Recounting this incident, he told me that as Sarnoff's eyes met his, it was like looking into the eyes of a tiger.

McKenzie writes to the same effect that "the fear of bringing down Sarnoff's wrath—which could strike like a thunderbolt as a result of some non-function—was strong in all RCA employees." He cites a story told by George Bailey, the retired executive secretary of IEEE, about Ray Guy, who was setting up a television transmitting antenna on the Empire State tower. Sarnoff asked when the station would be on the air. McKenzie continues:

> Guy said the time would be 9 A.M. Sarnoff expressed the hope that it would be a good show, because he was having some people join him in his New York City apartment at 5 P.M. It is reported that Guy began to worry after the station had made its debut on schedule. With Mrs. Sarnoff's collusion, he tried the main television receiver in the apartment. There was little or no signal. Additional antenna elements were quickly jury-rigged from the tower to get the television signal down to Sarnoff's apartment, and they remained there for years, according to Bailey. Sarnoff never found out about them.

This is impressive because around that time Guy was president of the Institute of Radio Engineers and a personage in his own right. Also, he was a phlegmatic type. With an ordinary management figure, he would probably have explained that the apartment was in a dead area and measures would be taken in due course to lay down a satisfactory signal there. Not with Sarnoff!

Intimidation is a frequently used means of getting things done in business. In its most common form, it is expressed in the high decibels. According to *Fortune*, aluminum magnate Arthur Vining Davis could be heard two stories below his office in the Alcoa Building in Pittsburgh when reasoning with a subordinate. With rare exceptions, that was not Sarnoff's way. He could make the guilty one cower inwardly by a few well-chosen words at normal conversational level, accompanied by a freezing look.

Still, none of this answers the question: why did we take him so seriously, aside from his power to hire and fire? Perhaps Rabbi Mandelbaum came up with a clue when he pointed out that Sarnoff spared no one, least of all himself. If Sarnoff had been a severe taskmaster but had indulged himself, he would have provoked resentment, perhaps even rebellion. But we knew—the evidence was always before us—that Sarnoff worked harder, and thought and planned more assiduously, than any of us did, or could do. That did not make us love him; nor did he care about our love. It did make us feel obliged to exert ourselves as he did, or come as close as possible, but we were always conscious that we fell short of our full capability, as he did not. Thus, when we failed him, we feared not only his contempt, but our own towards ourselves.

People outside of RCA were also subject to Sarnoff's discipline, and some knew intuitively how to get along with him. Some did not. McKenzie tells about an off-the-record press conference in the early fifties at which a reporter was rash enough to twit Sarnoff with a question about color television, at a time when monochrome television had not yet begun to pay. Worse, CBS was pushing a mechanical—as opposed to an electronic—system of color television which was so regressive and obstructive that it could have enraged a less impatient man than Sarnoff. The resulting scene, in McKenzie's words: "Sarnoff's face grew red and seemed visibly to swell. If his fist did not strike the table, the impact of his voice was almost frightening. 'Nobody,' he shouted, 'is going to stop the development of television!' There were no more questions."

Within RCA, there were disadvantages inherent in this stern management style of Sarnoff's. He was a strong man. To work for him at close quarters one not only had to be strong, but of a particular temperament —nerves of steel, invincible poise, and speed on the uptake. Sarnoff was so conditioned to contentious negotiation that any show of uncertainty or vulnerability on the part of people who were not contending with him for advantage irritated him, much as a top-notch athlete or mechanic cannot stand a clumsy performance in his specialty. He made no allowance for the fact that people not gifted with his business acuity were under a handicap in any intercourse with him. He was always the same, always at his best; they were at their worst.

Some RCA employees, as well as outsiders, insisted that Sarnoff was too dictatorial in his management techniques, and increasingly so as he grew older. Thomas Whiteside, interviewing him for an article, "David Sarnoff's Fifty Years," (*Collier's*, October 12, 1956) noted this tendency:

> In running RCA or anything else connected with his life, Sarnoff, it is clear, has a passion for economical organization. He has no time for waste motion or trivial matters. "I don't want to do what someone else can do," is the way he puts this. Sarnoff probably dictates no more than half a dozen letters during the average day. He never lets papers pile up. When he finishes with one, which he does quickly, he sends it away and then begins the next; so it is with people and ideas.
>
> Everything in Sarnoff's life is done by plan, everything in its proper sequence. . . . When a visitor to the 53rd floor of the RCA Building has gone through the ritual of being marched under escort from the outer reaches of the General's suite through deeply carpeted corridors and an impressive succession of inner offices, he is ushered in to see Sarnoff at almost the very second that the interview was arranged to begin. The General is all attention; when he has heard and said what he wants to, he closes the interview with firm and unmistakable finality and then, in the manner of a man tearing off a page from a desk calendar, he turns to the next piece of business.

All true and relevant, but also true and relevant was Sarnoff's view: "In a big ship sailing in an uncharted sea, one fellow needs to be on the bridge. I happen to be that fellow." Hence the requirement that memos addressed to him should be limited to a single page, which he would return with a yes or a no or some other equally laconic reply, or, in exceptional cases, "Pls see me," Nobody popped into his office with a question, and by some accounts a prearranged visit was more in the nature of an audience than a discussion between colleagues. Yet, two years before Whiteside saw Sarnoff, I asked for thirty minutes with him, and after an hour had passed and I had learned what I wanted to know and much else, *I* terminated the interview, for fear that I was unnecessarily taking up his time. He looked astonished for a second, then said amiably, "That shows what a good reporter you are."

After all, there were only twenty-four hours in Sarnoff's day, the same as in a bootblack's, and Sarnoff was, exactly as he said, the fellow on the bridge. And against the complaints of Sarnoff's stern rule, it is only fair to consider the fact that Elmer Engstrom, who worked with Sarnoff for nearly forty years, began a written account of his impressions of Sarnoff which I will later quote in full, with the simple statement: "I genuinely liked him."

Sarnoff's executive manner was the only one with which he could function as effectively as he did, but some executives operate in a softer way and nevertheless reach the top. One example was H. I. Romnes, who until his mandatory retirement in 1972 at age sixty-five, was president and board chairman of AT&T, a much larger corporation than RCA. His obituary in the November 21, 1973 *New York Times* included the comment that company employees agreed that he was the "best" chairman they ever had, which presumably means that they felt more rapport with him than with his predecessors. He was generally more liberal than Sarnoff:

> Among his favorite themes [according to the *Times*] were the ideas that even sudden change can be rationally managed; that taking time to know the other person better and to listen to him tends to diminish differences; that institutions have no rights except through performance; that long-term consequences are more important than quick results; and that even in a complex society, one man can make a difference.

But Romnes's success consisted in maintaining in good health, with a minimum of risk, a corporation which was already doing well when he took charge. Under his management there was expansion and technological progress, but he was not a radical innovator like Sarnoff—nor was anyone else in the five decades (1917–1967) during which Sarnoff did his work.

That work—a long struggle against industrial inertia—called for a consistently aggressive managerial attitude. In *Science and Government* (1961), C. P. Snow remarks on the importance of assurance in any crisis of action: "It is not so relevant whether you are right or wrong. That is a second-order effect. But it is cardinal that you should be positive."

One must, Snow adds, not only be certain of one's course of action, but be able to explain it lucidly. He could have been writing about Sarnoff.

Managerial positiveness may approach brutality at times, but there may be some excuse for the executive involved. Nor was Sarnoff the only offender. Patrick E. Haggerty is said to have reduced hapless employees to a "pulp" at big meetings of Texas Instruments executives, but the chances are that the victims had brought it on themselves by bluffing or trying to pull the wool over the boss's eyes which, as I have noted in relation to Sarnoff, was a suicidal error. In such cases severe reprimands are to be expected and may be a necessary part of managerial makeup and operating procedure. But that cuts both ways. The official cannot afford to publicly humiliate subordinates—or for that matter privately—without just cause. If he made a practice of chastising people for no good reason, he would speedily lose his best men.

Haggerty was more than a match for Sarnoff in several areas of RCA-Texas Instruments competition. In 1952, when transistors were still a novelty, though one with a promising future, Bell Labs held a conference for prospective licensees. The exposition was comprehensive and the terms were liberal—the big fellows had learned their lesson, in part from Sarnoff's excessive terms for licenses in the early days of radio broadcasting. Texas Instruments, a small instruments and geophysical exploration firm, took out a license. They were looking for a bonanza and they found it, though not without arduous efforts of their own. Starting with what Bell Labs gave them, they embarked on their own program of research, development and investment, amounting, according to Christopher Layton et al. (*Ten Innovations*, 1972) to an average of $4 million in each of the following four years. Within six years, according to Layton, they developed the silicon transistor, the germanium transistor, and the first integrated circuit. There may well be argument about who did what in regard to these devices; what is certain is that Texas Instruments secured a dominant place in the semiconductor industry with rapidly increasing turnover:

Year	Sales, in Millions
1953	20
1959	93
1969	832
1974	1,502*

It was a classical case of a small company with adequate financial resources making the right technical decisions with the right technical and managerial personnel and capturing a major part of the market— precisely because they were small at the outset. In contrast, RCA was already big, with its best managerial and technical talent spread thin, and concentrating just then on color TV. Layton credits Texas Instruments with "carefully disciplined creative energy which makes for success in transforming technology from invention into the market place."

Haggerty's success throws light on Sarnoff's success, both in the similarities and differences. Sarnoff prevailed in radio and TV broadcasting, as in wireless telegraphy earlier, by sheer perspicacity, assiduity, foresight, astute evaluation of researchers and the products of research, and other personal attributes which were in part intuitive. He had neither the time nor the inclination to formulate these attributes in print. In contrast, Haggerty's ideas on management are set forth quite systematically. He was aware that in management, as in any art, sound theory supports and guides practice. His papers on "Innovation and the Private Enterprise System in the United States" (1968), "Technology and the American Standard of Living" (1970), "Economic Growth and Quality of Life" (1974), far eclipse anything Sarnoff expressed publicly in these fields. This doesn't make Haggerty a Sarnoff, nor did he claim such distinction. The devices Texas Instruments developed were important but they served mainly to implement the fundamental ideas and devices developed by RCA under Sarnoff's management.

A crucial fact in research, development, investment, and marketing is that there are only so many first-rate managers around. Sarnoff, being one of the few himself, was well aware of this deficiency, and it was

*Based on first-quarter sales, preceding the recession.

no small achievement when he managed to recruit David E. Lilienthal, the first director of the Tennessee Valley Authority and later chairman of the Atomic Energy Commission. He worked for RCA as a part-time consultant for two years, most of the time directly under Sarnoff, with whom he had a cordial relationship.

From my viewpoint—that of an outsider but one with some knowledge of the circumstances and Sarnoff's mode of operation—I am practically certain Sarnoff was grooming Lilienthal for the RCA presidency. Nonetheless, this is a surmise on my part, a conjecture—it is difficult enough in writing biography to get the facts straight without stretching speculations, however plausible, into facts. Lilienthal heard the same report from people closer to the scene, but not specifically enough to either affirm or deny it.

In Volume 3 of his *Journals* (1950–1955) Lilienthal writes that when the time came to renew the consultant contract, Sarnoff expressed satisfaction with Lilienthal's association with RCA,

> but he also wanted to say that twice during the year he had been quite disappointed and somewhat puzzled. He had proposed projects for me to head, which would have put me in a strategic position to carry on the things which for years he had been carrying, functions for which there were no successors. . . . He said he had taken the precaution of checking all through the company and getting . . . enthusiastic approval for the idea of my heading up the color "field tests" . . . if I spearheaded these demonstrations it would put me in line to handle the function which he had been carrying—this relation between overall management and the technical people. . . . Yet I turned this down. I wanted something which RCA could not provide: capital gains . . ."

That was the sticking point. As head of TVA, Lilienthal's salary had been $10,000 a year. This isn't quite as bad as it sounds, since these were 1930 dollars; but it was bad enough to make accumulation of capital henceforth a necessity. Lilienthal solved the problem by founding the Development and Resources Corporation, a worldwide company which provides managerial guidance to underdeveloped countries, applying TVA methods of development to Iran, Brazil, and other countries. No doubt he would have done well in RCA likewise, but he might have become involved in the computer debacle, one in which no amount of experience and business acumen could avail.

Lilienthal's recollections of Sarnoff are peculiarly reliable not only because he was an experienced and discerning observer but at an early age he learned Gregg shorthand and made a practice of taking notes immediately after an interview or meeting. He was also careful to check other people's impressions against his own. He tells of an hour-and-a-half conversation in 1951 with an unnamed informant who knew Sarnoff well. This "X" said Sarnoff had no other interest than work—somewhat too sweeping but it approaches the truth. "X" went on to say that Sarnoff hated to hear bad news or to have people in RCA disagree with him. This may well have been true at the time and in relation to some of Sarnoff's subordinates, but it does not jibe with Lilienthal's own impression in the same paragraph: "a fascinating picture of a strong but very human man, a fighter, a pioneer, and not an easy man to understand—too complex."

Lilienthal did not have a close association with Sarnoff until the fifties, when Sarnoff was in his sixties. Earlier, when Sarnoff received bad news, it just impelled him to jump in and clean things up. As he said, when asked which was his favorite division in RCA: "the one that's in trouble." Lilienthal also writes, "Sarnoff's passion is on the research end of the business," and while that is true it is not the whole truth—certainly not in Sarnoff's opinion. A good many people said he was not sufficiently profit-minded; he denied the charge with some heat and could have replied that for some businessmen profits, no matter how large, are never large enough.

In color, at least, Sarnoff seems to have struck a good balance. Dr. Edward W. Herold, one of the prime movers in the crucial color project at Princeton, told me that when it first came up, in his opinion it was hardly of major importance—it might add 10 percent, say, to RCA's profits from TV. Actually it proved highly profitable, providentially at a time when prices of black-and-white TV sets were slipping.

Although Lilienthal's connection with RCA was relatively brief, indirectly he exerted considerable influence on the future setup on the 53rd floor of the RCA building. Except for Sarnoff, he regarded Engstrom as the best brain in the corporation. "He has a good executive's mind," Lilienthal wrote. "He analyzes things, knows how to move from where you are to the next station." Engstrom's title was senior executive vice-president, but he had been around so long that Sarnoff more or less took him for granted. In 1957 Sarnoff chose for the presidency John L. Burns, a senior partner in Booz Allen & Hamilton, a firm of management consultants which had done previous work for RCA.

Conflicts of policy and personality developed, and Burns departed four years later. Sarnoff then awarded the presidency to Engstrom, with whom he would have been better off in the first place. If, as I suspect, Sarnoff had Lilienthal in mind for the presidency and Lilienthal had accepted, Engstrom would presumably have retired as the topmost of the vice-presidents, and the succession of Robert W. Sarnoff to the presidency—and later to chairman of the board—would have been delayed. But more on that subject later.

Next witness: author of *Biography of an Idea: Memoirs of Public Relations Counsel Edward L. Bernays,* (1965). Bernays was deputized by Sarnoff to look over NBC, in charge of Lenox R. Lohr, appointed president after serving as general manager of the Chicago World's Fair of 1939. Sarnoff told Bernays that Lohr lacked *saichel* (Yiddish for shrewdness, capacity for quick understanding) and needed help in that respect. Bernays failed to establish rapport with Lohr but from other sources found in NBC "the internecine warfare between executives was always greater and more intense than their common action against the competition or to meet the problems the company was facing." Bernays asked Sarnoff for an organization chart of NBC so that he could determine who was responsible to whom, and for what. Sarnoff's answer was, "My dear Eddie, this is a company of men, not of charts."

Of course, in any business organization, an organization chart is only an approximation of personnel relations. The corporate imperialists expand in power and influence, the weak or failing sink below their nominal status. Apparently, however, Sarnoff had made up his mind that in an electronic show-biz hybrid like NBC, an organization schematic had little if any meaning. As a corollary, he was telling Bernays that he himself, or an appointee responsible to him, would make decisions extemporaneously. Nothing more was required in the way of a chain of command. When disputes about jurisdiction and power occurred down the line, if they were important enough they would come up to him, and he would decide. Insofar as there was an organization chart, it was in Sarnoff's head—or he would improvise one when there was need.

In Peter F. Drucker's *Management, Tasks, Responsibilities, Practices* (1973), we can view an RCA management failure from a different and instructive angle. Drucker points out that IBM, the outstanding leader in computerization for many years, was a Johnny-come-lately in that field. Univac, GE, and RCA were well ahead of IBM in electronic know-how. But leadership in engineering is not enough in business conflict. IBM's punch-card salesmen asked the right questions and got the right answers. With that approach, IBM could develop engineering from within or buy it from outside. The outcome of this difference in viewpoint was well-nigh catastrophic for RCA after David Sarnoff's death—a setback which will be treated in a later chapter.

Drucker also explains why RCA failed in the kitchen appliance business—ranges, refrigerators, etc. RCA had the engineering compe-tence and the distribution network. They had a solid base in living-room appliances—TV, radio, radio-phonograph combinations, etc. Their trouble was with the housewife, who saw living-room appliances as furniture and means of entertainment, while kitchen appliances were household machinery, like the boiler or furnace for central heating, except that the location was where she exercised sole authority if she chose to. She usually took advantage of her sovereignty, and was not impressed by RCA's prominence in electronics. After a few years of futile struggle, RCA was forced to sell its kitchen appliance business to a manufacturer with an established reputation in that field.

Sarnoff has received deserved praise for the seventeen years during which the NBC Orchestra, conducted by Arturo Toscanini, was on the air. Sarnoff's role in Toscanini's crack-up at the last concert has been less publicized, but a plausible version has come to light in George R. Marek's *Toscanini* (1974). Marek, an RCA vice-president and general manager of RCA Records, was an experienced biographer as well as a musician; a more reliable judge of what happened could hardly be imagined.

From a business standpoint, Sarnoff probably had no choice—the mismanagement was in the way Toscanini, then eighty-seven years old, was manhandled. The Maestro was in the habit of writing a letter of resignation towards the end of each season in a yes, no, maybe key. This time (March 25, 1954) Sarnoff had a letter of resignation drafted for Toscanini. On March 29, before Toscanini had affixed his signature, Sarnoff drafted a cordial letter of acceptance: ". . . I realize that after more than sixty-five years of absolute dedication to the art of music you have fully earned the right to lay down your baton." The correspon-dence was released to the press before the concert. However uninten-tionally, it became a sort of "Here's your hat, what's your hurry?" situation.

For a full minute during the concert, Toscanini was paralyzed, unable to continue. There was chaos in the orchestra, with one of the cellists preparing to take up the baton. Marek's version is that as he stood on the podium, Toscanini knew that "his artistic demise had been proclaimed that very hour, and it is reasonable to assume that this contributed to his malaise. . . . The whole matter was handled with consummate stupidity."

THE SARNOFF
WAY OF LIFE

While performing prodigies in electronics innovation and management, Sarnoff rewarded himself on the material side with the perquisites that customarily go with conspicuous success: spacious office suites, including a sumptuous private dining room; the town house in the most expensive part of Manhattan; the baronial quarters RCA provided for him at Princeton, etc. Seen in perspective, Sarnoff's life covered in succession all three of Marx's nineteenth-century concepts of the class structure of society: the proletariat living in excruciating poverty; the middle class or petty bourgeosie; and the grand bourgeosie or capitalists in possession of the means of production and living accordingly. That Sarnoff was more of a manager than a big owner of the productive machinery himself did not affect this progression. He could have been a major capitalist if he had wanted to, but he preferred to play that role by proxy, augmenting RCA's capital rather than his own. However, at a time when a single million was still a mark of wealth, or at least a promising start, he remarked to me: "I live like a millionaire, but I haven't got a million." He must have been pretty close to it, and in his later years he built an estate of a few millions, but that was all.

If he had been single-heartedly intent on making money, the scorecard could have been radically different. The estimate of his brother Lew—that David could have accumulated a personal fortune of $200 million, more or less, if he had put his mind to it—seems to me entirely plausible. Lew qualifies as a sound judge in such matters. He became a millionaire himself, without help from David although he conceded that the connection did him some good—businessmen are impressed by a family relationship with a prominent man. Lew made his money in businesses which lacked the glamour of broadcasting—like a messenger service which he turned over to a nephew, cleaning skyscraper windows when curtain-wall architecture was taking hold, and an early interest in the Diner's Club. The way he put it was that he always thought "downwards"—the existing mundane things that had to be done and ways of doing them efficiently, while David thought "upwards" towards new and far-reaching services which, for better or worse, (or both) changed the world.

Lew and David Sarnoff made their relatively modest fortunes the hard way, constructively. Compared with the nouveaux riches of today, they were pikers. *Fortune* (September 1973) listed more than a dozen Americans who in the last few years accumulated more than $100 million each, and at least two dozen more in the $50 million to $100 million range. The study, by Arthur M. Lewis, excluded everyone who had big money before 1969. An article in *The New York Times* (August 27, 1973) summarizing these data, showed a thirty-five-year-old; Leonard N. Stern, head of Hartz Mountain Corporation, whose wealth was estimated at between $500 and $700 million! (Hartz Mountain deals in pets, pet foods and accessories. The name comes from a species of canaries.)

Sarnoff's marriage to Lizette Hermant took place during the middle stage, when he was ascending in the Marconi Company and, having provided some security for his parental family, could afford to raise one of his own. The date was July 4, 1917, and the couple were married in the Bronx, which was then a respectable, mostly middle-class residential borough. The ceremony has been described as a typical modest Jewish wedding. If a cantor or other vocalist added to the solemnity or joyousness of the occasion (it will be remembered that as a boy soprano Sarnoff sang at Jewish weddings) I would assume that the vocal contribution was likewise unpretentious. At Sarnoff's funeral, fifty-four years later, the cantor was Richard Tucker, a friend of the family and a long-time leading tenor of the Metropolitan Opera, who had got his start in small Northern New Jersey synagogues. For Tucker, at the height of his career, and Sarnoff, at the end of both career and life, the compass of personal celebrity was the same; but within three years, Tucker, too, died.

Mount Vernon, where the couple lived during the early years of their marriage, was and is a predominantly middle-class, undistinguished Westchester County suburb. Scarsdale had not achieved its present grandeur in the teens and early twenties, but when the Sarnoffs could have afforded it they preferred to move in the other direction, to Manhattan. There, after a succession of apartments of rising size and status, when Sarnoff's salary was increased to $100,000 in 1937, they purchased the five-story twenty-eight-room house on 71st Street, between Madison and Park. If bought at the market, it turned out to be a wild bargain for anyone who could afford the taxes. The forty-foot frontage is nearly double that of many quite impressive mansions in the East Sixties, Seventies, and Eighties, a considerable number of the larger ones having been converted to foreign embassies and other nonprofit uses. Even multi-multimillion families like the Woolworths found it expedient to turn over their seventy-five-foot frontage at 2 East 63rd Street, just off Fifth Avenue, to the tax-exempt New York Academy of Sciences. The Sarnoff acquisition was only a couple of blocks from the supermansion which the steel magnate Henry Clay Frick had the architect design as a magnificent art museum for eternity, rather than a necessarily transitory residence for himself. Frick was able to afford a full-block frontage on Fifth Avenue with a lovely garden in front and extending back almost to Madison Avenue—nearly an entire square block.

The Sarnoffs lived in the 71st Street house for thirty-four years, so they got their money's worth out of it. And if, as the saying goes, living well is the best revenge, they did doubly well. When David died, at the age of eighty, it was for Mrs. Sarnoff the end of a marriage which was a success as remarkable in its way as Sarnoff's career in the exploitation of electronics engineering.

Yet, prior to this courtship and marriage, Sarnoff had a narrow escape. I have mentioned Nan Malkind, the first office secretary of the Institute of Radio Engineers. When Nan was young, it could be said—the lines are Pope's:

> If to her fate some mortal errors fall
> Look on her face and you'll forgive them all.

Or you could look at her figure with the same result. She came from Trenton, New Jersey, at the age of sixteen, with only a primary- and business-school education. Her lower-middle-class parents managed to equip her with that and then she was on her own. The qualities nature had given her, plus the vocational training, were more than adequate.

She had a good, practical mind and a realistic appraisal of people. For another of her qualities I cannot account: she had not lived among cultivated people, but by her speech she could not be readily distinguished from a graduate of Smith or Vassar. She was more than pretty, though not beautiful in the movie sense. She was discreet in her business relationships, but attractive to a variety of men for the usual reasons, enhanced by a gamine quality which was both amusing and sexy.

She was born in 1895, which would make 1911 the year of her arrival in New York, when Sarnoff was still a wireless operator. She must have had a job—or jobs—before she was employed by the Institute of Radio Engineers, since it was not founded until 1912. Sarnoff met her through the institute, of which he became an associate member in the year of its founding. By 1917 he was a fellow—a rapid rise paralleling his rise in American Marconi. In that interval he also served a term or two as the elected secretary of the institute. While Miss Malkind ran the IRE office as the one and only paid employee, she was subject to the orders of Sarnoff and the other elected officials, who, as in all professional societies, served without pay.

Sarnoff and Miss Malkind began going together four or five years before he met Miss Hermant. He was making about $40 a week, enough to get married on. His formal education was no better than hers; she had been born in the United States, the daughter of Russian immigrants, while he was an immigrant himself, so there was not the social gap which opened up later. He met her parents and brothers and sisters in Brooklyn: hers was a large family. It was all as decorous as tentative relationships between respectable young Jewish girls and men usually were at that time. If a conventional Jewish man wanted to seduce a girl, he had to find a suitable *shiksa.*

Some years later, when I got to know her well, Nan told me casually that he had wanted to marry her. I always found her completely truthful; even if in this case she exaggerated an interest which may have been only exploratory, marriage was a possibility. The chief obstacle was that Sarnoff did not attract her. He always smelled of tobacco, she complained; that distaste was probably a manifestation of something deeper and indecipherable. Moreover, there was competition from other men, perhaps more sophisticated at that stage than Sarnoff in the wiles and stratagems of courtship. One was a well-to-do Broadway haberdasher, another, Emil J. Simon, who left Columbia University during World

War I, made a million in radio manufacturing for the services, and lost it all in a gallant but premature effort to establish an intercity radiotelegraph service.

Miss Malkind would not have made a suitable wife for a man with a career like Sarnoff's ahead of him. This is apparent from the only letter of hers I ever kept, at a time when I had no idea that I would ever be writing about Sarnoff. I did not know I had it and came upon it only when I was embarked on this project and was looking for Sarnoff memorabilia. The letter is dated March 27, 1934, when Nan had a duplicating and mailing service in the Wall Street area and was married to a bathrobe manufacturer. I was working in Hollywood. The pertinent part reads as follows:

> Some friends of mine wanted an audition and knowing that I knew him [Sarnoff] asked me to intercede for them—a boy and girl team —so I wrote him and he phoned me and asked me to come up and see him. So I did, but I was snotty as hell. Told him I didn't know he was president—which I really didn't. Thought he was vice-president—and that I wouldn't want to be in his shoes, which came about thisaway. I asked him to take me to lunch when he was downtown sometime and he said, "What, take you to lunch! Why, I haven't taken a young lady to lunch for the past 15 years. I wouldn't dare. It would be in Walter Winchell's column and what-not if I were seen with a girl." So I said, "Well, I suppose you get compensated for not being able to do what you want, by being a big shot," and so on. I don't think he liked it very well. We talked about old times mostly. When I first came in he told me that anyone could get an audition and that if he gave me a letter to anyone in the studio it would only prejudice them against the people and they would be better off just taking their chances.

What I think is significant here is Nan's unmannerly lack of respect for Sarnoff, characteristic of her but I think exaggerated in this instance to show she wasn't impressed and perhaps—I am conjecturing—she now felt some regret that she hadn't grabbed Sarnoff when she had the opportunity. I knew her husband—a nice guy and successful in bathrobe manufacturing but. Still, while her choosing to be "snotty" was at least partly reactive, for her, Sarnoff remained a formerly eligible Jewish boy, now somewhat overweight and still smelling of tobacco, though of the finest Havana quality.

Even more than the generality of highly successful businessmen, Sarnoff had an expansive ego and often expatiated on subjects about which he didn't know much and lacked the intuitive "feel" which comes with experience. But he did not do this as naïvely as many industrialists do, nor as rashly as Edison did in his later years. Sarnoff always gave the impression of having given the matter some thought and, not infrequently, out of the blue he would come up with a piece of insight or a witty observation which not only showed understanding, but inspired it in others. As when, rejected for membership in a riding club, he exclaimed, more in amazement than in chagrin: "They'll take my horse but they won't take me!" That crack circulated about New York and skewered the WASP idiots who had blackballed him.

At the least, supplementing his absorption in corporate problems, Sarnoff's wide-ranging thinking, even when it was superficial, made his life more interesting, both for himself and others. It also had a psychologically prophylactic function. Sarnoff could never have found himself in the pathetic situation of a man like Harlow Curtice of General Motors, described in a biographical piece by Rush Loving, Jr. in the September 1973 *Fortune* about an atypical General Motors executive, John DeLorean, who quit long before retirement age. Curtice made $750,000 a year while he was boss at GM—about three times Sarnoff's average. He ran the company "almost as a monarchy" with spectacular success. Sarnoff ran RCA in the same way and with the same results, but there the similarity ends.

DeLorean told Loving he almost worshiped Curtice until after meeting him at a California golf club some years following the older man's retirement. Still impressed, he mentioned Curtice to the professional at the club. What followed was an eye-opener for DeLorean and one of the reasons for his premature retirement.

"That's the loneliest human being who ever lived," the pro told DeLorean. "He comes into my golf shop for a couple of hours every day and talks to me and my assistant about the automobile business. We don't know anything about the automobile business, but we listen to him. He just seems to want to talk so badly."

Sarnoff didn't play golf; that alone set him off from the accepted model of the American businessman. And he never lacked for an audience: he had extraordinary oral charisma even before he began talking. You only had to look at him to want to talk with him. Mrs. Sarnoff, of course, had maximal opportunities in that respect and she did not fail to take advantage of them. In her article, "My life with a

Genius," *Good Housekeeping,* June 1955, she paid her husband a rare tribute and, not realizing it, paid the same tribute to herself: "I have been fascinated for thirty-eight years; every one of those thousands of days he has made my life like being at a play, like sitting in a theater. I can think of no man who has given more to a woman."

She tells how, lolling in his bathing trunks on the beach (he could not swim) Sarnoff would be engaged in conversation by a stranger, shortly others would join them, and he would have a fascinated audience. He might be talking about radio or television, or about things not connected with his primary interests. When anyone else was talking, he paid close attention. He never interrupted, but in almost any gathering he was the center of attention.

While Engstrom was president of RCA, he and Sarnoff had a standing luncheon date once a week in Sarnoff's private dining room just below the executive floor. These lunches were three-hour affairs without benefit of martinis—Engstrom did not drink at all and Sarnoff drank very little, even in the evening. The verbal exchanges usually started off with the current problems of RCA, went on to general business matters, and finally to politics, national and international. Engstrom is a normally articulate, exceptionally thoughtful man; he looks and talks more like a professor than a top manager in a big corporation. I gathered that although he enjoyed these marathon sessions with Sarnoff, he found them rather overwhelming. Everyone who came in contact with Sarnoff marveled at his gift of discerning, forceful speech; but perhaps three hours at a single sitting was too much.

What was most astonishing was that English was not Sarnoff's native tongue and he was largely self-educated; yet he had this remarkable facility. Dr. Claude M. Fuess, the headmaster at Andover for many years, commented on this in his oral reminiscences recorded at Columbia University. In a discussion of the quality of teaching, Fuess said to a teacher, "You were rugged. You were, if I may say so, like David Sarnoff as an immigrant boy from Russia to this country, faced with hardship but able to take it."

All three Sarnoff boys attended Andover. It was a tough school, and almost certainly that was one reason Sarnoff sent his sons there. Perhaps also because he realized that Fuess was a truly educated man and a first-rate judge of both men and boys. He read *Anna Karenina* every year and compared *War and Peace* with Hardy's *The Dynasts,* which

I read with admiration in my twenties and never thereafter met anyone who had read it, with admiration or not. Sarnoff came up to Andover now and then to see how his sons were getting along. At a Sunday lunch at Fuess's house, Sarnoff and President James B. Conant of Harvard were guests. Fuess recounts:

> In the conversation that followed after lunch in my study, I remember watching those two faces, very interesting faces, both of them, and listening to the conversation. . . . No one could have told, listening to the two men, which one had had the very formal education through the various grades, and which one had almost no formal education. Mr. Sarnoff's adjectives and verbs and adverbs were just as good as those of Mr. Conant, and the ideas matched his perfectly. In other words, these were two highly educated men, highly cultured men, one of whom had a very formal education, the other had had almost no formal education at all.

Language was one of Sarnoff's implements of power. That, and that only, was why he acquired unusual facility in English—especially in spoken English, where the personality shines through more than in writing. He would not be regarded as well read, although he picked up an impressive amount of general information from one source or another. I never heard him quote—certainly nothing apropos—and I would be astonished if I heard that he read poetry—the most succinct and eloquent form of language. The beauty and grace of the language, the derivation of words and what it tells us about the human beings who created and re-create it, nor its imperfections—none of these were among his interests. He was fluent, discerning in his choice of words, incisive and often witty, but Fuess most likely got the idea that Conant and Sarnoff were alike "highly cultured" from a conversation limited to practical topics of interest. Not business in the narrow sense: if, for instance, Conant had happened to talk about the defects of secondary education, a subject on which he was an acknowledged authority, Sarnoff would have followed his argument and very likely contributed ideas of his own.

What we are dealing with is the development of a first-class mind under the adverse conditions of public education—to which Sarnoff was careful not to submit his sons. He spoke English admirably because, at the very beginning, when he knew only a few words, he realized that command of the American language was essential if he was to "better" himself, i.e., make a living for his family. Later, as the objective broadened, his vocabulary and verbal skill broadened proportionately. And of course, from his later twenties on, he was largely in the company of people who could serve as models in that respect.

The Sarnoffs divided responsibility between them—he ran RCA and she bore the children (Robert, 1918; Edward, 1921; Thomas, 1927) and ran the household. She not only brought the children into the world, but had far more to do with raising them than Sarnoff did. Not that it was a marriage on the pattern of Bismarck's relegation of women to *"Kirche, Kinder und Küche"*—church, children and kitchen. Mrs. Sarnoff had managerial ability of her own, and some of her husband's no doubt rubbed off on her. For many years she was on the board of trustees of the New York Infirmary, and during World War II she worked full time as chairman of the hospital's Red Cross Nurses Unit. After the war she continued to spend several days a week as director of volunteers. She survived her husband by a little over two years.

Sarnoff did not have time for anything but the big decisions. He told Lizette before they were married that her decisions would be of less gravity than his, but there would be more of them; and that was the way in which it worked out. In fact, she took over many minor matters that conventionally devolve on the male. Sarnoff was a stickler for elegance in dress at the office; this led him into an absurd declaration to the effect that you could judge the quality of a man's mind by the way he dressed. He forgot Einstein, Heywood Broun, and a good many other sloppy dressers who knew what the score was. Yet he could not dress himself in a style befitting his image of himself. Mrs. Sarnoff wrote in the *Good Housekeeping* piece that she bought all his clothes and neckties. Since his suits were tailor-made, presumably this meant she chose the fabric from a swatch. She complained that he always wanted the same suit over again, and the same color.

Sarnoff had other peculiarities. His inability to drive without making Mrs. Sarnoff nervous has already been mentioned. He seemed constantly to be fighting the machine, she said. Perhaps he was right, then, in abandoning the idea of making a career of engineering. Most engineers are good drivers, not by original nature but by the impulsion of their training to study the hazards of the road and become aware of their own deficiencies.

A different kind of idiosyncrasy was his reluctance to tip in cash. He was not a particularly democratic person—I have a good deal of evidence to the contrary. The evidence indicates he wanted to be democratic, but it conflicted with his predominant sense of order, efficiency, and corporate hierarchy. He tipped, and generously, Mrs. Sarnoff emphasizes, but annually, by check. He dealt in this way not only with his barber and manicurist, but when the Sarnoffs ate out he wanted always to go to the same restaurant, where he handled gratuities in the same way.

He was the least athletic of men. With a slight change, Damon Runyon's remark about some Broadway character fits Sarnoff perfectly. Runyon's friend kept his muscles limber by climbing in and out of taxicabs; Sarnoff by getting in and out of a chauffeured limousine. He not only did not play golf—a heresy in itself—but he did not bowl, play croquet, swim, or engage in anything that called for physical exertion. As a boy he had had no time for play; in manhood that pattern persisted, and may well have been a secondary requisite for his industrial achievements.

The one exception—horseback riding—was forced on him. General Harbord, like most army officers of his generation, rode; it will be remembered that at the very hour when the Japanese bombed Pearl Harbor, General Marshall was out on the bridle path. General Harbord disapproved of Sarnoff's physical lassitude and urged him to ride with him in Central Park in the morning. Sarnoff had no choice but to consent. He consulted his brother Lew, the cavalryman who had pursued Francisco ("Pancho") Villa in Mexico with Pershing. So David bought a horse, which he was permitted to stable at the riding club off Central Park West where he—the owner of the horse—was later rejected as a member.

Regardless of such contretemps, Sarnoff's heart was not in this manly exercise. Mrs. Sarnoff tells how he would get up early to keep his Central Park rendezvous with General Harbord, look out of the window, and say, "Good, it's raining. I don't have to ride today."

Sarnoff apparently had a feeling of guilt about his sons for which, distant from all this and viewing it from another perspective, I can find little or no basis. In the early fifties Dr. Bela Kornitzer succeeded in interviewing Sarnoff in connection with a book, published in 1952 under the title of *American Fathers and Sons.* Kornitzer went about his task carefully: first he interviewed the three Sarnoff boys, then the father who, in an atypical feeling of guilt, confessed that he had not been a good parent.

Well! Can a man of Sarnoff's authentic genius—though perhaps within narrower limits than he realized—can such a man be expected to double as an admirable parent in the conventional sense? One of Sarnoff's mistakes, he told Kornitzer in this rare mood of contrition, was that he had not found enough time to spend with his children when they were young. That was no doubt true, but does it follow that a man with Sarnoff's responsibilities must, to be a good parent, devote as much time to his children as a welfare client or a nine-to-five trust officer of a bank? And does it not often happen that a male parent obstructs the development of a bright child? And in the case of the Sarnoffs, since the mother had a good rapport with the children and the children had an unusual father, isn't it plausible that a somewhat tenuous relationship between father and sons was to the benefit of all concerned?

In a compendium of Sarnoff's feelings of guilt, Eugene Lyons quotes Sarnoff, "a sad smile playing about his lips": "Another mistake parents make—and that includes me, is the notion that the companionship you may have with your children while they're young you can make up later when you are older and have more time. A French philosopher, I think, has given the best answer to that and similar problems. He said, 'Happiness postponed is happiness lost.' "

Of course, and not only in the relations of parents and children. Despite the wording of the Declaration of Independence, the pursuit of happiness is not necessarily the proper aim of life, at least not for everyone. Achievement, more than happiness, was Sarnoff's aim; and in view of his abilities, it was a proper, even compulsive goal.

At Sarnoff's funeral the eulogists were Governor Nelson Rockefeller, the Rev. Dr. Nathan A. Perilman, chief rabbi of Temple Emanu-El, and the Rev. Dr. Bernard Mandelbaum, president of the Jewish Theological Seminary. Rabbi Mandelbaum's address began, "Dear Friends, I loved this man—not only for what he did—and is there anyone anywhere who has not benefited from this—but I loved him for what he was." So Rabbi Mandelbaum could be accounted an intimate friend, though the relationship was also a pastoral one. Among the laity, Sarnoff had innumerable friends—and no talent for close friendship. He could know almost anyone he chose to know and usually he knew people well—but they did not know him well, or if they did it was the result of astute insight, rather than anything Sarnoff was willing to disclose about himself. A gift for friendship requires self-knowledge, absence of vanity, willingness to reveal oneself, and the desire to know others reciprocally. These qualities mark a warm personality, yet are perfectly compatible with good taste and a reasonable degree of personal privacy. Sarnoff's desire for power and dominance impelled him to project an image of himself rather than the reality.

Sometimes he seems to have honestly deceived himself. A biographer who played down Sarnoff's faults, or neglected them altogether, slipped up in a few instances: in particular, he had the temerity to call Sarnoff "ruthless." I have it from an absolutely reliable source that this made Sarnoff "furious," and he blue-penciled the passage. I don't have the original text, but I am sure the writer did not say that Sarnoff was uniformly ruthless. He must have known that Sarnoff was sometimes kind and compassionate; he intervened from time to time on behalf of people down the line whose jobs were at stake, during the Depression, especially.

But he was also capable of summoning employees to his home after business hours for the express purpose of firing them. He was ruthless when he felt it was needed in RCA's interest. Does anyone believe that it is possible by the exercise of loving kindness to build up a company from a few hundred employees and no capital to speak of, to one with over 100,000 people on the payroll and assets of $3 billion? Sarnoff's wrath indicates that sometimes he was as capable of kidding himself as ordinary people are, or that he preferred to have himself depicted not as he was, but as an image of near-perfection.

Without question, however, he was genuinely liked—even revered —by an extraordinary variety of people. Ruling out RCA colleagues, among his admirers were Ferdinand Eberstadt, the banker, who had been among the assistants at the Paris confabulation with Schacht; Harold S. Geneen of ITT ("Hal" wrote that he accounted Sarnoff as one of the great men of our times); the publisher M. Lincoln Schuster; the surgeon Isidor Ravdin, who operated for ileitis on Sarnoff and President Eisenhower; Admiral Lewis L. Strauss, Eisenhower's Secretary of Commerce; Judge Simon R. Rifkind; Frank Stanton, president of CBS; Lyndon B. Johnson; Dwight David Eisenhower; Harry Truman; Judge Irving R. Kaufman; James A. Farley; J. Edgar Hoover; Arthur J. Goldberg; Bernard F. Gimbel; Samuel Goldwyn; Henry R. Luce; Bob Hope; Robert A. Lovett; and even professional critics of corporate ethics like Mrs. Wilma Soss and Lewis D. Gilbert. And this is only a small segment of the people who were more or less friendly with Sarnoff. Even if one questions the quality in the sense of real intimacy, he made up—or tried to—in quantity of cordial relationships.

A perhaps related peculiarity: Sarnoff was a man certainly not lacking in assurance and self-esteem, but these were not enough: he wanted proportionate public recognition of his achievements—and got it. He must have been one of the most practiced and graceful recipients of "kudos," as David E. Lilienthal refers to it, of the century. But Lilienthal says this in passing: he had genuine respect for Sarnoff as a person and a businessman.

BUSINESS AS USUAL

What would have rated as upheavals in any other industry were more or less routine for Sarnoff. A typical problem was the separation of the Red and Blue networks. Controlling both, NBC was a target for government intervention—the FCC questioned whether this dual operation under a single management was in the public interest. A key figure in this situation was Mark Woods, a handsome, cool-headed young man with a good business-oriented mind. He had been general office manager at WEAF and came to NBC as Popenoe's assistant. By the middle thirties, he was in operational charge of the Blue Network.

Woods had a more enlightened cultural view of broadcasting than most broadcasters. In the early thirties, sales messages in the station breaks were first introduced. "In my estimation," Woods said later, "it was that station-break announcement which really expanded the commercialization of radio, frequently to the point where it was really obnoxious." Network stations at first refused to carry these "spot" announcements, but local stations led off with the thirty-second hard sell and the networks finally gave in.

Of Sarnoff, Woods says he was "quiet and yet dynamic, with a great deal of poise." He showed superior judgment in conferences—"always seemed to know where he was going and what he wanted to do and always proceeded with great dispatch and courage." He pretty much kept hands off NBC until 1934, when he took over the chairmanship and directed policy from RCA.

In hearings before the FCC, Woods says "of course" he did his best to convince the commissioners that it *was* in the public interest for NBC to control both networks, although personally he was convinced to the contrary. Eventually the FCC ruled that NBC must dispose of one or the other network, and the Supreme Court upheld the FCC.

In this connection, Woods says, "Mr. Sarnoff never questioned my personal loyalty to him; he had no reason to."

I have said that Sarnoff did not nurse grudges, but he did in the case of James Lawrence Fly, who was chairman of the FCC at the time of its ruling for the separation of the Red and Blue networks, as well as when Sarnoff felt Fly had double-crossed him in connection with the 25,000-receiver television test. During a quiet conversation, when Fly's name came up, Sarnoff burst out with a furious remark about the "Flies and the fleas and the mice and the rats!" I laughed, but Sarnoff did not.

Woods, however, believes that Fly was sincere in his stand on the NBC two-network issue. He points out that Fly "had nothing to gain as a result of the separation except, possibly, antagonism on the part of a great many people; and great pressures could be brought to bear upon him to allow the status quo to remain."

From the first, NBC tended to favor the Red network; affiliates and advertisers were of the same mind. The Blue received more of the institutional and educational programs (not too many of the latter, in any case) and that made it less desirable from the sponsors' standpoint. The reference to it in the industry as the "dumping ground" of NBC Woods regards as unwarranted, but he concedes that "one was preferred over the other."

Niles Trammel was a highly regarded president of NBC whom Sarnoff addressed as "boss" in a rather heavy-handed effort to stress Trammel's freedom of action in NBC. Woods and Trammel wanted to buy the Blue network, with outside financing, as early as 1936, but at that time Sarnoff was unwilling to sell. In 1941, when disposal of the network had become mandatory, Sarnoff told Woods he would recommend to the RCA board that Woods be authorized to find a purchaser and to operate it in the meantime. An ad hoc committee was appointed: General Harbord, DeWitt Millhauser (an RCA director who was Sarnoff's principal financial advisor), and Woods. It was obviously a complex undertaking, since the Blue had to be profitable to be profitably salable; at the same time, the Red had to be protected in order to remain profitable.

Woods assured Sarnoff he would get a "fair" price for the Blue. I would interject here that the much-quoted doctrine of fairness in business is little more than a convenient fiction for purposes of bargaining. When it comes down to realities, a fair price is in between the most a seller thinks he might get, or proposes as an asking price, and the most a buyer can be persuaded to fork up. Woods put it more discreetly. He would get a fair price for Sarnoff (he had better!):

> On the other hand, I didn't want to pay more than a fair price for it, because it was my intention of going with the new company when I finally succeeded in finding a buyer. I wanted to be sure that the buyer didn't pay an excessive price, because I might be in an extremely difficult position in producing a fair return on his investment if he had gone too high.

A first approximation was in the $6–12 million range. Woods concluded that $8 million would be a fair price, and this was accepted by the other members of the committee and recommended to Sarnoff and the RCA board. Operation of the Blue Network Company under Woods began on this basis on January 1, 1942. The network was still owned by RCA, but it was no longer a subsidiary of NBC. Woods selected the entire Blue personnel from the NBC ranks, mostly the second men in the various departments.

There was no time limit on disposing of the property. The FCC and the Supreme Court had specified only a "reasonable period." However, difficult problems in regard to affiliated stations and advertisers arose. Among other questions, prospective purchasers wanted to know how RCA could guarantee that advertisers who were spending about $12 million a year with the network would continue with it.

Early in 1942, after fruitless efforts with no less than 115 individuals and institutions, Woods attempted to sell the network to Edward J. Noble, president of the Life Savers Corporation, a manufacturer of a popular candy in the form of a small white torus suggesting a life preserver. Aylesworth played some part in bringing Woods and Noble together and later claimed a finder's fee. Noble was not altogether new to radio; he owned the unaffiliated WMCA in New York. He listened attentively to Woods's presentation, but at the conclusion said he was not interested.

Woods got offers as high as $7 million. In the meantime the Blue continued on a modestly profitable basis—$66,000 after taxes for the first year. In the second year the profit was more impressive: $1.5 million.

A comical situation then developed, revealing Sarnoff's often imperious way of doing business. On June 1, 1943, the investment banking house of Dillon & Read agreed to form a syndicate with Woods to purchase at $8 million. At about this time Noble indicated revived interest through James McGraw, president of McGraw-Hill, Noble and McGraw to be equal partners. But their offer was only $7 million and was rejected.

Woods resumed negotiations with Dillon & Read on the basis of a maximum of $8 million purchase price, in exchange for 100 percent of preferred stock, together with 50 percent of the common stock. The balance of the common was to go to Woods for distribution among his employees and himself at his option.

This agreement being set down in writing, Woods attempted to reach Sarnoff, who was out of his office and would not be available until lunchtime. So Woods transmitted the offer to DeWitt Millhauser. In Woods's words:

> No one having offered $8 million for the Blue network and the highest offer being $7 million, we determined that we would offer $7 3/4 million in order to close the deal, saving 1/4 million for the new corporation, and still being 3/4 million higher than any other offer.

If challenged at $7.75 million, they were agreed that they would pay the other $.25 million. Millhauser offered no objection and indicated that since the offer was so close to the required $8 million, he would recommend acceptance to Sarnoff.

But as usual, Sarnoff had his own ideas. At 12:30 he phoned Woods. Sarnoff stated "that he would like me to come to his office to meet my new associates. I explained to Mr. Sarnoff that my new associates (Frederic Buradi and Dean Matley of Dillon & Read) were in my office with me, and I would like to bring them to his office so that he could meet them."

He said, "Well, there must be some mistake, Mark. I have just sold the Blue Network Company to Ed Noble and James McGraw."

Woods asked how much they had paid and Sarnoff said, "They agreed to pay eight million. They are in my office. I would like you to meet them and we'll close the deal."

And so the deal was closed—by Sarnoff. Apparently having forgotten that Woods knew Noble and McGraw very well, he introduced Woods to them. After having assured Woods of the presidency of the new company, Noble said to him, "Well, you've just cost me a million dollars!" Woods said, "No, I haven't cost you a million dollars, Mr.

Noble. The price was eight million and whoever put up the price of eight million and were people that could carry on the public responsibility of operating a network, were to get it. You have put up the eight million, so it's yours."

"Well, I still think you've cost me a million dollars in bidding against me."

Mark Woods said, "That's extremely unfortunate, Mr. Noble. Frankly, if I'm going with this new corporation, I want to go with it on a basis where I'm not under suspicion of having cost anyone a million dollars, so I will get you a million dollars right now!"

Turning to Mr. Sarnoff, he said, "Mr. Sarnoff, we have been attempting to sell the Radio Corporation on putting on an hour-program on the Blue network. Time costs on that program will run to about $650,000. The talent for programming it will run to about $350,000, so it will cost just about a million dollars to put a full-hour program on the Blue network for a year. I would like to ask you if you would approve such an expenditure. I will tell you that we have submitted this program to your manufacturing company and it has their approval; but every time it comes to you or to the board of directors of the Radio Corporation for approval, it's turned down. I want it now. Will you do it?"

Without the slightest hesitation, Sarnoff said, "Is that what you want, Mark?"

Woods answered, "Yes!"

Sarnoff said, "It's done!"

"For fifty-two weeks under the ownership of Edward J. Noble, we had a one-hour program from the Radio Corporation of America—a program with the finest talent. Actually, it cost them $1,110,000, but that deal was lived up to, and I've always had the highest admiration in the world for David Sarnoff's never hesitating one instant in going along with such a proposal of mine. Of course, it was a good program and the Radio Corporation got great advertising value out of it; but nevertheless they put up the money for it. I think it pleased Noble a great deal. . . ."

Before the deal was consummated, McGraw withdrew for reasons of health. Noble put up the entire amount: $4 million in cash for 100 percent of the new company and a three-year, $4 million bank loan which was liquidated when it came due. Under Noble's ownership the Blue Network Company, subsequently the American Broadcasting Company, went through a difficult period, with Noble asserting his rights as proprietor and interfering with Woods's management. Woods finally abandoned broadcasting and went into the less hectic and very successful business of selling Florida real estate.

Reading about Sarnoff in the biographical studies he approved and circulated among his friends, and which reached the public as substantially complete and objective accounts, one would suppose that under his direction RCA miraculously avoided such unpleasantness as labor trouble, blacklisting, and the like. As a matter of fact, as early as 1936 the RCA Victor plant was subjected to an organizing strike (a strike to gain recognition). Julius Emspak recorded the union's side of the dispute in 1959 and 1960 in Columbia University's Oral History project.

The thirties Depression was the heyday of the sitdown strike, and the RCA Victor dispute (which did not involve occupation of the Camden plant) was preceded by one against General Electric where the men held the Schenectady works for two weeks, sitting-in in three shifts. No attempt was made to evict them. A month later, in June 1936, RCA Victor was struck, despite efforts by Emspak and James B. Carey, president of the United Electrical, Radio and Machine Workers (UE) to reach a settlement with Sarnoff, and despite an effort to avoid a strike by John L. Lewis through informal negotiation with Sarnoff, which was resented by the leaders of the UE locals at Camden—leaders who were close to the rank and file.

Aside from what it tells us about Sarnoff, the character of the negotiations at RCA Victor reveals both similarities and dissimilarities when compared with such major labor-management negotiations as those of the United Auto Workers with General Motors, Ford, Chrysler, and American Motors today. The unions are established now and there are many other differences over an interval of almost forty years, but the maturity of an organization, such as UE, is never entirely dissociated from its infancy, despite the fact that Emspak, the narrator in this case, was accused by the legislative Red-hunting committees of the fifties of being, or having been, a Communist.

Carey and Emspak had several meetings with Sarnoff. They were accompanied by representatives of the Camden locals, who had not the slightest idea of how to negotiate with someone with the status and dignity of a man like the president of RCA. Nor does Emspak himself seem to have been well qualified for this assignment. He was honest and zealous, but inexperienced and tactless; and the leaders of the locals who accompanied him were worse:

It was an express elevator [to the 53rd floor of the RCA Building, Emspak explains]. No stops. After all, you don't stop on the way up to God. . . . His [Sarnoff's] attitude was that of God, too. . . . He had cigars, a full box, passed them around. . . . I suppose there were eight or ten people. . . . I suppose they were a bit childish, decided to annoy Sarnoff, and cleaned out his cigar box, taking handfuls of cigars. Carey and I didn't like this especially. . . ."

If there had been any chance of arriving at a settlement, these antics queered it. The leaders of the Camden locals could not be expected to know about Sarnoff's insistence on protocol, not only as a matter of his sense of self-importance, but as a means of civilized discourse and possible reconciliation of differences. That Carey and Emspak didn't like this raiding of Sarnoff's cigar box "especially," was not enough. They should have had control of the delegation and not have allowed to descend to a juvenile level what was, after all, a serious meeting involving issues of national importance.

Afterward, they tried to retrieve the damage. The cigars Sarnoff had offered, they noted, were Edens, presumably a superior brand. They went out and bought a box and mailed it to Sarnoff. A secretary called and asked what was in the box. "I suppose," Emspak comments, "he thought we were trying to blow him up. . . ." He probably didn't, but what with the pervasive bitterness and anxiety of the Depression, there was some reason for taking precautions.

According to Emspak: "The company imported [in the classic union-busting manner] some several hundred strikebreakers, the dregs of the slums of the metropolitan area of New York; [the company] used several well-established strikebreaking fink agencies. They had these thugs in the plants . . . armed with clubs, just intimidating the people."

But also to prevent occupation of the plant—this Emspak still did not recognize in his account of 1960. As he saw it:

Sarnoff, in his arrogant manner—at which he's an expert, and I'm sure most of the employees who work for him day to day will confirm this—said he saw no reason, nor would he continue to negotiate with a gun at his head, meaning the threat of a strike. We of course countered this with the fact that people had clubs in that plant— these thugs and bums and killers and dope fiends, these fink agents he'd hired to break the morale of the people . . ."

At this unpromising point in the negotiations, Sarnoff exploded a bombshell. He said that Mr. Carey (who was not present at this meeting) had talked with Mr. Lewis, who had assured Mr. Sarnoff there would be no strike.

The negotiating committee immediately adjourned the meeting and returned to Camden to confer with the local committees representing the rank and file directly. At Camden they were told to find out from Lewis "what the hell he said, and why, and how come? . . . Who's Lewis to be telling Sarnoff something we don't know about. This is *our* union."

Emspak and another union official thereupon tried to track down Lewis. It turned out that he was in Hazleton, Pennsylvania, at a convention of anthracite miners. Failing to get him by phone, they started out for Hazleton in an old car Emspak's brother had lent him. They had trouble on the rough mountain roads, including a tire blowout, but finally reached Hazleton at midnight and, checking in at the hotel, met Lewis checking out. "Well, we met him in the lobby, so we bearded him."

Lewis did not deny he had talked to Carey and to Sarnoff, but asserted that Sarnoff had no right to say what he had said to the union negotiators. Emspak's conclusion was, "Partly evasive, partly on the level, because he certainly didn't deny discussing that stuff with Sarnoff." In Emspak's opinion, what Sarnoff had told the union negotiators was probably implicit in what Lewis had said to Sarnoff.

The discussion in the hotel lobby lasted ten or fifteen minutes and ended with Lewis saying, "Well, boys, sit on the lid and organize." Emspak commented after Lewis had left that the lid was halfway up to the sky and they were wondering when they would slide off it.

This was on a Friday. The two of them went to bed, sharing a room. Saturday morning they hot-footed it to Camden, where they had a meeting with the union board and the strategy committee. The strike began on Monday.

Lewis supported the strike. As Emspak put it: "He was operating in the manner he knew how. The tradition of the Mine Workers was that he was the boss; therefore he'd talk to Sarnoff, the boss. That wasn't the operation of UE, though. Then and now we firmly operated on the basis of the members running the union."

The UE was only three months old at the time. Emspak asserts that the International Brotherhood of Electrical Workers played a strike-breaking role. That is possible, because in a strike in Hollywood in which I tried to mediate between the RKO management and the soundmen's union, the IBEW furnished ad hoc union cards to strikebreakers, most of them unqualified for sound work. In the Camden situation, Emspak says a company union, strikebreakers, and the local police were also involved. The strike lasted four weeks and there was rioting, violence, and much hardship for the strikers, many of whom were jailed. Lewis furnished assistance from the Mine Workers legal department. The New Jersey Civil Liberties Union also aided the strikers.

Emspak admits that "a good many people scabbed"—the UE did not represent a solid front of the RCA Victor employees. Nevertheless it was an important strike. General Hugh Johnson, who had served as head of the National Industrial Recovery Administration until the Supreme Court declared it unconstitutional, came to New York, put up at the St. Regis, and talked to the UE people and Sarnoff. The strike was finally resolved on the basis of a National Labor Relations Board election which the UE won by 60 to 1, or some such lopsided figure, although a majority of the workers did not vote. The upshot was that the UE wound up with a collective bargaining agreement, so it is fair to say that they won, though at a considerable cost in lost wages, bail bonds, physical injuries in the rioting, and so on. For his part, Sarnoff could claim that he had averted occupation of the RCA Victor plant.

Asked by the interviewer to define the issues in the strike, Emspak summarized:

> "Well, we were all brash young men . . . we had the enthusiasm, and I suppose courage, that goes with youth. . . . We made decisions that said our organization's objective would be to go after the big ones first, and then the rest would fall in line. There had to be that fight to convince the company to use the federal machinery that was available when the strike broke. . . . [The strike] established the union as a functioning and growing outfit."

Labor executives are counterparts of management executives and, with some exceptions, aspire to the same way of life. This doesn't sit too well with the nut-tightener on the assembly line, so a prudent labor official will take care to retain membership in the local union in which he was originally a rank-and-file member. Thus, symbolically, he remains, say, a plumber, although he may no longer know one end of a pipe wrench from the other.

Sarnoff was different. His first significant job was that of a telegrapher, and a telegrapher he remained, with one of the most admired "fists" in the business, and ability in code reading to match. He spoke in Morse—where every letter must be transmitted in dots, dashes, and spaces—with precision, rhythm, speed, and clarity. People who are familiar with artistry in the manipulation of the keys and pedals of a piano by a concert pianist may be surprised to hear that there can be artistry in the manipulation of such a simple device as a telegraph key, but it is a fact. Sarnoff was admired for his style in sending by the sodality of old-time wireless operators, who could recognize him by his touch on the key almost as unmistakably as by hearing his voice over the telephone.

In later years he still had a telegraph key in a top drawer of that immaculate desk of his. The key and some receiving equipment were connected with the main RCA telegraph office at 66 Broad Street, enabling Sarnoff to send and receive via RCA telegraph facilities all over the world. This resulted in occasional surprises, as when George Milne, an NBC engineer who later became chief engineer of the Blue network, was supervising a special event—a ship disaster off the New Jersey coast. The network had a plane on the scene which communicated its observations to NBC headquarters through a relay station in an Atlantic City hotel. Milne was using radiotelegraph facilities, which under the circumstances were more reliable than radiotelephone.

Suddenly a "beautiful fist" broke in, requesting the latest information on the disaster. Puzzled, Milne asked, "Who wants to know?" The answer came back swiftly: a dash and two dots, followed after a short space by three dots, "DS"—Sarnoff's personal call letters, as well as his initials. Milne nearly fell over backward but, rallying, supplied the requested information in his own best Morse. Sarnoff said, "Tks," and left the circuit.

On another occasion Sarnoff was on an ocean liner en route to Europe with Louis Kirstein. A day or two out of New York, he went up to the radio room, fraternized with the operators, introduced Mr. Kirstein, and asked if he could take the watch for a while. The operators sat him down at the transmitter control and deposited a sheaf of westbound messages on the table in front of him. Sarnoff put on the headset, listened a minute to familiarize himself with the latest abbreviations, called Chatham, the RCA marine station on Cape Cod, then tapped out the ship's call letters, signifying he had traffic to get off. The Chatham operator said, GA DS ("Go ahead, DS") and Sarnoff proceeded to dispatch message after message, getting an RD ("Received") after each one and finally, 73 DS ("Our compliments, DS").

Kirstein was rightly impressed. The Chatham staff most likely didn't know Sarnoff was on the ship, but one of them—probably the chief operator—immediately recognized his legendary "fist." It reminds one of Queen Elizabeth's (the original Elizabeth, an early feminist) challenge to her privy council. She needn't be queen of England, she told their lordships—she could earn her living as a seamstress in any capital in Europe.

When high-speed machine sending came into vogue on the international radio circuits, Sarnoff delighted in reading the words orally for admiring colleagues, but since he did not use the typewriter he could not copy. (The limit for legible handwriting is not much over 50 wpm.) The champion in copying code was an operator named Ted McElroy, who was noted also for his fluent profanity. George Bailey was present at a contest with ten starters, when McElroy won the world's championship by copying on a typewriter at 72 words per minute (five letters constituted a word). At 72 wpm, the only other surviving contestant dropped out.

"You made one mistake," the chief judge said to McElroy.

"I did not!" McElroy shouted, with a string of choice expletives. "The tape said, 'seed' when it should have said, 'seem.' "

The tape was rerun at low speed, and McElroy was proved right.

Sarnoff, like all virtuosi, was proud of his virtuosity, and a trifle envious of anyone who could better him, although now as an operator he was more of a legend than a performer. He invited McElroy to visit an RCA installation with him, where they stopped at a relay which was emitting what to the untrained ear sounded like a continuous buzz.

"Can you read that?" Sarnoff asked. "That's sending one hundred twenty-five a minute."

"I can read some of it," McElroy said, "But it's more like ninety a minute."

"A hundred and twenty-five," Sarnoff repeated.

"Ninety," McElroy insisted.

Getting angry, Sarnoff sent for the engineers. "The speed is ninety-one and one half," he was told.

"What's it saying?" Sarnoff asked McElroy.

"It's sending stock quotations with fractions," McElroy said nonchalantly.

In business, likewise, Sarnoff occasionally met his match. Commander Eugene McDonald of Zenith was at loggerheads with Sarnoff since Zenith became an RCA licensee in 1927 and some thirty years later won a $10 million verdict against RCA on monopoly charges. On Sarnoff's side, it must be noted that to make money in big business one must go to the brink at times, and anyone who goes to the brink often enough is bound to go over it sooner or later.

As McKenzie pointed out, Sarnoff was not infallible either in his visions of the electronic future. He had too many visions to be always right. In 1919 he suggested that radiotelephony might make telephony by wire obsolete. It proved to be supplementary, rather, and mainly for special applications, such as microwave relay circuits for television. Yet a few years before his death, Sarnoff took another swipe at AT&T. What with satellite communications, he said AT&T was sitting on a powder keg.

In 1947, as part of an effort to interest the movie producers in television, Sarnoff predicted that TV would prove to be a great boon to movies by presentation of TV programs on theater screens. The idea was sensible enough, but it came into use only for heavyweight championship prizefights, where there was enough fight-fan interest to justify the expense of big-screen TV in movie theaters, and the admission could be high enough to make these special events profitable.

In an article, "By the End of the Twentieth Century," *Fortune*, May 1964, Sarnoff included among a melange of forecasts under subtitles such as food, raw materials, health, genetics, defense, travel, air and space, some remarks on energy. He pointed out the long-known fact that one pound of fissionable uranium the size of a golf ball had the *potential* energy of nearly 1,500 tons of coal, and added that "the supply of nuclear resources is greater than all the reserves of coal, oil, and gas." All of which may be true, but it does not follow, as Sarnoff predicted, that "atomic energy will be a major power source particularly in the underdeveloped areas." Aside from the fact that only a small percentage of the energy can be extracted, at present serious and possibly irremediable difficulties are being encountered in the design and operation of nuclear power plants burning fissionable fuel, the only type practicable at present and in the foreseeable future.

Nuclear power on the scale Sarnoff envisioned may have to await the development of nuclear fusion, and whether that will be available, even by the year 2000, is uncertain. It may never work at all. Sarnoff does not mention the hazards of fission power. These may be overcome, but Edward Teller is dubious and would allow fission power plants only at underground sites. Within the Atomic Energy Commission, there was continuing controversy regarding the danger of radioactive emission from plants as then designed and located, if something should go seriously wrong in operation. Sarnoff's views in this field carry no special weight.

On the subject of communications, however, Sarnoff was an authority:

> Through communication satellites, laser beams, and ultraminiaturization, it will be possible by the end of the century to communicate with anyone, anywhere, at any time, by voice, sight, or written message. Satellites weighing several hundred tons will route telephone, radio and television, and other communication from country to country, continent to continent, and between earth and space vehicles and the planets beyond. Participants will be in full sight and hearing of one another through small desk instruments and three-dimensional color-TV screens on the wall. Ultimately, individuals equipped with miniature TV-transmitter receivers will communicate with one another via radio, switchboard, and satellite, using personal channels similar to today's telephone number. Overseas mail will be transmitted via satellite by means of facsimile reproduction. Satellite television will transmit on a worldwide basis directly to the home, and a billion people may be watching the same program with automatic language translation for instant comprehension. Newspaper copy, originating on one continent, will be transmitted and set in type instantly on another. Indeed, by the year 2000, key newspapers will appear in simultaneous editions around the world.

Some of this is already clearly in prospect, and some of the ideas are attractive, although they rest on the supposition that by the end of the century the dream of "one world" will have come true. Even without the full realization of that ideal, transmission of overseas mail by satellite facsimile seems both feasible and desirable. But about the degree of interaction among people that Sarnoff seems to regard as a valid objective I have my doubts, and I am sure I will have plenty of company. To be able to communicate with anyone, anywhere, at any time, is the opposite of being a recluse, and seems to me just as undesirable. Shouldn't we spend more time with ourselves, in meditation or reading, both of which afford a certain privacy of thought, a communion with oneself, which surely has value as great as the give-and-take of two-way communication, whether for business or pleasure. I have an idea that in this extrapolation Sarnoff was influenced by his own temperament and managerial role, with its necessary concentration on decision making, which in turn required more communication than would be healthy for most people, or for society as a whole.

Nevertheless I am reluctant to end this chapter on a critical note, because though Sarnoff was sometimes wrong, when he was right he was remarkably right, with vision far ahead of his contemporaries, whence came his success and the momentous effects of his enterprises. As one instance, in 1951 Dore Schary, who was in charge of production at Metro-Goldwyn-Mayer, was in New York conferring with Nicholas Schenck, the head of the parent company, Loew's, Inc. Schary, whose early life bore some similarity to Sarnoff's, suggested that MGM might do well to explore possibilities of a merger with TV interests.

"Dore, my boy," Schenck said, "five years ago David Sarnoff, sitting where you are sitting now, made that same proposal to me."

"And?" said Schary.

"And I asked him, 'What have you got to offer us?' And I ask you: What have they got to offer? *We've* got the pictures."

Schary's comment when I interviewed him was that Schenck was getting old. Fifteen years earlier, he might have been more receptive; now he didn't want to be bothered.

Again the difference between Sarnoff and a run-of-the-mill entrepreneur is obvious. The result in this instance may be seen in the present state of television, which with all its defects and troubles, is top dog in mass entertainment, and the present subservience of Hollywood. Loew's is still a big corporation, but now only a subsidiary of a conglomerate with massive interests far removed from movies, while MGM is a feeble enterprise compared with what it was when Nick Schenck said, *"We've* got the pictures."

TRAGEDY

The annual meetings of great corporations are a mishmash of publicity for the corporation, a basis, however transparent, for the fiction that the horde of stockholders own and control the corporation (the stockholders who really count may not even show up unless there is a proxy contest) and, though an occasional sound criticism is voiced, an opportunity for a handful of exhibitionists to attract attention to themselves. The 1935 annual meeting of RCA, with Sarnoff presiding was an important exception, although few in the audience realized it at the time. At a certain point in the proceedings, Edwin Howard Armstrong, the largest stockholder, rose to his feet.

> I didn't come here to make a speech [said Armstrong]. I didn't come here to get into a row. I have been a stockholder since 1915, since the days of the old Marconi Company. I have seen the inside of radio from the beginning to the end. I want to say that the man who pulled this company through during the difficult times of the General Electric, Westinghouse, RCA mix-up with the government was its president, Mr. David Sarnoff. [Applause] I think you would have been wiped out if it hadn't been for him. I know what I am talking about. I tell you, I wouldn't have his job for $500,000 a year. I don't agree with everything, for I have a row on with him now. I am going to fight it through to the last ditch. I just wanted to tell you what you owe to Sarnoff.

Sarnoff was deeply moved, with good reason. Armstrong was as honest a man as a modern Diogenes, equipped with a 500,000-candle-power lantern, could hope to find. He wrote Armstrong the next day, inviting him to lunch and expressing a sentiment matching Armstrong's in sincerity: "Doubtless I have made many mistakes in my life, but I am glad to say they have not been in the quality of the friends I selected for reposing my faith."

Whether they met for lunch doesn't matter. The differences between them, which the audience at the annual meeting knew nothing about, were impossible to resolve by compromise, given the deeply rooted values and interests of the two men. Reduced to its elements, Armstrong had developed a system of frequency modulation which, from an acoustic standpoint, was demonstrably superior to the existing system of amplitude modulation. On first listening to it, noting the silent background and the purity of reproduction, Sarnoff had called it "revolutionary." For that reason, among others, it is understandable that Armstrong concluded that FM should entirely supplant the conventional amplitude modulation—what might be called the establishment system—within a reasonable time.

But business considerations are not the same as technical considerations. Nor is AM inferior for *all* applications: small transistor radios, for instance, though unknown when Armstrong got going on FM, are still tuned to AM transmitters. The two systems now exist side by side, and all but the cheapest table radios offer both FM and AM reception.

The conflict between Sarnoff, the practical man, the entrepreneur, and Armstrong, the dedicated engineer, was even more irreconcilable than differences involving current and future applications and the existing investment in thousands of AM transmitters and millions of AM receivers. Armstrong was fixated on radio, intent on transmitting the best possible sound—he was looking ahead to high-fidelity reproduction—while Sarnoff was convinced—and rightly so—that there would be far more popular interest, and more profit for RCA, in television: picture plus sound. Consequently, after field tests of Armstrong's system from an RCA antenna on the Empire State Tower, and endless disagreement between Armstrong and his aides on the one hand and pro-AM RCA–NBC engineers on the other, and World War II intervening, RCA politely evicted Armstrong from the Empire State location on the ground that it needed the space for TV tests. In no pleasant humor, Armstrong sold a block of RCA stock and got an FCC license for a powerful FM station on the Palisades at Alpine, opposite his old home in Yonkers. By the summer of 1938 he had a 400-foot tower of his own to climb and help chip off ice on wintry days. He operated that station, broadcasting mostly classical music and other high-grade program material, at great expense, even for an owner who was reputed to be worth $8 million.

Again, as with De Forest's oscillating audion, he found himself in litigation, and that was expensive, too. The receiver manufacturing industry was riven, with RCA, Philco, Crosley, Emerson, and other large producers manufacturing FM receivers without benefit of Armstrong licenses, while General Electric, Westinghouse, Zenith, and Stromberg-Carlson, as big or bigger and spurred by ancient enmities as well as current interests, lined up with Armstrong and became his licensees. Armstrong and his allies contended that the RCA-type FM receivers were strictly ersatz. The nonlicensees retorted that most of the improvement in quality was a matter of better microphones, amplifiers etc., which could be achieved just as well on AM as on FM.

Not a little casuistry enters into engineering controversies, especially when large commercial stakes are involved. In retrospect, there is no doubt that with FM Armstrong succeeded in reproducing sound with a fidelity and freedom from disturbance previously unknown and not excelled since. The patent position, however, was not as strong as his technical and ethical position, and when Sarnoff extended the hand of compromise it held only a lump sum of $1 million—and no royalties. It was another illustration of the well-known fact that Sarnoff liked to collect royalties—not to pay them. Armstrong spurned the offer.

Armstrong's basic patent on FM was issued in 1933; the system was brilliantly demonstrated at an overflow meeting of the Institute of Radio Engineers in November 1935. The war intervened and was followed by acrimonious contention centering on wavelengths to be granted by the FCC. Finally, in July 1948, Armstrong brought suit against RCA and NBC in the U.S. District Court in Wilmington, Delaware, charging that the defendant companies had conspired to discourage FM, had attempted to persuade the FCC to allocate to it an inadequate number of suitable frequencies, and had illegally obstructed an application of Armstrong's in the Patent Office. In 1953 and early 1954, he filed additional suits against numerous manufacturers of radio and television receivers.

By this time his erstwhile friends had become hopelessly alienated. Testifying before a special master in federal court in Delaware, Sarnoff said:

> Now my view was that the way for FM to be accepted widely and to be introduced commercially was to make it a supplement or an

accompaniment of television, and I had been thinking in terms of television not only in 1935 but as early as 1925. . . . If you went to the public with a new service that combined sound and sight . . . and you offered it to the public at prices that it could afford to buy, no one could accuse you of trying to obsolete a complete system just because there was some degree of improvement in sound as between FM and AM as used at that particular time.

The issue could not be stated more clearly from the RCA viewpoint. As for the personal relationship, Sarnoff answered a question of Armstrong's lawyer with equal clarity and intransigence:

I don't know what I did. You assume that the only purpose in life I had was to just deal with this FM thing. I was a busy man at the time [circa February 1936]. I left the negotiations and the explanations to my subordinates. I am not in the habit of asking them to report on what he said and she said every time they have a conversation.

I did not find any necessity for associating myself or disassociating myself with anything, because Major Armstrong knew me well. He knew he was always welcome. It was as much his obligation to call on me as anything else, and if he kept away, why, I kept away.

By the summer of 1953, the suits against RCA and NBC had dragged on for five years. Armstrong, an acknowledged genius in electronics, was spending most of his time on legal strategy. Obsessed by the justness of his cause, and more and more embittered, he was dangerously overtaxed. Mrs. Armstrong tried to persuade him to taper off. That was one thing Howard was incapable of; the other was dishonesty in engineering, including its forensic side. As his troubles accumulated, he became difficult to live with; difficult, also, in relations with Alfred McCormack, who had been his lawyer since 1928. McCormack should be remembered not only for his service to Armstrong over the years but because, as a colonel in Intelligence in World War II, he saved Kyoto, the cultural heart of Japan, from bombing—the only Japanese city so spared.

Howard's millions had melted away, and he was left with barely enough to tide him over for another year. Complex litigation, especially where patent rights are involved, is more time-consuming than Hamlet —in his reference to the law's delays—ever dreamed it could be. Sarnoff's depositions alone make a book three inches thick. Howard was still living in his accustomed style, in an elegant apartment on Sutton Place, but at sixty-four, he looked ten years older than he was. Sarnoff, the same age, looked younger. He had worked just as hard as Armstrong; it was a matter of temperament.

On January 31, 1954, a Sunday, Mrs. Armstrong was in Connecticut. There were three servants at the Armstrong apartment; they left shortly after preparing Howard's lunch. Howard wrote an affectionate letter to his wife on two sheets of yellow paper. It ended with "God keep you and may the Lord have mercy on my soul."

Sometime during the night, Howard put on his hat, overcoat, and gloves, as if he were going for a walk. Instead, he jumped out of the thirteenth-story window. He fell to a third-floor terrace. No one heard him. The sun rose a few minutes after seven. The body was found about three hours later.

When I saw Sarnoff, he was his usual direct self. Looking into my eyes, he put both hands on his chest and said, "I did not kill Armstrong." I said I didn't think he did and, as a matter of fact, the thought had not entered my head: the tragedy was not as simple as that. At this distance, my feeling is that Sarnoff was not at all generous in his dealings with Armstrong. The NBC–RCA suit was finally settled for the million Sarnoff had originally offered. That was RCA's contribution to a total of $10 million from the radio-TV industry. Considering the cost of the litigation and the capital cost and operation of the Alpine transmitter, which was shut down shortly after Armstrong's death, the net proceeds could have been only a fraction of the settlement.

Sarnoff could not have anticipated that the litigation would lead to a fatal outcome. There was no longer a personal relationship: the only communication was through judges and lawyers. And even if friendship had endured through such stress, what practical difference could it have made? Sarnoff was the chief executive of what had become—largely through his efforts—a great business enterprise. His legally enforceable duty was to his stockholders. Being the man he was, he was also bound to pursue his own vision of the future in electronics, as in the past. Television was the wave of the future. Sarnoff saw that, as no doubt did Armstrong, but in the role he chose to play he threatened the huge investment and revenues of AM broadcasting—revenues which Sarnoff needed for the further development of black-and-white television, and later color.

Death, being universal, is not tragic per se. Sarnoff's death seventeen years later, however painful to his family and friends, I cannot see as tragic. He had done his work and found it good. Armstrong's death was tragic because he was so agonizingly frustrated that he was driven to take his own life, and I don't think he ever understood what was happening to him. I wrote at the time that here he was, a revolutionist only in technology—in politics he was one of the most conservative of men—bucking the economic and political system which placed the interest of the financier before that of the inventor, yet which had made him rich as an inventor. He was trying to act like one of those eighteenth- or nineteenth-century industrialist-inventors who, before the era of big business, started their own industries in an atmosphere of total freedom: freedom from both governmental supervision and the network of existing financial and corporate interests; while Sarnoff adhered to a consistent and unswerving policy, oriented toward a medium with far greater mass entertainment potential, and promising proportionately greater profits, than any improvement in sound alone could expect to achieve.

Today all television sound is frequency modulated: in that sense Armstrong has the last word—from beyond the grave. Not only that, but FM is the mainstay of the radio portion of high fidelity. None of which alters the fact that from a business standpoint Sarnoff's argument in federal court—that the most practicable way of introducing FM was by way of television—has withstood the test of time.

COLOR

Sarnoff's explosion when a reporter twitted him about pushing color TV while black-and-white had not yet begun to pay off, was not merely the reaction of a man easily provoked by criticism. Sarnoff was willing to answer sensible questions, but he was sorely beset at the time and responded to a gratuitous taunt with an angry reiteration of his determination to push television—black-and-white and color both—come hell or high water. Sarnoff did not suffer fools gladly, and this was a particularly bad time to provoke him. Though things got better shortly on the technical side of "colorization," for a decade and more RCA was not out of trouble.

About ten years after bawling out the reporter, Sarnoff told Walter Guzzardi, Jr. that he never doubted, even in the hard years, that it would all come out well in the end. "I never got butterflies," as he put it (*Fortune*, October 1962). A characteristic statement, and true—fearlessness was a primary factor in the authority Sarnoff radiated. Still, the statement requires interpretation. It does not mean that Sarnoff was never free from anxiety, although he may not have recognized it as such under the overlay of his determination. His fearlessness was akin to that of the professional soldier in a fast-moving combat situation. He knows that he is responsible for his men and the commands on either side of his, and that he is personally in danger. But he appraises the situation coolly; he does not tremble.

In establishing color, Sarnoff needed all his personal and corporate resources—self-confidence, sangfroid, ability to analyze the situation and assess the future probabilities, and, not least, lots and lots of money. At the outset he was overconfident. The RCA stand—and I find it plausible—was that CBS's color system was brought forth in order to retard the commercialization of black-and-white TV, in which CBS was far behind RCA. The CBS system, a modernized version of the obsolete mechanical systems, was noncompatible—incapable of receiving black-and-white pictures. That alone ruled it out as a serious solution. The viewer interested in color would have had to start all over and buy a separate color receiver while keeping his old receiver, since the bulk of TV broadcasting for at least the next few years would necessarily be in black-and-white. The system had only one merit: the color picture was quite good, hence suitable for publicity-motivated demonstrations.

This was in 1945 and, according to Barnouw in *The Golden Web* (p. 243) Sarnoff told Harry M. Plotkin, of counsel for the FCC, that in six months RCA would demonstrate an electronic color system compatible with black-and-white. Plotkin asked how Sarnoff knew the engineers would have it ready. Sarnoff replied, "I told them to."

It took more like six years than six months. In 1949 Sarnoff spurred the RCA engineers into a premature demonstration for the FCC commissioners and their technical staff which was a complete fiasco—in Sarnoff's words, "The monkeys were green, the bananas were blue, and everyone had a good laugh." At the demonstration there was nothing else to do, but when the RCA color developers got back to Princeton, we can be sure nobody laughed.

Dr. Elmer W. Engstrom (he had just got his first honorary degree, a Sc.D. from New York University) was in charge at Princeton at the time. Dr. Edward W. Herold was one of the top research engineers. Aside from the color triumph, his account is instructive about research and development in general—activities which played an indispensable part in Sarnoff's achievements. Let Herold take the story from there as he told it nineteen years later to a group of RCA engineering managers, many of whom had not been with RCA when these events occurred:

> I remember vividly that day in 1949—it was September 19—when Elmer Engstrom called me to his office. He told me that the entire RCA case before FCC rested on our ability to show the feasibility of a single color-picture tube. He didn't know of anyone who had a really workable idea, but it was a task we couldn't shirk. We had to try, and we had very little time to do it in.
>
> ". . . Elmer asked me if I would coordinate a major company effort, a crash program so to speak, and show within three months that a

color-picture tube was possible. He promised top priority to the project—all the manpower we could use, and "money no object," i.e., essentially unlimited funds. I don't know whether he thought I was too ignorant of the difficulty to object—after all, I wasn't a picture tube expert, and I wasn't even close to this work. In fact, however, I knew the job was just about impossible. But I also recognized a standard Engstrom technique in running research, one that I had always admired. This was that you never get anywhere sitting around waiting for a desired invention. You have to get to work on it, and the results are usually proportional to the effort. So here was a chance to use unlimited effort. Could unlimited effort reach an unattainable result? To be truthful, I didn't think so, but it sure was a challenge to try.

The first thing Herold and his colleagues did was to take stock of the extant ideas, and to enlist every expert who had some related skill. None of the ideas was promising, so the inventive minds in the organization were asked to help. This is my comparison, not Herold's, but asking an inventor to invent ad hoc is a little like asking the poet laureate of Britain to produce a poem for some royal occasion. He can do it all right, but no one expects it to be a great poem. However, after two weeks of organizing, this team was in possession of five separate and different approaches.

The most remarkable part of the story is that four of the five ideas worked. The preferred one was the three-gun shadow-mask, the basic idea for which is credited to Dr. Alfred N. Goldsmith. Herold ascribes its practical success largely to Dr. Harold B. Law, who had always tended to work on a do-it-yourself basis, in which he personally carried out every step. I suppose in this respect he resembled the great British nuclear physicist, Ernest Rutherford (1871–1937) who, with his assistants, constructed much of the apparatus they used in their work.

In two months, Law got a result described in Herold's notebook: "A three-gun tube with H. B. Law's shadow-mask screen . . . was demonstrated by L. Flory . . . about 4" by 5" . . . excellent registry in the center . . . good rendition of colors, and adequate brightness made this demonstration outstanding."

This tube had three electron guns, each of which could excite—cause to glow—a phosphor of one of the three primary colors which together make up a color picture. The mask is a thin sheet of perforated material so positioned behind the viewing screen that the gun associated with the appropriate phosphor could not excite the other two phosphors. A variant of the principle used only a single electron gun. The principle sounds simple, but that it could be made to work with the speed and accuracy required is little short of miraculous—until somebody does it.

After weeks of sixteen-hour days, seven days a week, and participation of other departments of RCA, the Princeton people brought to Washington for the edification of the FCC, the industry and the press, four complete receivers. Let Herold summarize the results of the demonstration, which took place on March 29, 1950.

> We showed three sets; the center one was a black-and-white receiver to show compatibility, and the one on the right was the three-gun receiver, the one on the left the one-gun set. . . . Here's a quote from the April 1, 1950 *TV Digest:* "Tri-color tube has what it takes: RCA shot the works with its tri-color tube demonstration this week, got full reaction it was looking for . . . not only from . . . FCC . . . and newsmen, but from some 50 patent licensees. . . ."
>
> So impressed was just about everybody by remarkable performance that it looked . . . as if RCA deliberately restrained its predemonstration enthusiasm to gain full impact.

Summarizing, Herold points out that the supposedly unattainable project was finished in six months, at a cost of seventy man-years and under $2 million up to that point. They chose the three-gun shadow-mask tube as the best bet for the future, but had three other usable types. Herold told me that personally he did not think color was all that important—that it might add, say, 10 percent to the market for television receivers. But color turned out to be a terrific money-maker, and Herold reaches this conclusion: "In my opinion, it was one of the most successful of David Sarnoff's visionary projects, using Engstrom's policies on research: if you work hard enough at it, and don't tie up people with financial strings and red tape, the impossible does *not* 'take a little longer'."

It must be emphasized that Herold's figure of $2 million did not encompass production of a commercially available picture tube. It took many millions more for product development and factory facilitation before RCA could reap rewards in the way of a salable product. It is a long way, in any branch of engineering, from the devices that work in the laboratory to the commercial product to be sold to the consumer who has no interest in what came before and no interest in what comes after the product is in his hands, except the cost of service and the amount of downtime of what he has bought.

The shadow-mask tri-color tube triumph typifies the Sarnoff-RCA research and development approach to the market. At this stage of the game Sarnoff needed this particular device and he had to have it fast. He impressed the urgency of the situation on Engstrom, reinforcing what Engstrom already knew: "Money is no object." Engstrom selected as the coordinator of the effort an engineer who had no specialized expertise in the problem area—therefore was free of fixed preconceptions and open to new ideas—yet was well acquainted with the experts and had unusual clarity of mind and a broad view of electronic technology. The result was a venture into the unknown, or only partly known, which was pursued with intellectual efficiency of a high order and reached an intricate objective with time and ideas to spare.

Sarnoff never failed to take full political advantage of an RCA technological advance; the engineers served as his springboard. In this instance he appeared before the FCC and in an opening statement, delivered on May 3, 1950, gave the quietus to the rival CBS system, which he denounced as retrogressive. In contrast, RCA was asking the Commission

> to adopt color television standards which will permit the utilization of an all-electronic, compatible-color television system which does not have those defects and which has picture quality at least equal to that provided by existing black-and-white standards. . . .
>
> Let me emphasize that black-and-white and color television are not separate arts. Color is a further step along the television road which has been blazed by RCA. RCA was for television when that was a solo effort. The 100 successful manufacturers of today, the more than 5,000,000 set owners, the many additional millions who are daily enjoying television programs, all bear witness to the fruitfulness of RCA's original concept and pioneering in this art. . . .
>
> CBS has asked the Commission to adopt a system which would saddle an all-electronic art with a mechanical harness. You are being urged by CBS to build a highway to accomodate the horse and buggy when already the self-propelled vehicle is in existence and has been demonstrated.

Sarnoff's statement included a tribute to the engineers who had developed the shadow-mask tube:

For myself, I cannot say enough in praise of the RCA engineers and technicians who have so brilliantly and successfully created the RCA all-electronic color-television system and the RCA direct-view tri-color tubes. . . . I have watched the development of radio and electronics for more than forty years and never before have I seen compressed into a single effort so much ingenuity, so much brain power, and such phenomenal results as are represented in these new developments.

Even so, Sarnoff still had his troubles in putting color TV over commercially. Many experienced industry people felt that color was too complicated to survive. Zenith called the RCA system "a Rube Goldberg contraption." Ralph Cordiner, head of General Electric, broadcast his opinion that if you had a color TV receiver, "you've almost got to have an engineer living in the house." As it turned out, Cordiner was wrong, but he was no irresponsible commentator, and that well-publicized remark may have cost RCA millions of dollars in delayed sales.

Sarnoff was in a different position from the rest of the industry. He had so much capital invested in colorization that he could not afford the wait-and-see attitude of other industry interests, most of whom had made no contribution and were doing well with black-and-white. Financially, he was past the point of no return. For a time it looked as if the companies that favored a wait-and-see policy had him over a barrel. In fact, what with lawsuits, a Sherman Act violation suit by the government, and other complications, color TV did not turn the corner until well into the sixties. The sales curve remained flat at a low level until 1963, then began to rise, slowly at first, then steeply. A combination of retail economics, public demand, and publicity served to put it over. Sales of black-and-white sets dropped from 7.4 million in 1955 to 5.1 million in 1958 and a large proportion of the latter were second sets, low-priced and with scanty profit margins. As always, dealers were interested in "big-ticket" items—color was ideal in that respect.

As color was plugged and caught on, its appeal spread not only by reason of its actual merits but by social contagion. Aside from the people who could easily afford it, to some extent the boom was a repetition of 1947, when slum families bought expensive black-and-white TV on time. In the early sixties, in lower-middle-class suburban developments, an appreciable number of householders already had a color receiver. Part of this was keeping up with the Joneses, part the ingrained or induced American desire for the newest gadget, part enjoyment of color, even though that enhancement was not matched by improvement in the programs.

By the end, of 1968, 20 million color sets had been sold and a quarter of American homes had color sets. That fall, color outsold black-and-white for the first time. Sarnoff had had to wait a long time for the fulfillment of his dream, the one which turned out to be his last.

Much else could be written about the ascent of RCA into the ranks of the twenty topmost American corporations, but it would add little, if anything, to an appreciation of Sarnoff. The problems and solutions of big-time corporate managers are not in themselves interesting—except, of course, to big-time managers. Sarnoff had his troubles right along, not only with TV and computers, but, as we have seen, with transistors. Recalling Sarnoff's snap answer to the question, "What's your favorite division?" "The one that's in trouble," the transistor people must have got a lot of his attention, but it is doubtful that they relished it. Even after Sarnoff's troubleshooting, RCA never became a leader in transistor production.

An outright failure of near-disastrous proportions occurred in electronic data processing, but in the sixties, with David Sarnoff remaining in charge, the outlook still seemed hopeful. Guzzardi wrote in *Fortune* that by RCA's own estimates the computer effort would not turn profitable before 1964. It never did turn profitable, and in the fifties and sixties the company was carrying the burden of heavy concurrent losses. Color TV cost $130 million (spread over thirteen years, or the load would have been unbearable) and data processing cost $100 million from 1958 to 1962 alone. RCA was saved by its diversity (for the entertainment market, records, radio and TV sets; components, such as tubes, including TV picture tubes, for industry, including in some instances RCA's competitors; sales to the U.S. government, for defense and space; NBC's large and consistent profit from advertising; and the commercial communications end of the business) and by its size (at the beginning of the sixties it was already No. 26 in *Fortune's* ranking of the 500 largest industrial corporations, with sales of more than $1.5 billion and working capital of more than $370 million). Sarnoff believed that a company smaller and less diverse would have gone under. The effort he had put in over a span of forty years in achieving independence and prodigious growth was what saved it in the clutch.

THE COLD WARRIOR

Under the prevailing circumstances, the cold war was inevitable. Senator Harry Truman probably echoed the sentiments of most Americans when, before the United States entered World War II, he declared that if the Nazis appeared to be winning, we should aid the Russians; if there was danger of a Russian victory, we should aid the Nazis. World War II, with the United States and the Soviet Union perforce allies, was only an interlude. The two were far from friendly before the war, and outright hostility followed it. The fire eaters and militarists on both sides fomented the atomic arms race. Senator Arthur Vandenburg, a relatively sober citizen, told Truman, "I see no help for it, Mr. President, but to scare the hell out of the country about communism."

Sarnoff ran with the hounds. If he had followed the example of Cyrus Eaton, the steel magnate E. T. Weir, and a number of other level headed capitalists and military men, he could have served the country well. But that would have required independence of mind, which—in politics—Sarnoff lacked. He was a political conformist and follower, and everything conspired to his following the wrong people—in particular, Henry R. Luce.

It was a mutual attraction. Luce was impressed by Sarnoff, the electronics tycoon; while Sarnoff respected Luce for his accumulation of wealth, and, even more, for the influence he wielded through his magazines. That influence was immense. In his critical biography, *Luce and His Empire*, W. A. Swanberg quotes Robert M. Hutchins: "Mr. Luce and his magazines have more effect on the American character than the whole educational system put together." While Luce was alive this was unquestionably true, and it applied to Sarnoff as well as to the average reader. *Life*, before it was done in by television, had 18 million readers; *Time* about 6 million. Swanberg shows how the policy of the

Luce press bordered on fascism. In the thirties, Laird S. Goldsborough was not only foreign editor of *Time* but also a friend of Luce. During Goldsborough's tenure Leon Blum was always referred to as "Jew Blum," while Leon Trotsky was tagged "né Bronstein." These are only small samples; Swanberg tells the whole story, and it is not a pretty one.*

Another linkage between Sarnoff and Luce can be traced through *Time*'s cover portraits and the associated biographical stories, which were said to be worth more than a million dollars to a featured business-man. Sarnoff received this accolade twice (July 13, 1929, and July 23, 1951). He did not, however, approach the record holder, Benito Mussolini, a favorite of Luce and his editors—and admired also by Sarnoff. Sarnoff's friendship with Marconi was not disturbed—rather enhanced —by Marconi's status as a member of the Grand Council of Fascism. In 1934 Sarnoff acted as Marconi's advisor and advocate in drafting a new employment contract Marconi was negotiating with British Cables and Wireless, Ltd.

> Sarnoff in this connection, reported to the RCA board of directors: it is interesting to mention the personal affection which Mussolini holds for Marconi as evidenced by the fact that Mussolini sent his personal counsel with Marconi to London in order to help the inventor with his problem. Marconi introduced me to Mussolini's counsel who was naturally in favor of the suggestions I made.

The entrance of the United States into World War II turned Sarnoff around for the time being. At a March 1942 dinner meeting of the Economic Club of New York, of which he was president, he introduced the Soviet ambassador, Maxim Litvinoff:

> Whenever men's minds turn to the spirit of mass heroism, to unfaltering resistance to aggression, and to what made the intuitional Adolf run, they must pay homage to Russia. If others had underrated the mighty power of the Russian nation, the indomitable purpose of her people, the prepardness of her heroic armies after the first shock, it is a comfort to think that so did Hitler.

---

*At the same time, Swanberg gives Luce a fair break. Referring to Luce's last speech (at Santa Barbara, early in 1967) Swanberg describes it as "the last of his lifelong efforts involving how much thought and study, how many plane rides, how many hotel rooms, handshakes and drafty halls, never charging a fee, all in his errand of alerting America to her greatness and her world mission!"

Meeting the full flood of the Axis tide with a vast human dike, Russia has forced the Nazis to change their plans and their timetable, and has destroyed the myth of their invincibility.

At first, even after the cold war was well under way, Sarnoff was cautious in switching his views. In April 1947 his address on "Science and Society" before the American Physical Society in Washington was moderate in tone:

The advance of social science, no less than that of physical science, calls for the creative imagination of a Newton or a Maxwell, an Edison or a Marconi. Obsolescence is a factor in social as well as in industrial machines. In society as in industry to stand still is to go backward. . . . But a study of the social strains and stresses in the world today points toward a clearly defined objective which should be the immediate goal of social science. That goal should be to achieve economic justice, peace, and prosperity in a free democracy.

These admirable sentiments shortly withered in the miasma of the cold war. Sarnoff did not go all the way, but he was not far behind Luce, who was prepared to wage nuclear war against the Chinese as well as the Russians. In an italicized paragraph in *Life* (July 10, 1950), Luce laid it on the line: "Someday, a president of the United States will have to take a fighting stand against Communism somewhere west of California. It will be better to do it today than tomorrow. It would have been better to do it yesterday than today. And a lot better day before yesterday."

Luce had already made it clear that the "fighting stand" would entail the use by the United States of atomic weapons. The danger was aggravated by Luce's Presbyterian piety, which he shared with John Foster Dulles. They were Gott-mit-Uns men, much like Kaiser Wilhelm II in World War I. Sarnoff agreed in general, except that he left out Jesus.

Other influences tending in the same direction included Winston Churchill, who launched the cold war definitively with his "Iron Curtain" speech at Fulton, Missouri, in 1946. Churchill was one of the few men to whom Sarnoff deferred. Both were men of action, and Sarnoff was not satisfied with waging the cold war merely in words. Even before World War II, Sarnoff had been on the lookout for Russian aggression, and he took countermeasures in his own field. When short-wave broadcasting became feasible in the twenties, he feared Communist propaganda might undermine the sturdy American commitment to capitalist enterprise. This apprehension proved groundless: shortwave propaganda has never acquired an audience worth considering in the United States. In the thirties, however, it was having some effect among the neutral and underdeveloped nations, and Sarnoff entertained the idea of using it for counterpropaganda. U.S. government officials were slow to act on the suggestion: FDR had established diplomatic relations with the Soviet Union and the current headaches of capitalist democracy made it difficult to sell.

The cold war finally made the idea timely and Sarnoff renewed his proposal, which came to fruition in the Voice of America program, adopted in late 1947. A parallel idea—an international broadcasting system to be known as "The Voice of the UN"—based on the principle of "Freedom to Listen," failed to find favor, nor did Sarnoff's addition of "Freedom to Look" (by television) fare any better. However, by way of consolation, the United Nations presented Sarnoff with a testimonial for his contribution to the general principle of freedom of information, which has been totally ignored in the communist states and equally in American client states, and as late as the seventies fared none too well at the hands of top government officials in the United States itself. What gives meaning to American freedom of the press is not so much government permissiveness as the activity of courageous and competent investigative reporters.

The cold war did not gather full momentum until the 1950s, with the emergence of Senator Joseph R. McCarthy from senatorial obscurity to power so great that even the President of the United States refrained from directly challenging him. Though he never supported McCarthy (nor antagonized him either), Sarnoff similarly did not get into the thick of cold war action until Eisenhower was in the White House. John Tebbel in his biography, *David Sarnoff*, wrote;

> The general is constantly thinking up new ways to fight Communism. In April 1955, he submitted a memorandum to President Eisenhower urging the government to adopt a bold "Program for a Political Offensive against World Communism" that he had devised. It soon became one of the most widely reprinted and discussed plans in the cold war, appearing as required reading in numerous college courses and in military officer training programs. This and other statements he made in support of his belief that "the best way to prevent a hot

war is to win the cold war" have made him one of the private citizens most often quoted on the floor of the Senate and House.

Sarnoff dictated a memo summarizing his contribution at a high-level luncheon meeting in a private dining room at the Capitol in June 1955. Present besides Sarnoff were Vice-President Nixon; Senator Lyndon B. Johnson, majority leader; Senator William F. Knowland, minority leader; Senator Karl E. Mundt; Representative Walter Judd; Represenative Francis E. Walter; Nelson Rockefeller, special assistant to the president; and Allen Dulles, director, Central Intelligence Agency. Sarnoff's memo follows:

> As we can freeze to death as well as burn to death, the best way for us to prevent a Hot War is to win the Cold War which the Communists are prosecuting vigorously on all fronts.
>
> I expressed the opinion that Russia has not the slightest intention of abandoning the Cold War. What Russia seems to be working for now is the combination of a Hot Peace with Cold War. If we touch their hot stove we get burned, and if we sit on their cake of ice we get frozen. . . .
>
> The idea that we must win the Cold War was shared by all present.

Considering the participants, the conclusion is hardly surprising.

In his formal addresses after World War II, Sarnoff showed all the élan and energy of his earlier years; only the vital elements of originality and objective judgment were missing. After 1948 his performance resembled that of an aging athlete or virtuoso: the magnificent instrument still existed, but it no longer functioned as it had in its prime.

In Sarnoff's case passion overrode judgment. He saw only one side —the one that coincided with his prejudices, which grew increasingly strident. The Soviets were bad enough in respect of civil liberties, freedom of political and artistic expression, and tolerance of religious beliefs; the effect of Sarnoff's intemperate attacks was to make them even worse. When they showed some tentative inclination to let up, Sarnoff became still more furious. He threatened them with World War III, in which the industrial might of the United States would destroy them. Flying in the face of all experience, he seems to have thought he could convert them by verbal violence, or perhaps he was merely throwing his weight around, like the vociferous protestors at a town meeting. In speech after speech, he used the same uninspired metaphor: we could freeze to death or we could burn to death—we had to win the cold war or perish. From the time he got up to the time he sat down, everything he had to say was predictable, almost as if on tape.

Going beyond verbiage, Sarnoff proceeded to practical measures. Quoting the Henry Luce *Life* maxim that one picture is worth 10,000 words (never mind what words—the Bible comes without illustrations) he advocated big-screen units in black-and-white and color, to be used, together with mobile film units, in "backward areas." A more ambitious idea involved mass distribution of cheap, lightweight radio receivers pretuned to the frequencies of powerful CIA-financed propaganda transmitters based in West Germany, and similarly inexpensive hand-operated phonographs to be supplied with a single record explaining American policy and inciting the enslaved Russian masses to rebellion. These devices were to be dropped by the million from cargo-carrying airplanes.

Probably President Eisenhower would never have acquiesced in any such hazardous, not to say harebrained, schemes, but the U–2 Gary Powers incident put the quietus on one and all. Besides, Eisenhower's intelligence sources failed to support Sarnoff's conviction that the Russian people were yearning to overthrow their rulers, presumably under CIA leadership. The Soviet Union was not Iran, where a Mossadegh could be knocked over in a three-day CIA-managed uprising. The radio receiver scheme was tried out later in Vietnam, but it seems to have failed to win the hearts and minds of the people.

The point may be raised that Sarnoff swung so far to the right because of the iniquities of Stalinism. These may well have contributed, but why did he assume such a high moral stand against Russian tyranny while, earlier, admiring Mussolini's dictatorship? A more plausible etiology—though possibly likewise incomplete—is that he became such an ardent crusader because at a certain point his personal inclinations coincided with those of the power elites—military, political and economic—in all of which he now held full membership, and outside of which he no longer had much association, except insofar as RCA's needs required his attention.

I am not in a position to say it was this much of one and that much of the other, or to what effect other factors played a part. What does seem certain is that, convinced by his own metaphors, with Communism as the overwhelming menace to peace and freedom, Sarnoff neglected the more immediate threat to the internal cohesions and moral defenses of American society of a quarter-century of cold war, culminating in the plunge into the quagmire of Southeast Asia, which apparently met with his full approval.

In one phase of Sarnoff's personal cold-war crusade, however, a serious injustice has been done him. It appears in Alexander Kendrick's otherwise admirable *Prime Time: The Life of Edward R. Murrow* (1969). Describing Sarnoff's program for ringing the Communist world with fixed and mobile broadcasting facilities, distributing propaganda-laden radios and phonographs, etc., Kendrick comments, "By happy circumstance RCA . . . was in the radio set and phonograph record business."

I did not know Sarnoff intimately, but I knew him a lot better than Kendrick did—enough to convince me that the ascription of a venal motive is unfounded. It was a foolish scheme, but devoid of any commercial motive. I have no doubt that in this matter Sarnoff was the crusader—also to some extent the social climber—but it was not a business scheme. He wanted to impress Eisenhower, Nixon, the Dulles brothers, and other leading cold warriors with his dedicated anti-Communism. He had some prototypes of these devices built by his engineers, but if it had come to production, I believe he would have preferred to have the contract turned over to other companies. If RCA undertook manufacture, it would have been on a nonprofit basis.

By the time Nixon had made it to the presidency, Sarnoff, dying, was spared the pain of seeing Nixon tentatively modify the policies which had endeared them to each other. By that time, also, Moscow and Peking had been at odds for nearly twenty years. Sarnoff's cries of alarm about worldwide monolithic Communism were as outdated as skirts on women's bathing suits.

An observation of David Lilienthal's indicates that Sarnoff's overwrought hostility to the Soviet Union may have resulted in a missed opportunity which might have changed the course of history and saved countless lives. In an October 1951 talk with President Truman, Lilienthal suggested that Sarnoff might be useful in negotiations with the Russians if the time ever came for some sort of rapprochement. Truman agreed. "Yes," he said, "Sarnoff comes down here for a talk now and then and I think very well of him." Lilienthal commented that our career people in State were "too reasonable and rational in their approach to the Russians when they set out to exasperate and wear us down—which they usually do. The General would do some wearing down of his own, and he is as smart and intelligent as they come; needs more depth, and as an antagonist and cusser, at that stage he would be very good." Lilienthal conveyed this idea to Sarnoff and he seemed "intrigued," but nothing came of it.

It is hard to see how anything could have come of it, with Sarnoff's prior record. If, rather, it had been one of judicious condemnation and conciliation, he might have had a chance of assuming the role Lilienthal had in mind. As it was, the Soviet rulers must have regarded Sarnoff, plausibly enough, as an irreconcilable enemy.

Possibly Truman changed his view of Sarnoff later. Merle Miller, in *Speaking Plainly*, 1974, relates a gratuitous taunt by Truman when the two met by chance in an elevator of the Beverly Hills Hotel. Sarnoff's right foot was bandaged. "Well, General," Truman said, "looks as if you'll have to kick people in the ass with the other foot now." Sarnoff got off the elevator.

THE BLACKLISTERS

The vulnerability of the broadcasting industry, based on business sponsorship and the axiom that no sizable section of the public was ever to be offended, was demonstrated well before World War II. In the thirties Alexander Woollcott, drama critic, journalist and radio raconteur and commentator, was broadcasting a weekly Sunday evening series titled "The Town Crier," sponsored by Cream of Wheat. Woollcott took off after Hitler and the Nazis, who were openly preparing for war and the extermination of European Jews. Woollcott's sponsor asked him to desist. Woollcott refused and the sponsor cancelled the series. Woollcott said that anyone with the courage of a sick mouse would have done what he did. Had he lived to see what went on in radio-TV after the war, he would have changed his mind.

Blacklisting in its mature phase, peaking synchronously with the cold war, spread from the movies eastward. The theater offered the most resolute resistance, radio-TV the least. There was also less excuse for the TV tycoons, since they had early warning from Hollywood and could have prepared an effective defense, if they had been so inclined —as a few were.

The invasion was led initially by three former FBI men who were alert to the opportunities afforded by their version of the free enterprise system. Starting without any connection with the broadcasting industry, Kenneth K. Bierly, John G. Keenan, and Theodore C. Kirkpatrick quickly acquired the power to bind and to loose. Financed initially by Alfred Kohlberg, a millionaire importer who doubled as a supporter of Chiang Kai-shek and a variety of anti-Communist causes, the three inquisitors operated through a weekly paper: *Counterattack: The Newsletter of Facts on Communism.* A year after it first went on sale, *Counterattack* was grossing $100,000. A principal source of derogatory information, yielding even more pay dirt than the files of the House Un-American Activities Committee and other congressional sources, was the *Daily Worker*. To be mentioned in the *Worker*, except in an unmistakably hostile context, was tantamount to vocational oblivion, unless the suspect could clear himself before a *Counterattack* kangaroo court by expressing contrition, exposing fellow culprits, and subscribing thenceforth to the tenets of American Legion-Veterans of Foreign Wars patriotism.

A reporter from the New York *Daily News*, itself no mean scourge of Reds, remonstrated with Kirkpatrick: "I have been reading in *Counterattack* that Communists cannot be trusted, that they are devious, that they are full of intrigue and so forth. And yet you can sit there and tell me that you take these things out of the *Daily Worker* and do not check them. . . ."

Kirkpatrick's answer was that if the *Worker* printed something that *Counterattack* reprinted and it proved to be false, the injured party's recourse was to the *Worker*.

Week after week *Counterattack* tossed about the terms of excommunication, ranging from the sparingly used, outright appellation of "Communist," to its libel-proof derivatives: "Quislings," "dupes," "pinkos," "fifth columnists," etc. Having purged the industry of the most conspicuously "liberal," "progressive" or insufficiently flammable anti-Communists and terrorized most of those still on the payroll, the *Counterattack* group followed up their initial success with a handbook, *Red Channels: The Report of Communist Influence in Radio and Television*, published by a *Counterattack* subsidiary, American Business Associates, Inc. *Red Channels* listed 151 of the leading creative people in the industry and allied fields, including Leonard Bernstein, Marc Blitzstein, Morris Carnovsky, Lee J. Cobb, Marc Connelly, Aaron Copland, Clifford J. Durr, Olin Downes, Richard Dyer-Bennett, John Garfield, Ruth Gordon, Ben Grauer, Uta Hagen, Dashiell Hammett, E. Y. Harburg, Lillian Hellman, Langston Hughes, Lena Horne, Marsha Hunt, Burl Ives, Sam Jaffe (the actor, not the agent-producer), Burgess Meredith, Arthur Miller, Garson Kanin, Pert Kelton, Gypsy Rose Lee, Philip Loeb, Margo (the one-name actress), Zero Mostel, Jean Muir, Dorothy Parker, Edward G. Robinson, Hazel Scott, Pete Seeger, Irwin Shaw, William L. Shirer, Howard K. Smith, Lionel Stander, Louis Untermeyer, and Raymond Walsh.

For the complete list, see *The Golden Web*, p. 266. Barnouw also lists the citations against the 151: they had opposed Franco, Hitler and Mussolini, tried to help war refugees, combated race discrimination, campaigned against poll taxes and other voting barriers, opposed censorship, criticized the House Committee on un-American Activities, hoped for peace, and favored efforts toward better U.S.-Soviet relations. Many had been New Deal supporters.

Barnouw concludes that the compilation could be seen as a move to pillory the liberal impulses of two decades as traitorous.

It was only at this point that Senator Joseph R. McCarthy came into the picture. On February 9, 1950 he delivered before an audience of receptive ladies in Wheeling, West Virginia his famous "I have here in my hand" speech. McCarthy did not initiate blacklisting in the entertainment field, but his activities greatly enhanced the power of internal cold war propaganda, including that of *Counterattack* and its derivatives. Conversely, when McCarthy rashly attacked the army and was finally "condemned" by the Senate (Vice-President Nixon, as president of the Senate, reduced "censured" to the milder "condemned") the blacklisting subindustry gradually lost its virulence.

In my opinion, Sarnoff and NBC were more culpable in the institutionalizing of radio-TV broadcasting than William S. Paley, Frank Stanton, and CBS. Forming a united front, with or without ABC, the two leading networks probably could have stopped the invasion at the outset. Instead, both collaborated with the invaders, with only the difference that the CBS procedure was more candid and somewhat less destructive of morale among those blacklisted.

The CBS operation was in charge of vice-president Daniel T. O'Shea, whom I have known for many years. He was in charge of RKO's legal affairs during my tenure as recording director; later he was David O. Selznick's principal assistant. He is an astute and fair-minded lawyer and show-business executive and while I wouldn't have touched his job as CBS's clearance man with a barge pole, that is only because I agree with Dore Schary's statement before the Un-American Activities Committee: "Up until the time it is proved that a Communist is a man dedicated to the overthrow of the government by force and violence, or by any illegal methods, I cannot make a determination of his employment on any other basis except whether he is qualified best to do the job I want him to do."

That was how Schary, the head of the MGM studio and RKO

studios (at different times) saw it. O'Shea saw it as a public relations problem for the network, of protecting itself against accusations that it was hiring communists which, in the cold war climate of those days, could have been damaging. Paley and Stanton, Sarnoff likewise, felt that in the existing state of public opinion a broadcasting company, always under scrutiny by interests and organizations hostile to Communism (and to left-wing liberals but *not* to their equivalents on the right) should, simply as a matter of sound business practice, hire only people whose background was nonpolitical or whose inclinations were safely slanted toward the right. Why take chances with actors, writers, etc. who could inspire damaging publicity, boycotts, lawsuits, and the like when, as always in show business, people were available of substantially equal competence to whom no one could object. With the far-reaching political consequences of this basis for employment and unemployment, neither Paley, Stanton, nor O'Shea were vitally concerned, Sarnoff even less so.

All four were personally opposed to McCarthy. In O'Shea's case I have direct knowledge; all the evidence indicates it for Paley and Stanton; Sarnoff is entitled to the benefit of the doubt. But, consistent with their practice of blacklisting, they were necessarily cautious in their opposition—at first. They must have known that the CP never had any identification with the workers, that it was stigmatized as in effect an agency of a foreign power, and that the great majority of active, "card-carrying" members did nothing but sometimes attend meetings, maybe subscribe to the *Daily Worker,* pay their dues, and talk about a "better world" in the distant future. In a few cases, they stood on street corners handing out leaflets (never in Hollywood—that was for the humbler and less affluent members in downtown Los Angeles). The rank and file never thought of spying or doing anything illegal. They, and "fellow travelers" close enough to the party to fall under suspicion of membership, were blacklisted not because they were a menace to the Republic, but because an assortment of American Legion-Veterans of Foreign Wars vigilantes, racketeers, religiously motivated anti-Communists, and hatemongers had found a collective scapegoat incapable of fighting back.

Ah, but what about Whittaker Chambers? He was indeed made of sterner stuff, he acted as a spy-courier, and when he switched, was equally fanatical in his anti-Communism. He was not unique in that respect—in America rational anti-Communism was never enough to satisfy a Communist renegade. As for Alger Hiss, maybe he was framed, maybe not—but I read somewhere when his case was being discussed that the information he had allegedly furnished to the Russians was about *Japanese* military dispositions in Asia and never had anything to do with U.S. military strength in any part of the world or about U.S. military plans. If that was all that Hiss did, he is to be extolled—he saved American lives in the ensuing conflict. As far as I know, the Department of Justice has never revealed what information Hiss was supposed to have transmitted to the Russians; he was convicted of perjury on Chambers' say-so, never of spying.

Dan O'Shea was in sole charge for CBS—he took the job on that basis—and worked openly in his blacklisting. The accused could see him or his assistant, and if they could satisfy them that they were falsely accused or had repented (repentance, however, involved "naming names") he gave them the okay. When a director or producer asked for a certain actor or writer, clearance had to be obtained through O'Shea's office. Clearance might be given, or the answer might be, over the phone, "Sorry, we can't clear." If the director (or producer) asked why, the answer was, "That does not concern you."

I know nothing about the procedure at NBC; the clearance group there was faceless. And I have been assured that RCA–NBC public relations will never let anything out of that bag. Sarnoff could safely have been as liberal as, say, Dore Schary, who was a friend of his and a fellow member of Rabbi Mandelbaum's ethics class. He did not choose to be that liberal, or to be liberal in any sense. He simply switched.

Schary's Americanism is the real thing, not a counterfeit. He is that rarity—a genuine principled liberal. His beginnings were much like Sarnoff's, though less harsh. He was born in Newark, New Jersey, the son of immigrant parents, and raised in an Orthodox Jewish environment. As a youth he did anything for a living—wrote a play, sold stock and Christmas cards, opened a restaurant with his mother, a woman of great courage, like Sarnoff's mother. And, like Sarnoff, he was a nil desperandum sort of fellow. "I always had the feeling I could make a dollar," he said later. "If things got too bad, I could drive a cab or something. I could manage to live, if my health held out."

Schary rose from a pitiable $100-a-week junior writer in Hollywood to head of production at MGM, the proudest post in Hollywood. He was fired a few times on the way up, but he always got a better job.

In a Republican milieu, he was a New Deal Democrat, but as a writer and producer of inexpensive but good pictures he overcame that handicap. He was anti-Communist but not bigoted about it. At one time he taught playwriting at the League of American Writers, knowing it was a left-wing outfit, a "Communist front." He liked teaching playwriting, and there was nothing political about it. The comrades never bothered him until they asked him to sign a philippic against FDR. Schary balked and quit.

When the right-wing attack on Hollywood came to a head, the opposition in Hollywood, nominally led by Humphrey Bogart, at first resisted vigorously. It looked for a time that they might win out, but the top movie executives in New York overruled those studio heads who were against intimidation by the American Legion and kindred organizations. The studio people who sided, on principle, with the Bogart group (which included the Hollywood Ten who later went to jail) were Schary, Walter Wanger, and Sam Goldwyn. At the crucial meeting at the Waldorf Astoria, they defended their position; but all the other movie magnates favored purging Communists and those identified with them. Schary, Wanger, and Goldwyn were out-voted.

In *The Time of the Toad: A Study of Inquisition in America*, 1972, Dalton Trumbo, one of the Hollywood Ten and a first-rate movie scriptwriter (and not confined to movie writing) identifies Schary as "a man of higher intellect and morality than those [producers] with whom he had been cast." Trumbo quotes Schary's personal views on blacklisting, then complains: "Yet it was this man, upon his return to Hollywood, who accepted the chairmanship of the producer committee to enforce the blacklist. Asked by a *New Yorker* reporter why he had changed his mind, he replied with stark simplicity that he had done it to hold his job. . . ." Schary says that is not true. He quotes Casey Stengel: "You could look it up."

I agree that Trumbo's stand was a nobler one than Schary's, or O'Shea's, and certainly Sarnoff's, but Trumbo was not head of a studio, or a show-business lawyer, or chairman of the board of RCA. He was, I assume, a Communist; I know beyond a doubt that he was a decent, honest, admirable citizen. I think he and the other victims of the Red hunt were ill treated and that the nation is the worse for it. To show in what way, let me quote from Alexander Woollcott on Paul Robeson, who was persecuted as a Communist, and deprived of health and livelihood:

> . . . Of the countless people I have known in my wanderings over the
> world, he is one of the few of whom I would say that they have
> greatness. I do not mean greatness as a football player or as an actor
> or as a singer. . . . I do not even have in mind what is, I suppose, the
> indisputable fact that he is the finest musical instrument wrought by
> nature in our time. I mean greatness as a person.

I have taken this from a column of Pete Hamill's in the *New York
Post* of April 11, 1973. It is from Woollcott's *While Rome Burns.* I
append Hamill's comment:

> It is not clear, even now, whether Robeson actually became a Com-
> munist; certainly, his closest friends were Communists; he loved the
> Soviet Union, and sent his son Paul Jr. to school there for a while;
> later, he won the Stalin Peace Prize. It really isn't important. What
> everyone forgot at the time was that if Robeson, a free man, wanted
> to be a Communist, it was his business. Picasso, Sartre and many
> others were Communists. Nobody went after them the way the
> American government went after Robeson.
>
> But then Robeson was not feared in America because he was a
> Communist. He was feared because he was black, because he was a
> man, because he refused to become a "house nigger" for anyone. He
> was feared, more than anything else, because he was an artist.

But to return to Schary and Sarnoff, and my belief that it was a good
thing that Schary stayed at MGM. Among liberals Schary was the real
thing, as Sarnoff never was. In the David Sarnoff Library there are
laudatory citations from the American Legion; Schary incurred the
hostility of the Legion. He told me how he recruited Darryl Zanuck
and some other studio heads in a project to make a film showing the
services of the movie industry to the nation in World War II—the
numerous movie people in military service; the educational films produced at Wright Field and in Hollywood; the combat film unit in New
York, sales of bonds, public relations contributions, etc. The American
Legion was to be taken to task for its campaign against Hollywood.

The Producers Association finally vetoed the idea, but the Legion
got wind of it and Schary received a call from an American Legion
official who wanted to see him—alone. Schary insisted on having another MGM executive present and selected Eddie Mannix, one of the
top people. The American Legion man, O'Neill, also had somebody
with him. Schary cited a post at Saugus, not far from Hollywood, with

not a single Jewish member and the fact that American-Japanese combat veterans, who had taken the risk of being killed through mistaken identity by their own comrades at night, had to form a post of their own.

Schary said to O'Neill: "We don't interfere in your business, however repugnant in may be to us: why do you think you are privileged to interfere in ours?" The Legion campaign against the movie industry was attenuated to the point where it ceased to be troublesome.

In 1966–67 Schary recorded his reminiscenes at Columbia University. The record shows how, a liberal, he took a pasting from both sides. In reference to his stand at the Waldorf conference (he was head of production at RKO at the time), he said:

> I took the position that all the industry was to have taken, which was that you could not deny employment to a man because of his political beliefs. I maintained that position, because I believed in it. Some of my colleagues in production at the time did not maintain it, because they got a little worried and frightened. So I inherited the whirlwind; the Hearst papers in Los Angeles had big headlines saying, "RKO Chief Says He Will Hire Reds.". . .
>
> I recognized very quickly that to have, let's say, known Communists on your payroll at two or three thousand a week might create a couple of problems for you—one, in terms of job relations and, two, in terms of what your own attitude as a citizen might be. But I said, "Let's take our time. This is a very important issue." And this is the position that Sam Goldwyn and Walter Wanger took. But there was nothing we could do about it.

Later, when an MGM picture was picketed with placards reading, "Don't go to Metro pictures, Dore Schary is a Red," Schary's comment on this and on a leading actor, now deceased, is the following:

> They [the placard carriers] were crackpots, totally unimportant. But we went into court and got a secondary injunction against them, and it killed them. . . . They're nothing now.
>
> . . . I have no respect for——'s political opinions whatsoever. I think he's an absolute dullard and I think he's stupid, politically. But I employed him. Have I spoken to him on politics? Oh, no . . . it's a waste of time, he's an idiot. . . . Anybody who really believes that there is a possibility of a Communist revolution in America is crazy. He's as politically naïve as the Communists, but no use saying I

> wouldn't employ him—I employed him. I employ many people I don't like socially, that I can't stand, who bore me, whose morals I hate, whose point of view about everything I hate. I've employed people that I'm positive were anti-Semitic. . . .

Schary then refers to a writer who argued that he was being denied employment because he was anti-Communist: "He's always complaining he has no employment, but he hasn't written anything. And he wants to stay unemployed at a very high salary—[$4,000 a week]."

The movie experience with blacklisting antedated television blacklisting by three years. Yet Sarnoff and Paley seem to have learned nothing from it. The most outrageous case involved NBC and Jean Muir, a screen star who had been chosen for the role of the mother in the TV version of "The Aldrich Family," after the show's eleven years on radio. Three days before the scheduled premiere, set for Sunday, August 27, 1950, the Young and Rubicam advertising agency announced she would be playing the role. Then the premiere was postponed for a week, and Miss Muir was fired and offered a cash settlement. The decision not to let her play the role was made at the highest echelons at General Foods, the sponsor, and at NBC. The case was so widely publicized that both David and Robert Sarnoff must have known about it. Robert, however, was not yet in a position of power, where his approval or disapproval meant much.

Miss Muir was not anything remotely resembling a Communist— but she had been cited in *Red Channels.* One of her offenses was that she was a student of the Stanislavski acting method and had signed a cable of congratulations to the Moscow Art Theater on its fiftieth anniversary. General Foods, Barnouw says in *The Golden Web:* "made no investigations, asked no explanations, claimed no disloyalty on her part. It merely asserted the need to avoid 'controversial' people on programs it sponsored."

CBS had embarrassing incidents, too. Late in 1953 AWARE, Inc. got into the same business as the *Counterattack* group, with Vincent Hartnett, who had written the introduction to *Red Channels,* as a top official. AWARE was allied with Lawrence Johnson, a Syracuse, New York supermarket owner and volunteer Red-hunter. In January 1956 John Henry Faulk, a premier CBS disc jockey and occasional panelist, took office as vice-president of the American Federation of Television and Radio Artists. Faulk was anti-Communist, but also anti blacklisting and anti-AWARE. Although Faulk had never been on any blacklist, AWARE denounced him, alleging "Communist" activities. Johnson urged Faulk's sponsors to drop him, which they did.

In June 1956 Faulk brought suit against AWARE, Hartnett, and Johnson. CBS kept Faulk on for a while without sponsorship, then fired him. Edward R. Murrow was outraged and sent Faulk a check in the amount of $7,500 so that he could retain Louis Nizer as his attorney. AWARE had no case to speak of, but the suit dragged on for years. In June 1962, while testimony was being taken in New York, Johnson died, apparently of an overdose of barbiturates, in a Bronx motel. The court ordered that Johnson's estate be substituted for Johnson. The jury awarded damages of $3,500,000 to Faulk, more than he had asked for. A five-judge appellate court held that the actions of the defendants had been proved to be "as malicious as they were vicious," but scaled down the damages to $550,000. It had taken six years for Faulk to get himself vindicated.

Sydney W. Head (*Broadcasting in America,* 1972) sums up the lesson:

> With the benefit of hindsight one can find a number of indications to suggest that their sense of economic vulnerability made advertisers, networks, and agencies give in to a tyranny which would have collapsed in the face of a firm commitment to normal American standards of evidence, due process, and fair play. The Faulk verdict came too late to be of practical help to the chief victims. But it did expose the incredible flimsiness of the professional blacklisters' ramshackle guilt-by-association edifice. . . . What made them seem monstrously powerful was the response of men in the advertising companies, agencies, networks and stations, who simply surrendered to pressure without firing a shot.

To CBS's credit, but more to the credit of Edward R. Murrow and Fred W. Friendly, were the CBS TV broadcasts which set the stage for the Army-McCarthy hearings, which began on April 22, 1954, and continued for thirty-five days. NBC and CBS used only excerpts. ABC–TV, a poor third in the ratings and without daytime programs to distribute to its affiliates, had little to lose and carried the hearings in full. The close-ups of McCarthy and Roy Cohn murdered McCarthy.

The crucial difference between a man like Schary, and Sarnoff, comes down to this: Schary was an anti-Communist in a rational way, while Sarnoff became an anti-Communist crusader and, as chairman of RCA, permitted its subsidiary, NBC, to become allied with some exceedingly dubious characters, and thereby put his own status as an enlightened citizen in question. To his further discredit, there was no need for all this cruelty, injustice, and assault on the Constitution, in a moral if not legal sense. He should have exerted his powerful influence to preserve the good name of the media which he had done so much to create. If he had done that, or something resembling it, I would never have had occasion to write this chapter.

DEAR DAVE,
DEAR DICK

Those of us who knew Sarnoff early in his career were confident, despite his lack of political experience and the handicap of his foreign birth, that in some future crisis he would play an important role in American politics. When he accompanied Owen D. Young and the rest of the American delegation to Paris and took over the negotiations with Schacht, we were confirmed in that expectation. There were others of the same opinion; although in their view Sarnoff's expanded role was not necessarily political, they shared the impression that RCA, big as it was, was incapable of containing Sarnoff in the full amplitude of his powers.

Rabbi Mandelbaum did not say so explicitly, but it was a clear deduction from his statement at Sarnoff's funeral, "I loved the man," that the inspiration could not have come from Sarnoff's position as the chairman of the board of a corporation, however great and powerful. Joseph H. McConnell, a lawyer and business executive who was president of NBC, 1949–52, regarded Sarnoff as an "idealist" who caused considerable trouble for NBC in Washington with his outspoken views. McConnell's own opinion seems to have been akin to Herbert Hoover's, harkening back to the early controversies about how radio should be supported—that broadcasting, being invested with the public interest, should not be a business at all; but as long as it was operated as a business, and he was associated with it, he would do his best to make it profitable. But he did not stay long; he left for the presidency of Colgate Palmolive.

Lilienthal's view is the most persuasive on the subject of Sarnoff's idealistic germination, for all that Sarnoff kept this aspect of his character well concealed most of the time. In one of his conversations with Sarnoff in which they digressed from business matters, Sarnoff avowed his belief in God as a "Great Intelligence," but even if no such Supreme Being existed (and though at this time Sarnoff expected a world-devastating nuclear war) he felt it his duty to "plant seeds in the minds of fellows who have a bean" (like Lilienthal), do the best job he could, and live happily from day to day.

Sarnoff was "full of fire and quite moving." When he had finished, Lilienthal said, half to himself: "What a great rabbi, what a prophet you would have made!" This "rather caught" Sarnoff. He said for the past several months he had been reading the entire Talmud, in an English translation.

So, what came of all this promise of an almost messianic role? The ironical result was an alliance between David Sarnoff and Richard M. Nixon. While Sarnoff was more intimate with Nixon, he also repeatedly warned President Eisenhower of the dire consequences of American defeat in the cold war, an improbable outcome which seems to have kept Sarnoff awake at night. At the end of an April 1955 memo to Eisenhower, Sarnoff wrote:

> We have only a choice between fighting the Cold War with maximum concentration of energy, or waiting supinely until we are overwhelmed. . . . Our current posture shows the weakness inherent in all defensive strategy. . . . *Our duty and our best chance of salvation . . . is to prosecute the Cold War to the point of victory. To survive in freedom we must win.* (Emphasis in the original.)

From 1954 through 1961, Sarnoff carried on an extensive correspondence along these lines with Vice-President Nixon on a first-name footing, combined with a political-social relationship. Their conversations dealt mostly with the cold war and military and propaganda projects. In a memo dated June 17, 1960, Sarnoff discussed weapons systems designed to launch missiles against ground targets from spaceships orbiting several hundred miles above the earth. Sarnoff dictated this memo after dinner at Nixon's home, where the subject had been discussed, though neither man could possibly have had more than a superficial knowledge of a highly technical subject. Thus qualified, they were apprehensive that the Russians might develop such a system targeted on U.S. fixed nuclear installations, with bombs flying over the South Pole, where we had no antimissile defenses and early warning systems. Why the Russians should go to all this trouble, with its inherent inaccuracies, was not explained; but both sides were dreaming up all sorts of weird schemes (and still are) in the battle of the budgets. This idea may have appealed to Sarnoff's indomitable faith in research: at the end of the memo, he wrote, "We may find ways to remove the present perils, but we must not ignore those in the making, for we cannot disarm the human mind."

Under date of August 10, 1960, Sarnoff sent Nixon a 23-page, 7,000-word draft of a proposed speech by Nixon on the meaning and menace of the cold war, obviously in preparation for the approaching election. The title, "We Can Prevent a Hot War by Winning the Cold War," did not reveal any startling new ideas. Under the caption, "Our Patience," Sarnoff could not contain his indignation at the perfidy of the enemy:

> Certainly no one can accuse our country or its allies of lacking patience in dealing with the Communists. We have bent over backwards, on occasion almost breaking our backs, to persuade them of our peaceful intentions. We have shown our readiness to negotiate on any diplomatic level despite the dismal Soviet record of violations of previous pledges, agreements and treaties.

All to no avail. "The spirit of Teheran, of Yalta, of Geneva and now of Camp David, all, all, have been wrecked by the Communists." (Sarnoff did not mention Gary Powers's U–2 reconnaissance flights over Russian territory in May of the same year as having a possible connection with the wrecking of the spirit of Camp David.) "Free world patience has been repaid with betrayal and total disregard of the facts and the truth. The cold war must be won," Sarnoff concluded. "We must not delude ourselves. Defeat would be catastrophic, final, beyond retrieving, perhaps for centuries. As one American summed it up: 'Whether we freeze to death or burn to death, our civilization would be equally finished.' " Sarnoff was that clairvoyant American.

Sarnoff quickly followed up the August 10 speech he wrote for Nixon with one under date of August 16 which he delivered in person at an Advisory Policy Group lunch at the Mayflower Hotel in Washington. This body was assisting Nixon, who was present, in his 1960 campaign for the presidency. Sarnoff made the familiar points: we must win the cold war, accelerate our military strength, adopt a meaningful civil defense program, avoid the snares and delusions of Communist-proposed agreements on disarmament and stop at nothing short of victory, the terms of which he did not specify.

The Advisory Policy Group was a body of nineteen influential and mainly wealthy Republicans directed by James Shepley, a writer on leave from *Time*. If elected, Nixon proposed to continue the group in existence and seek their counsel and criticism during his presidency. All this came to naught at the time, and when, eight years later, Nixon, having mastered TV and adapted it to his peculiar style in appealing to the voters, won the presidency, he adopted a monarchial type of rule which, had it not been for his rash insistence on taping the incriminating conversations in the Oval Office, might have enabled him to establish a larvated rightwing dictatorship behind a presidential facade.

This was certainly not Sarnoff's objective. By the time Nixon was running for the presidency in 1960, Sarnoff had moved far over to the right, but he did not envision a dictatorship; nor does he seem to have been in any way connected, after Nixon's first term as president, with the White House-Watergate gang. His participation ended with the Soviet-baiting phase of the cold war, support of the Vietnamese war, and other actions which, however they might be rated morally, were in no way illegal.

A valid question, however, is why and how Sarnoff was so easily taken in by Nixon. For one thing, in serving Nixon, Sarnoff believed he was serving Eisenhower. Another factor was that his cold war activities kept Sarnoff in the limelight and enabled him to play a dramatic political role, although one of no real importance—even big-time Red hunters and Soviet baiters were a dime a dozen during the cold war. Probably the chief reason for Sarnoff's gullibility, or acquiescence, was that it suited his purpose: He was satisfied with his influence in Washington, atop his industrial power. That this had become his permanent political bent was shown by his blacklisting activities in radio-television.

In retrospect, it seems questionable whether Nixon was ever such a hotshot anti-Communist as he wanted to appear before the country. During the cold war, fervent anti-Communism was the royal road to preferment for a young politician. Probably that was Nixon's overriding motive from the time he clobbered Jerry Vorhees and Helen Gahagan Douglas in California until, after his rise to the presidency, he decided that the Red hunt was running out of steam and henceforth more mileage might be obtained from a transition to what in his earlier phase he would have denounced as "soft on Communism."

If Sarnoff had been unbiased he could have sized up Nixon as a politician devoid of principles and scruples—as single-minded an adventurer and as sordid an opportunist as could be discovered in the upper reaches of American politics. Sarnoff could readily have ascertained the facts, but he was not interested. Those who were interested were on to Nixon from the start. Though more complex than Joe McCarthy, he was no enigma. William V. Shannon, of the editorial staff of *The New York Times*, says that when he watched the "Checkers" broadcast of 1952 he knew for a certainty that Nixon was no more than a con man, unusual only in his success up to that point. Twenty-two years later, the *Times* pointed out editorially that since Nixon extricated himself on that occasion by a well-staged TV playlet, he had used the same formula whenever a major difficulty arose in his climb to the highest office that a majority of his purblind or indulgent fellow-countrymen saw fit to bestow on him. The formula was "to evade the substance of the problem as much as possible and yield as little information as possible and yet seem to be baring one's soul."

In recalling Sarnoff's associations with Nixon, I am not engaging in "guilt by association." Sarnoff was not hauled before a congressional committee, charged with conspiracy to teach the overthrow of the government. His career was not in jeopardy, he was not in danger of going to jail, he was not held up to contumely and ridicule, he retained all his honors and emoluments and was honored the more for his defense of the country against totalitarianism (the leftist kind—Nixon was preparing to establish the regressive kind). No one had the power to blacklist him. Blacklisting was left to the industry in which he was the leading figure, and the network he controlled exercised that power in ruthless disregard of democratic principles and elementary fairness, ruining careers without the slightest compunction and often giving employment to a corps of stoolpigeons and racketeers.

As Lilienthal observed, Sarnoff was a very complex man. If he were alive today, he would probably regret the Nixon interlude, perhaps also the blacklisting, perhaps even his failure to join the Pope in asking clemency for the Rosenbergs. He would almost surely look back on our atrocities in Southeast Asia with compunction. Even when the effects of his actions were evil, his intentions were not; and while this must have been small comfort to the innocent, often admirable people whose lives were ruined by the persecutions in which he participated, there is room for forgiveness when malice is not the motivating force. Gross errors were made in those years even by men whose essential good will and moral courage were later demonstrated. Among the contributors to the disgraceful *Collier's* "Occupation of Russia" issue of 1951, in which the Soviets were obliterated as a military power, perhaps down to the last civilian, were Stuart Chase and Edward R. Murrow!

Sarnoff's qualities of fairness and foresight, though overlaid by the exigencies of business and politics, never wholly left him. In the middle sixties he tapered off on his Red hunting and addressed himself to the political and social implications of direct broadcasting from country to country via satellite. The October 11, 1965 *The Nation* ran an editorial praising Sarnoff's speech on "Law, World-Wide Communications and World Peace," delivered before the Conference on World Peace through Law. Carey McWilliams, the editor, sent Sarnoff a copy of the editorial and Sarnoff acknowledged it under date of October 7. (The date of the letter antedates that of the editorial because, like magazines generally, *The Nation* postdates its issues.) No doubt Sarnoff meant what he said in his letter to McWilliams—just as he meant what he said in his frenzied denunciations of the U.S.S.R.

One World

In 1916, David Sarnoff, then 25, submitted a memorandum on a proposed "radio music box" to his superiors in the Marconi Wireless Telegraph Company of America. The company officials, though already aware of Sarnoff's ability, considered this scheme so hare-brained that they did not bother to reply. They had second thoughts in 1921, when broadcasting burst upon the Radio Corporation of America, which by that time had absorbed the Marconi Company. Within a few years RCA's sales of broadcast receivers had eclipsed its marine and transoceanic wireless telegraph business, and in another few years Sarnoff was president of the company.

Last September 17, Sarnoff, now 74, delivered an address at the Conference on World Peace Through Law on "Law, World-Wide Communications and World Peace," which people familiar with his career consider fully as prognostic as his radio music box idea. We are already in the era of satellite communications, but heretofore the experts have surmised that intercontinental television would continue to require elaborate facilities like those of the Communications Satellite Corporation, which would channel picture and sound to the TV networks for distribution to home receivers. Thus governments and giant corporations would decide what the viewers in each country could see and hear—and what they were not to see and hear.

Sarnoff, who naturally has access to the latest technical advice, now tells us that this is not the way it is going to be. Within five or ten years, he believes, nuclear-powered satellites will transmit TV and radio programs directly to home receivers. Only the home antennas will require modification, and that presents neither technical nor economic problems. It may be added that with the waves coming in at a steep angle there should be less difficulty with "ghosts" than with the present system, where tall buildings, bridges, etc., often cause multiple images.

But it is the political implications that are most disconcerting, or exciting, depending on the viewpoint. Sarnoff asks: "When, for example, a Russian satellite can broadcast directly to a Kansas farm, or an American satellite can broadcast directly to a Hungarian collective, what will be the reaction in both countries? . . . What rules of conduct are to apply, and who is to establish them? This question evades the jurisdiction of any established body, yet it will affect the welfare of all nations and all people." He adds that "it would be a travesty on the hopes of humanity if this immense force for enlightenment, understanding and social advancement were to be subverted to narrow national ends, or become discredited by the failure of nations to agree upon its beneficial uses."

Not so long ago, Sarnoff's views on the cold war were indistinguishable from those of John Foster Dulles. At the request of President Eisenhower, he prepared a report on psychological warfare measures, using existing means of communication which, had they been applied, could only have worsened U.S.–Soviet relations. Now, both the forum he selected and the tone and content of the address indicate a more sober frame of mind. Sarnoff envisions summit conferences, scrambled or open, in which the principals would confer face to face without leaving their respective capitals, television by the United Nations, international educational programing and, in general, areas of communication designed to "strike a chord of response in civilized man regardless of his nationality or ideological allegiance." For the moment, at least, world peace has supplanted the cold war in Sarnoff's thinking. The outlook for the survival of mankind would be more hopeful if peace should become for him a lasting preoccupation, and if other powerful industrialists and politicians were to follow his lead.

Mr. Carey McWilliams
Editor
The NATION
333 Sixth Avenue
New York, New York 10014

Dear Mr. McWilliams:

Thank you very much for sending me, with your note of October 4, a copy of the October 11 issue of The NATION, containing the marked editorial—"One World." I have read it with much interest and thank you sincerely for your generous observations.

Men of good will may have different ideas of how peace can best be maintained but such men cannot differ on the fact that the paramount issue of our times is world peace. If I could make any contribution toward that goal, I would regard it as a greater accomplishment than anything else I may have been able to achieve in my lifetime.

> With cordial greetings,
> Sincerely,
> (David Sarnoff)

Yet, unless we believe that everything is foreordained, could it not have been otherwise? Sarnoff's success was essentially commercial and overrode the latent idealism that impressed Lilienthal and others. In many of the greatly successful, the element of idealism was totally obliterated or reduced to an imperceptible level; but in Sarnoff enough remained so that he could be exhibited as not only a beneficiary of the land of opportunity but as a philanthropist, which he was not, except on a modest scale. In a sense, he was Americanized too thoroughly, in that business became his preoccupation; when he turned to politics, all he had to offer was to the advantage of the already dominant hawks and predatory business interests.

It would be pointless to expect of Sarnoff the kind of Americanism that marked the career of Carl Schurz, but something of Schurz's political nobility was what Sarnoff's admirers would have liked to see in Sarnoff. Schurz, it is true, had every advantage. He was an educated German with early experience in revolution: he was forced to flee after the collapse of the uprisings of 1848–49. He was twenty-three years old when he came to the United States and prepared for a new career. He was soon prominent in politics.

He campaigned effectively for Lincoln and was rewarded with the post of minister to Spain. When he realized that the war would be prolonged, he resigned from the diplomatic service and was appointed a brigadier general of volunteers, later promoted to major general. He fought at Chancellorsville, Gettysburg, and Chattanooga, and at the end of the war was with Sherman in North Carolina. His subsequent career in politics and journalism was consistently in the country's interest. He was not hobbled by an RCA to run in his productive years nor anything else to hamper his political and social understanding and freedom to act. Those who expected political preeminence from Sarnoff had some grounds for their hopes: it crops up now and then, as in the conversation which inspired Lilienthal's wistful evocation. But, however understandably, the liberals deluded themselves. The basic reason for Sarnoff's political sterility was simply that he did not want to be what the liberals desired. What they desired was not in Sarnoff's makeup when he reached maturity, nor in the times in which he lived. The Civil War was a national tragedy of the first magnitude, and like most such upheavals it released both moral and immoral forces of great magnitude and brought to the fore men of corresponding stature on both sides. The basic issue was one which every Union and Confederate soldier could understand; in the American Revolution, the issues were even clearer.

Neither of the great wars of the twentieth century had that character. The first had little character of any kind; the notion that the world was growing better was proved an illusion. The second was necessary, but only because the first had spawned a Germany subservient to Hitler and Nazism. Sarnoff produced communications equipment for the first and organized communications—mainly civilian but including some important military circuits—for the second, and so established a relationship with a future president and a place for himself in the cold war. He supported the Korean and Indochinese wars; the latter brought to power a president consonant with the moral deterioration of the times. In the meantime, technology had produced armaments capable of destroying all mankind, if not all higher life; the radiation-resistant cockroaches might inherit the earth.

Sarnoff could have tried to mitigate the cold war, but he went along instead and contributed to the propaganda on the American side, which emulated in crudity and mendacity the propaganda on the Soviet side. Personally, he was satisfied with the conventional rewards of business success on a grand scale—money and power, mostly, in his case, power, and the satisfaction of leaving behind him a complex of new industries. But he also wanted lasting fame, and that RCA, much less his political activities, could not give him.

It was within his reach, though at a cost. All he needed was a fraction of the clear thinking that had served him in intra- and intercorporate conflicts, and the courage to apply it in politics. He would have carried a good many important people along with him, made some new friends; and lost some old ones—possibly Eisenhower? But Ike remained friendly with E. T. Weir, who circulated polemics against the cold war. If Sarnoff had lost Nixon, would that have been bad? For the moment Sarnoff would have been involved in controversy—perhaps acrimonious—but he could hold his own in that quarter. Above all, he would have gained what seemingly he wanted most; he would have been remembered not only as an industrialist but as the highest type of patriot—the type that doesn't run with the crowd.

Sarnoff must have heard later of General MacArthur's advice to President Kennedy to get out of Vietnam, to get out before worse should befall, and how Kennedy was greatly troubled and determined to end the Vietnam embroilment, but he felt he had to wait until his second term, and there was no second term. Instead, there was death: for Kennedy, for 55,000 Americans, for hundreds of thousands of Indochinese; and for the United States, shame in place of the respect it had gained in two world wars.

I would caution again that we must differentiate between Sarnoff's alliance with Nixon and the corresponding, but much attenuated, relationship with Eisenhower. Like any president, Eisenhower had to be polite to a great many people whose advice he listened to but did not act on. Also there was advice he did act on and, although he was a mediocre president (far better than Grant, ho·vever), either he acted on good advice or on his own initiative when he appointed Earl Warren Chief Justice of the United States. For that appointment (although he is said to have regretted it later), his sins, if any, may be forgiven, if not by God, for whom we cannot speak, at all events by men of goodwill.

What Warren thought of Nixon has been disclosed in a piece of Alden Whitman's in the April 1975 *Esquire*. Warren was one of those great Americans who, because they were never associated with a clash that threatened to disrupt the Republic, will probably not be given their due in the history books. Yet they don't come any better, nor any more objective in their judgment of their contemporaries. And here is what Warren said about Nixon to Whitman: "Tricky," he said, "is perhaps the most despicable President this nation has ever had. He was a cheat, a liar, and a crook, and he brought my country, which I love, into disrepute. Even worse than abusing his office, he abused the American people."

This condemnation postdates Watergate, but the Nixon who was a friend of Sarnoff was the same Nixon who was forced out of office in 1974. There are quite a number of things Nixon will never live down; this evaluation of Warren's is one. Inevitably some of it sticks to Sarnoff, too.

RCA'S EDSEL

When I heard of David Sarnoff's retirement, I knew for a certainty that he was dying. Only grave physical incapacity could force him to relinquish control of the corporation which he had created personally to a degree perhaps unmatched, and surely not exceeded, in American industrial history, and which he had dominated far beyond the customary retirement age. When Robert W. Sarnoff, David's eldest son and heir to the RCA empire, presiding at the 1969 (1968?) annual meeting, expressed hopes for his father's recovery, it was clearly one of those pious wishes with which we try to soften the inevitable.

Robert advanced to the center of the stage at this point because three years after he took over the chairmanship, RCA was forced to withdraw from the computer field, with a pre-tax loss of $490 million —a quarter of the company's net worth. Inevitably he took the brickbats and there were calls for his resignation from Wall Street wise guys who knew little or nothing of the circumstances, and from some insiders who did. Actually, the write-off was the culmination of a situation that had been developing for more than twenty years; and while some fault may fairly be found with Robert in connection with the debacle, he was less responsible for it than David. And on David's behalf, much may be said in extenuation. Chance often plays a decisive role in the affairs of big business, as in the ups and downs of individual lives; in data processing, RCA not only made mistakes but had more than its share of tough luck.

In 1948, at age thirty, Robert Sarnoff was a minor or middling executive in Cowles Publications, publisher of *Look* and other magazines and newspapers. His salary is said to have been a paltry $15,000 a year.

Largely on the recommendation of his uncle, Lew Sarnoff, Robert was hired at NBC, starting as an account executive. He moved through a number of departments, gaining knowledge of NBC personnel and job functions along the way, and overriding suspicions of nepotism. By 1951 he was a vice-president and by 1955 president. From 1958 to 1966 he was NBC's chief executive.

A speedy rise, to be sure, and it seems a safe assumption that with a different surname it might have taken him more than ten years to make it to the top; after that, he might have languished in NBC for the rest of his life. However, there is nothing to show that his father exercised undue influence on his behalf. It seems more likely that he was testing Robert at a time when changes in the top management of the parent company were imminent. Robert's performance was adjudged so satisfactory that when he moved over to RCA as president in 1966, within two years he succeeded his father as chief executive.

Actually, by normal American business and social standards, both father and son were unduly worried by imputations of nepotism. Nothing is more common in American business than primogeniture, or some variant, according to circumstances. If David Sarnoff had been a Rockefeller, a Thomas Watson, a Mellon, a du Pont, a Schiff or a scion of any one of hundreds of leading families of varying degrees of wealth and prominence, he would have been less squeamish. Wealth and status are retentive by nature.

However one looks on these peripheral matters, one thing is certain: RCA had to go into electronic data processing (EDP). Technologically it was RCA's bailiwick far more than IBM's. Can one conceive of David Sarnoff, a business imperialist proud to the point of vainglory and confident of his ability to manipulate technology to his company's profit, yielding a promising new field to these electronic arrivistes? And without a fight?

Nor was Sarnoff alone in the decision to accept the risks. John L. Burns had perhaps as much to do with the decision as Sarnoff, and Engstrom, no rash entrepreneur, described the situation with his usual lucidity:

> In business we never order things up according to our own timetable. We knew we had to go into the field. And we had to come in during the growth period. So we had this dual experience: color not having arrived yet, and data processing taking heavy investments and expen-

ditures. But not getting into the market when it was beginning to move would have been seriously to restrict our own growth. Now, nothing in the past will plague us.

Robert Sarnoff might have demurred on Engstrom's last point, but it was valid in the sense Engstrom intended: it followed from the foregoing reasoning. Again, when David Sarnoff turned RCA over to Robert, he could have advised him to cut RCA's losses and get out of EDP. That he did not give such counsel was, in hindsight, a mistake. So what? In the industrialization of technology David Sarnoff was rightly acclaimed a genius, but even a genius makes mistakes or, as Sylvia Plath pointed out, he would be a god.

RCA's major mistake in computerization was underestimation of IBM's background in business machinery. Thomas J. Watson was corny as hell, but no one ever denied that he was a first-rate salesman; and IBM followed his lead in that respect. It had developed a highly trained, customer-oriented sales force. The IBM salesmen asked themselves, "What does the buyer expect to get out of this elaborate machine?" "How will it help him reduce costs and increase profits?" "What type of computer will he buy (or lease) and how much will he pay?" They asked the right questions and they got answers which enabled them, and the IBM engineers, to corner a share of the market so large that little was left for the competition. Under Robert Sarnoff's direction, RCA would have been satisfied with 10 percent of the market—and it never got anywhere near that.

Early in data processing, when investment requirements were modest and the General was still in full charge, there were signs of trouble ahead. Loren F. Jones III was an RCA engineer charged with looking for promising new projects for management to consider. He sensed the profit potential of EDP early and in 1951, before the crucial decisions were made and RCA was deeply involved, he undertook to put the situation in historical perspective for David Sarnoff and members of the executive council on computers. He traced the history of RCA industry through the era when communications was the main line of development, then broadcasting, first of sound alone, then picture and sound, and into the era of EDP. The progress made since 1950 was an indication of what would follow. The pioneering electronic computer, ENIAC, built by the Moore School of Engineering of the University of Pennsylvania and put in service in 1946, was a kind of *Great Eastern* of computers: it had 18,000 vacuum tubes, weighed 80 tons, occupied 1,500 square feet of floor space, and required 150 kilowatts of power for operation—yet it was the answer to an ordnance man's prayer.

In Jones's view of the RCA–IBM rivalry at that stage, it was not so much a matter of RCA getting into IBM's business as the reverse. To get started, RCA needed $10.6 million, a ratio to later costs comparable to Zworykin's estimate in 1929 of $100,000 as the cost of developing a black-and-white TV system. Sarnoff no doubt sensed what he was letting himself in for, but he was also convinced of the possible benefits for RCA. He said, "If I approve this project and submit it to the board, it will be because of the concept that computers will be the next 'estate' in electronics." The project was approved and the board met in Camden, so that Jones and others could present and illustrate briefings on present and forthcoming developments. At this stage, Jones says, IBM was much concerned and ranked RCA as a more formidable competitor than UNIVAC and the other starters in the electronic data processing race.

No matter what wisdom is dispensed at the Harvard School of Business Administration, the American Management Association, and other repositories of commercial wisdom, no matter how well intentioned are the efforts to make high-level management more of a science than an art, risks, often of terrifying magnitude, are unavoidable when a company ventures into a new field. At a certain point in the RCA computer development, for all its unmatched strength in electronics, RCA management realized that it would be safer not to persist in going it alone, but instead to hook up with an IBM-type company of moderate size. After some abortive attempts, an RCA-Burroughs Corporation alliance seemed to be in the works. If that hookup had gone through, RCA's disaster of 1974 might have been avoided, or at least minimized.

But blind chance intervened. Within RCA full approval was achieved, and Burroughs' president, Coleman, gave assurance that his company was in compliance on all major points. But before the deal could be concluded, Coleman had a heart attack. Myocardial infarctions are not a rarity among topside businessmen: two or three weeks in the hospital and usually the victim is up and about, and shortly thereafter back in the rat race. Coleman's seemed a routine case: Folsom and other RCA people were allowed to visit him while he was laid up. But he had another coronary shortly after the first, and this one was fatal.

Coleman's successor had other ideas and the deal fell through. Sarnoff took a hand but to no avail. Loren Jones feels that RCA's management, as well as the new Burroughs management, might have been at fault. But the whys and wherefores are of no consequence after all these years—only the results—and these did not seem as momentous at the time as they later turned out to be.

Loren Jones had nothing to do with the failure of 1974; he feels it could have been averted. He had something to say about Sarnoff, however:

> I was impressed by his excellent command of diction. On one occasion he had me help compose a letter to President Truman. He not only improved significantly on my wording, but inserted every punctuation mark with a skill and exactness unsurpassed by the most erudite. I benefited greatly by my association with him and only wish it had been more frequent.

All of which jibes completely with the formal eulogies in the next chapter, and with other impressions from people of various vocations and educational status.

It was perfectly clear to Robert, after his father's death, that *his* RCA could not be his father's RCA, if only because neither he nor anyone else had David Sarnoff's qualities. He told William S. Hedges that he was well aware that he would have to do with such abilities as he had —an attitude both becoming and to his credit as a businessman. David Sarnoff's managerial style, with RCA virtually his personal empire, ended with David's life. Not that the new RCA would not retain traces of the original one, but the whole climate of business and politics had changed too, and RCA had to change with the times to survive. Whatever may be said in criticism of Robert's management of the transition, RCA not only survived, but was never in real danger.

The sale of RCA's computer assets to the UNIVAC division of Sperry Rand was not the only big computer deal of the early seventies; there was also General Electrics even bigger deal with Honeywell, involving 7,000 computers that GE had in the field, while RCA had only 900 computers on lease or service contracts.

The sellers fared differently in the exchanges, and the profit figures of the buyers tell part of the story. Before Honeywell bought out GE's computer business, it claimed 5.5 percent of the U.S. market. After the sale, it had over 9 percent. UNIVAC increased its market share from

5.6 to 8.9 percent. In terms of profit, Honeywell's computer profits climbed from less than $3 million in 1970 to a gratifying $30 million in 1972. UNIVAC's profit went up from $30 million to $48 million. Whatever has happened since, what with the disturbance of the recession (or depression), both the figures and the pronouncements of the buyers indicate that GE did pretty well in shedding EDP, while UNIVAC got RCA's computer business almost on a fire-sale basis. UNIVAC's negotiators knew RCA's financial situation, perhaps better than RCA's own people—including Robert Sarnoff—knew it until they were forced to face the facts. Both GE and RCA each needed expenditures of $500 million or more to stay in EDP. GE could have swung that, but, all things considered, it was wiser not to. For RCA it was just too much, and it would have been almost impossible to borrow the money, even before interest rates began soaring. Robert waited too long before taking the bath, as they say in Wall Street.

More important than this particular episode is the change in the character of RCA which the company's forced withdrawal from the computer field signified. Once Robert was on the bridge, he had no choice but to change course in accordance with changing business conditions. David Sarnoff's success and his place in American industrial history, rested squarely on his astute exploitation of the creativity of electronics engineers. At that lunch in 1913 with Marriott, the elder statesman, Sarnoff was not only mapping his own career, but foretelling the future of the RCA which did not yet exist. That the prophecy, suitably extrapolated, was good for fifty years was remarkable enough. But it required periodic technological breakthroughs, and the time came when none was in sight. RCA could no longer exist as an exclusively technologically based concern. It had now to adjust itself to the market, in contrast to David Sarnoff's RCA which had largely *made* the market by its own research and development. Robert's RCA was still doing a good deal of that, as in development of a computerized supermarket checkout system, but it had been converted from a purely electronic company into a conglomerate, scrambling for profit through subsidiaries engaged in car renting, carpet manufacturing and selling, TV dinners, book publishing, etc., all remote from the traditional RCA interests.

At the same time, the new RCA abandoned several fields which it had originated or in which it had held a prominent place. The electronic microscope is an important scientific tool which Sarnoff's RCA developed; RCA no longer manufactures it. In the old RCA, we broke our necks to achieve what is now known as high fidelity in receiver manufacture; but the profit potential of hi-fi ensembles is not enough to interest a corporation of RCA's size and it has left that field to smaller companies. By and large, the sales-oriented RCA is less creative than the earlier RCA, and Robert Sarnoff is not likely to have his biography written, but the nearly $483,500 (plus $79,338 in dividends, totaling $562,838), that he pulled down as chairman of the board no doubt will console him for that neglect.

This stipend ended as of the end of 1975, after Robert, following what the reporters called a "palace coup," retired and was succeeded by RCA's president, Anthony L. Conrad. For the first time in fifty-seven years RCA was left without a Sarnoff—if we except Thomas, the youngest son, who remained in charge of NBC's West Coast operations.

31

OTHER VIEWPOINTS

When a man writes a biography, in a sense he *lives* with his subject, through the events of that other life as he—the writer—has seen, narrated and judged them. I think I have been fair to Sarnoff—certainly I've tried—but I want to give him and myself some margin, first, by getting into print the picture of Sarnoff as others saw him, then by recounting some benevolences of his that did not fit into earlier portions of the book, and some notes on his attitude toward "science."

I could have garnered many more evaluations of Sarnoff, but those which follow are representative. These are eulogies rather than evaluations, since all express the views of fellow members of the "establishment," that loose confederation of political and commercial interest in which Sarnoff held a prominent place. Dr. Alfred N. Goldsmith, late honorary Vice President and Consulting Engineer, RCA Corporation.

> Only those who were close to David Sarnoff and who followed his career in detail could be fully aware of certain of his personal characteristics which contributed greatly to the success of his career. David Sarnoff was almost incredibly tenacious of purpose and unlimited in his energetic support and promotion of any idea or plans which he judged worthy of support. He had an extraordinary sense of values and of the public reaction to new services or devices. This was a formidable combination of capabilities. Long after others might have prematurely abandoned a project, David Sarnoff was still vigorously supporting it and continuing to promote it with almost incredible determination and energy.

Dr. Elmer W. Engstrom, former president RCA Corp.

I genuinely liked him.

He had strong likes and dislikes for people.

He pushed himself hard and expected others to do the same.

He was not tolerant of poor performance.

He had a strong intuitive sense of what was right in business—and what the public desired (and would buy) in a product or service.

In a tough business or competitive situation he was resolute and fearless.

He tended to lead or dominate in any group gathering.

He was always interested in the views of others regardless of the station in life of the person expressing his views.

He had about him the air of a person who sensed that he was destined for greatness.

He always had the objective before him to improve, to better, to uplift, to innovate.

Rear Admiral Lewis L. Strauss, late chairman, Atomic Energy Commission, late secretary of commerce.

David Sarnoff was very possibly the last of the rare men who have figured so importantly in American industrial history in the years since 1850. Brought to the New World as a child of Jewish immigrants in the wave which left the Russian ghettos eighty years ago, equipped with an insatiable curiosity and a capacity to learn and then to apply his knowledge, doors magically began to open for him early in his career. Without a reverse, he mounted from one success to another, pursuing such once visionary concepts as a box in the home which would talk (radio) and a box with a picture that would talk (television and color television) to the point where he made these dreams become realities. In the course of his career he sought out and encouraged inventors like Marconi, musicians like Toscanini, and built a company which, starting from nothing, became one of a dozen largest and most prosperous in the nation. The times were right for his character and combination of qualities which led to the opportunities that he discovered and so successfully developed. Even before his death, he had become a legend. His success never turned his head, and his humble beginnings and his Jewish faith were a cause for pride. David Sarnoff's

life is a landmark of success in the great American tradition.
3 November 1972

William S. Hedges, past vice-president National Broadcasting Company; past president National Association of Broadcasters; International Radio and Television Society; Broadcast Pioneers.

David Sarnoff was a great man!

He was a proud man—one who liked to see his efforts bear fruit, which was his reward for a lifetime spent in the field of electronics.

His initiation in radio was its utilization as a means of safeguarding life at sea. Indeed, it was this function upon which the first federal laws pertaining to radio were enacted.

Sarnoff's concept of radio covered not only safety measures, but the opening of doors to the vast resources of radio for the benefit of mankind. He visualized bringing the finest of music into people's homes, and the best of entertainment and public enlightenment. Education by means of radio he especially desired, and priority was given to the dissemination of news—keeping the public informed of the important events occurring daily throughout the world.

To accomplish these things, it was necessary that the stations and networks be adequately staffed with program personnel possessing the requisite expertise to provide a constantly improving schedule of service. Likewise essential to the success of broadcasting was the pooling of the best brains in electronics, so that the equipment which went into receivers and transmitters would meet the highest technical standards. Sarnoff was fortunate in his choice of scientists and engineers: they established a level of excellence for the entire industry.

He was aware of the importance of competition not only to the scientific and manufacturing fields, but of even greater importance to the public was competition for the attention of listeners. This competition has paid great dividends to the audiences, while enabling broadcasting to remain on a solvent basis.

While competition was desirable, in many situations cooperation was of paramount importance. Recognizing the necessity of teamwork in solving some of the industry's problems, Sarnoff fostered the work of numerous trade associations, including the National Association of Broadcasters; the Radio Manufacturers Association; the International Radio and Television Society and the Broadcast Pioneers, who with Sarnoff's help established an industry reference library in Washington D. C.

While I say that David Sarnoff was a great man, I am sure he would have been the last to claim himself to be infallible. Some of his choices in executives to carry the burden of developing broadcasting did not measure up to his expectations, but his average was among the highest for any industry. I would not claim a close relationship with him but, beginning in 1923, I was in an advantageous position to observe his operations and his use of men and resources. This opportunity seems to me as great a reward as the material compensation received by those who worked for him.

Eulogy by Governor Nelson Rockefeller at Temple Emanu-El, December 15, 1971.

Who was this man? What was he? Above all, he was a genius, a brilliant, creative genius. His genius lay in his capacity to look at the same thing others were looking at—but to see far more. Others looked at radio and saw a gadget. David Sarnoff looked at radio and saw a household possession capable of enriching the lives of millions. In others, the word "visionary" might mean a tendency to see a mirage. In David Sarnoff the word "visionary" meant a capacity to see into tomorrow and to make it work.

Not to be omitted is a statement by an anonymous competitor of RCA: "Bucher, I have been fighting Sarnoff for three years, but I must confess that he has something on the ball which I think we all need. He lifts you out of the world of petty bickerings, animosities and tempers. . . ."

Sarnoff did good deeds, but he was not a philanthropist in a big way. Rev. Dr. Nathan A. Perilman, chief rabbi of Temple Emanu-El, suggested that when it came to philanthropy in the narrow sense, probably Sarnoff felt he could not "compete." I certainly would not hold Dr. Perilman to that term, much less psychologize on it, but at the moment it seemed to me exactly right.

This does not rule out benefactions to the Educational Alliance, which Sarnoff served as a trustee, but under the pressure of other business could not often attend meetings. Nor did he neglect targets of opportunity. One such is described in *A World to Care For: The Autobiography of Dr. Howard Rusk.* Dr. Rusk tells of a program to aid the handicapped which originated at the end of 1955 in connection with the cold war mission of General William Donovan to Thailand. The Rusk program involved a system of training fellowships in the

United States for foreign physicians, financed largely by American corporations through the World Rehabilitation Fund. At the outset, a fellowship cost only $5,000 a year—it rose as the pay of American residents and interns rose. Every physician who took the training course subsequently received, four times a year, a packet of the latest literature to keep him up to date in his specialty.

Then a more ambitious idea occurred to Dr. Rusk: why not establish a shortwave station to broadcast, all over the world, a monthly symposium by rehabilitation specialists? Since radio was involved, Rusk went to see Sarnoff, who had been a sponsor of the program and a member of the board of directors of Dr. Rusk's rehabilitation institute, connected with University Hospital in New York. "I thought he would never stop laughing. 'Howard,' he said, 'you may know a lot about rehabilitation, but you don't know a thing about communication. I'll send you one of our experienced people. Tell him what you want and we'll see what he can work out.' "

A few days later, a senior RCA vice-president came to the institute and explained the almost insuperable difficulties of shortwave broadcasting, even for commercial and propaganda purposes. But there was a practical alternative. RCA had a tape recorder and playback machine with two-hour unerasable tapes. Record the symposium here, the RCA man said, and send the tapes abroad.

But, Rusk objected, those doctors around the world don't have machines with which to play back what we record. The vice-president was sure General Sarnoff and RCA would take care of that difficulty, and in fact they provided 126 recorders and all the tape that would be needed for three years. Dr. Rusk continued:

> With this we started a program of recorded clinics on every possible subject. Whenever an expert in a special field happened to be in New York, we would ask him for a taping session. He would make a presentation; then a panel of our fellows would ask him questions. Those tapes went all over the world, were translated into almost every language, and are now the real foundation on which rehabilitation is taught in many countries. We have also made more than 100 films on every subject from management of paraplegics to treatment of bedsores.

In other incidents, Sarnoff showed his human side. One occurred in the thirties, when an elderly middle-management employee who had known Sarnoff from the early days was suddenly fired by RCA Victor. The employee was within three years of receiving his pension. He was an urbane, likable, fashionably dressed, extremely handsome man with a wife and adolescent children.

The victim—let's call him Horowitz because he was not Jewish—telephoned Sarnoff and was reinstated and subsequently permitted to retire with his pension rights intact. We were friendly and he told me the story, ascribing his abrupt aborted dismissal to the desire of the RCA Victor management to reduce payrolls during the Depression. What actually happened, however, was more complex: also it tells something about business hazards in connection with sex, hazards which are aggravated in bad times, when any pretext for firing people will do.

Horowitz had attended a convention of RCA Victor dealers and distributors at which General Harbord was the principal speaker. Ordinarily Harbord would not have made an appearance at an affair of this sort, but the public was not buying, and it was necessary to inspire the dealers to greater efforts with forthcoming models of radio receivers. At one of the dinners or luncheons at which inspiration was imparted, Horowitz was seated next to the good-looking wife of a dealer and apparently an animated—perhaps flirtatious—conversation took place. In itself that would not have led to complications, but the next day Horowitz telephoned the lady at the hotel where she was staying with her husband and asked her to lunch. She declined amiably; perhaps Horowitz had not made as much of an impression on her as she on him, or prudence prevailed over the spirit of adventure. Still no harm would have been done, but the lady, possibly to enhance her attractiveness to her husband, told him of the telephone call. Lots of husbands would have let it go at that, but *this* husband wrote a letter of complaint to General Harbord, no less. Harbord, of a puritanical temperament himself, passed the letter down the line, and the firing followed.

Ordinarily Sarnoff would not have interfered in any disciplinary action that the officials of an RCA subsidiary saw fit to take, but he did in this case. Among all the people involved, his was the only urbane, humane action. He reinstated Horowitz and saw to it that he retired with his pension rights intact. To that observation I will add a general one—he has only a feeble knowledge of the mores and manners of business, big and small alike, who has not seen it in action during a catastrophic depression. It would take a Jonathan Swift to do justice to the subject, but if Sarnoff would not be rated among the

Houyhnhnms in that area, he was surely much closer to them than to the Yahoos.

If Sarnoff showed his benevolent side in the case of Horowitz, it is even more manifest in this letter from the late Guy Endore, a wise and civilized writer who died a few years before Sarnoff.

> Dear Carl:
>
> I'm going to have to buy the Sarnoff book you just reviewed, not because of your review which I enjoyed reading as I do everything you write, but because my brother-in-law asked me if I would get it for him. Some years ago when my brother-in-law, who for many, many years sold newspapers at the corner of 5th and Main in L.A., told me he was going to retire and go on Social Security, he informed me that he had just written a letter to General Sarnoff. Why? Well because as an immigrant he had to satisfy the S.S. people that he was really sixty-five years old. "General Sarnoff will know me," he said. "We come from the same village, Uzlian. We came to America together, on the same boat. He'll remember. And they'll have to believe General Sarnoff." Sure enough, a few days later he had a very nice note from General Sarnoff who said he was glad to hear from his old friend and that he would vouch for his age with the authorities. "You see," my brother-in-law pointed out to me: "No trouble. He remembers me. His cousin Eugene Lyons knows me too."
>
> "Have you been corresponding with them?" I asked.
>
> "No," he said. "Never wrote to him before. Why should I write to him? He's a busy man."
>
> It seems they both started to sell papers when they came to the United States at the age of ten. But my brother-in-law had a quality that Sarnoff lacked. He had stick-to-itiveness. And he stuck to selling papers for the rest of his life. In New York, and then in L.A. And his attention to his business paid off. He earned himself a modest competence, and when he retired he bought himself a pretty little bungalow and garden. . . .

And a final anecdote in letter form, showing a side of Sarnoff which he kept very much to himself:

> January 24, 1974
>
> Dear Mr. Dreher
>
> . . . Many years have passed since my first contacts with Mr. Sarnoff but I will try to give you as much information as possible.
>
> Around 1912 another kid and myself were wireless buffs. My friend

Fred O'Brien, a white-haired kid of about my same age spent all of our time winding coils, buying Crystals, trying to build sets and sticking our nose into every problem.

O'Briens Mother ran a boarding house and one of her boarders was a Paddy McIntyre who worked for John Wanamaker Co. as a freight elevator operator and handyman in the New York store. We knew there was a wireless station at Wanamakers. We connived with Paddy to get us up to see the wireless station on the roof of the building and spent every Saturday and Sunday afternoon and any days we could get off from school hanging around the shack. Mr. Sarnoff was in charge of this station. He knew us as Johnie and Whitehope and was always kind and considerate to us two kids, would let us listen in and we spent many hours sitting outside or on the floor of the wireless room, going to the store with a tin bucket for milk and buns which he would share with us. At one time he helped us to wire up a key and buzzer to practice the code. This to the best of my recollection lasted for at least a year. He gave me a note to a Mr. Cohn, Manager of the Western Union office at 125 East 34 Street so that I could get a job as a messenger and make it possible for me to associate with operators and learn the code. This job kept on till time to go to High School and we lost contact with Mr. Sarnoff.

Having obtained my License in 1918 I went to Sea as an operator and in 1922 was employed as a Shift Engineer at the Tuckertown New Jersey Transmitter, WCL and WGG, Alexanderson Alternator Plant. One day, I seem to remember it was the day President Harding was buried, Mr. Thomas Rossi of RCA Construction visited the plant with Mr. Sarnoff, when Mr. Rossi introduced him I mentioned I had met him years ago, told him about the kids at Wanamakers and he remembered Johnie and Whitehope. Mr. Rossi had to leave to go to Toms River the county seat and Mr. Sarnoff decided to stay and visit with me. We spent a pleasant afternoon talking about old times and he advised me at that time to get into broadcasting and to let him know if I wanted to change jobs. As he wanted this to be only a social visit he requested that I do not call the Plant Chief Engineer and on Mr. Rossi's return to the plant they left for Atlantic City.

In 1927 I decided to leave Tuckerton and wrote to Mr. Sarnoff, though I did not hear from him direct I did get a letter from Mr. Rossi advising me to come to his office in New York as he had a letter for me to deliver to Mr. O. B. Hanson of NBC. This I did and was employed by NBC as a Transmitter operator at WEAF in New York City and later moved on to WEAF at Bellmore.

Early in 1932, Mrs. Flynn was hospitalized for what was to be a normal child birth. Every thing went wrong and she was in Amityville Hospital for 5 weeks, bills piled up, no insurance or money to pay for them. The Hospital dunned hell out of me and one day toward the end of her stay I was advised that her bill, approx $900 was paid in full. Just who paid this bill I could not find out from the Hospital and did not learn who paid it until our Dr. Thomas Newsom told me that he and the Hospital had been paid by Mr. Sarnoff. Just who told Mr. Sarnoff of my predicament I do not know but when I did find out and tried to contact him and thank him I was told by his Secretary Miss Guy that I was to forget it. One act of kindness I will never forget.

In 1953 I met General Sarnoff in the elevator at Radio City, he recognized me, got off at the 5th floor with me, asked about my well being and family, laughed about our early days and out of the dim past remembered and asked for Whitehope.

This was the last time I ever saw the General but did receive a kind and gracious letter from him on my retirement from NBC in 1963. Much has been written about General Sarnoff as a great man but I will always remember him as a kind and good plain man and a real good friend.

This I know has been long and probably useless to you and I may have gone into too much detail but it's the best I can do.

Regards and Good Luck.
John M. Flynn

George McElrath, for many years operating engineer of NBC, met John Flynn at a gathering of broadcasting pioneers and put me onto this. I asked Mr. Flynn to write it up himself, rather than filter it through a telephone interview.

Sarnoff did for Flynn substantially what Jack Irwin had done for Sarnoff, in enabling him to get into radio. The 1932 hospital/medical payment makes one wonder how many other hidden benefactions Sarnoff was responsible for.

Miss Guy, mentioned in the above letter, was Ray Guy's sister. Their employment with RCA–NBC dated back to WJZ, where Helen was Popenoe's secretary. She was not connected with this incident. Flynn must have confused her with one of Sarnoff's RCA secretaries.

Like the man in the street (and most journalists), Sarnoff habitually referred to engineers as "scientists." He knew the difference well enough; it was just a matter of convenience. Though he forsook engineering for business, his thinking remained in large part that of professional engineers. It had to be: his industrial role was based on exploiting the work of engineers—using the term in its benign sense of turning to practical account. In general, he had a good rapport with engineers, but I don't think he ever had any deep comprehension of the philosophy of science and its ethical basis. After escaping from Hitler's Germany, Lise Meitner, a close associate of Otto Hahn and codiscoverer of the fission of heavy nuclei, declared that one ought not to gauge the value of science by its applications "but rather by the traits of self-abnegation, humility, and truthfulness to which it educates." No doubt Sarnoff would have agreed that science can have this effect, but he said nothing, so far as I have been able to ascertain, against the use of napalm, among other products of technology, to burn and maim native patriots, military and civilian, who resisted American aggression in Southeast Asia.

Sarnoff felt that everyone should know how a telephone, an airplane, or an electric motor works. I think here he misread the popular mind: most people are interested in the services such devices render, not in the machinery. Anything new and spectacular, like a spaceship, will attract attention, but even such grandiose achievements are soon taken for granted. The Victorians were more interested in science than we are. Faraday's lectures were attended by Prince Albert, Queen Victoria's consort. Gifted popularizers like John Tyndall and T. H. Huxley had large audiences. We have some science writers on the same intellectual level—astronomer Carl Sagan and Isaac Asimov, for instance— but most current science journalism deals with medicine. The readers are interested, next to sports, in their health, and the editors print what they have conditioned the readers to want.

On the plus side, Sarnoff, in common with everyone who makes use of scientific techniques in his thinking, was immunized against superstition, such as the inextinguishable, if only halfhearted, faith in astrology. Nor, I am sure, would he have taken any stock in the practice of exorcism, which probably reached its peak in 1974 and made a lot of money for some writers and movie producers while it lasted. One could always rely on Sarnoff's native good sense.

THE SUMMING UP

Sarnoff's stark achievement was the expansion of advertising by the creation of a new mass advertising medium, with a corresponding increase in the number of people exposed to advertising, and a rising potential for moving certain types of merchandise, though usually at a higher unit cost. Obviously no sponsor would pay for displaying a $2,750 digital wristwatch on television—the medium is for selling over-the-counter hypnotics (proved to be spurious), detergents that make clothes whiter than white, if you credit the advertising, dog food that almost makes you want to be a dog. Broadcasting is mainly for products for which the mass feels, or, more often, can be induced to feel, an urgent need. The publicity incentive is also important, especially on radio, where advertising breeds advertising: if the New York *Daily News* buys time on radio, *The New York Times* had better buy it too; and there is nothing like television to celebrate the efficiencies of Exxon while gasoline prices zoom.

If that were all to Sarnoff's life-accomplishment he would have hardly more claim to historical attention than any well-publicized Madison Avenue executive. The electronic media, however, also have great social impact: the entertainment field is only one example. Sarnoff likewise had higher ambitions than mere huckstering; he wanted radio —later television—to elevate the national cultural level while, of course, not neglecting the profit aspect. Starting in the twenties and continuing well into the sixties, he sprang to the defense of broadcasting like a fireman responding to the alarm gongs. An early instance was an article in *The Nation* (July 23, 1924) in which he wrote of radio broadcasting as so powerful an "instrument of public good" that it must be kept from "partisan manipulation." Simultaneously he was busily engaged in propagandizing to keep broadcasting under the control of the secretary of commerce, with a minimum of government regulation. He was, in fact, partly responsible for deferring the establishment of an effective Federal Radio Commission until 1929, and the enlarged Federal Communications Commission until 1934, under Franklin D. Roosevelt's first administration.

On one occasion when broadcasting was under fire, Sarnoff said he was not convinced that "bad" broadcasting was actually harmful. The weight of the evidence is on the affirmative side, especially in the conditioning of children to violence, but that is not the point here. Sarnoff was standing pat on the status quo, while making little, if any, effort to diminish the proportion of "bad" broadcasting—including commercials—and supplanting it with something better.

Pauline Kael, film critic of *The New Yorker,* did not have a TV network at her disposal; hence she harbored visionary ideas:

> I think enormous harm has been done by television commercials telling ghetto children they should go to school because their earning capacity would be higher. They never suggest that if you're educated you may go into fields where your work is satisfying, where you may be useful, where you can really do something that can help other people. . . .

In a footnote, Ms. Kael referred to a series of films in which she was the interviewer, dealing with people who had achieved some form of recognition in their respective occupations. The series was for showing before ghetto children. It turned out that the most admired subject was a three-part lawyer, real estate broker, and accountant, who showed off his possessions. About his work, he was unable to talk. The least popular subject was a distinguished black sculptor who showed his work in loving detail and spoke of it enthusiastically—to no avail. Ms. Kael concluded with the observation that "the children were avid TV viewers and remarkably knowledgeable about the commercials of the moment."

Nevertheless Sarnoff was by no means personally insensitive to the social and cultural side of broadcasting. In this and much else, he was not a simple man whom you could lambaste without qualification. In Volume 3 of Lilienthal's *Journals,* Sarnoff complains of that "damn bunch of hucksters, who let the advertisers run things. . . ." This was still in the radio era, but with television in the offing. Sarnoff expressed the fear that television would go the same way, "if something wasn't done." (It seems a fair question that if Sarnoff—and CBS's Paley and other TV moguls—didn't "do something" who would?) Lilienthal comments that if an outsider said such things, Sarnoff would have "climbed his frame."

Sarnoff did just that when the December 1958 *Fortune* carried a piece by Richard Austin Smith, "TV, the Light that Failed," which at first Sarnoff seems to have regarded as a stab in the back by Henry Luce, who was taking the sun in Arizona and apparently had nothing to do with the story. Sarnoff wrote a long, vehement defense of television in which he denied he had ever compared broadcasting channels to a pipe laid by a plumber, who isn't responsible for what goes through the pipe. At one point, Sarnoff went so far as to threaten suit against Time, Inc. The matter was finally adjusted with the publication of Sarnoff's letter, but it is revealing of Sarnoff's sensitivity on the subject and the wishful thinking into which he was led by his ambivalent position.

The following roundup of the goods and bads of broadcasting must be prefaced by the reservation that no group of men—much less one man —can be held solely responsible for the state of affairs in any mass-oriented industry. In electronics, Sarnoff (and others, but he was the protagonist) injected broadcasting into a preexisting society with con-gealed mores and institutions, avid for the new but clinging to the old. When one man is largely responsible for the introduction of a social invention, he cannot be blamed individually for the evils it propagated any more than he is entitled to personal credit for all the benefits it brought to humanity. A protean social invention like broadcasting must be distinguished from innovations in medicine, for instance—though even in that case, the problems of an overcrowded world may be one of the side effects. We must beware of making scapegoats of innova-tors; we must also bear in mind that in a sense all innovations are products of society—especially in fast-moving situations like electronics —broadcasting would inevitably have burgeoned within a few years had neither Sarnoff nor Conrad been born. Personal attributes, however admirable, are only part of the story.

Another word of caution: we must not take the United States, with its three TV networks, numerous independent stations, and millions of TV receivers, as typical. Even in the other industrialized countries, there is nowhere such a density of TV viewing as we have, while worldwide, radio is far more important than television. It is a matter of income. In countries of the Third World, a peasant or tribesman may have the means to own a small radio and keep it in operation, or there may be communal arrangements. A TV set is out of the question except for the elite.

In poor and rich countries alike, radio has the advantage of speed in the dissemination of news; hence the establishment, though so far to a minor degree, of all-news stations, pioneered by Westinghouse with transmitters in New York, Philadelphia, and Los Angeles. Such stations are more popular than profitable; they are expensive to operate because the collection of news is much more costly than phonograph music. Even WINS, the Westinghouse outlet in New York which has been on an all-news basis for years, has been casting about for a less expensive source of news, such as the audio news services of the press associations.

Actually, in TV news broadcasts, the contribution of the picture is usually secondary. For every live broadcast of the shooting of a Lee Harvey Oswald, the picture is usually of little consequence. Stop looking at it and the sound will give you all the essential information. The picture plays a more prominent role in the commercials. Apparently millions of Americans could not be persuaded to medicate themselves on the present scale ("Geritol Every Day") without an actor (or more often an actress) exhibiting a package to view while delivering the correlated spiel with appropriate gestures and grimaces. Or by showing a victim in misery, then the application of the miraculous remedy, clinched by the final sequence in which the actor is blissfully cured.

Not that television's defects are all there is to it. Just as it is, it is an immense blessing for shut-ins and hospital patients. Anyone who doubts that should talk to the house staff of the older city hospitals with their large wards. Things are not much different in more private accommodations, whether in municipal or voluntary hospitals. Television offers escape for the patients from the tedium of sickness, at least for the majority who are not in serious trouble. To claim a directly therapeutic effect would be absurd, but television lightens the load of interns, residents, and nurses, and thereby enables them to provide better care. That it would prove to be an important adjunct to medical practice was an unforeseen fringe benefit.

From a cultural standpoint, the bulk of television is bad, and its potential benefits are only fitfully realized. Its deficiencies call for continuous public monitoring and the application of pressure wherever it gives promise of being effective. But it is futile to expect quick results.

Most people are—and in the calculable future will continue to be—members of the uncultivated majority. Anyone who persists in holding their innate inclinations against them is taking on a large order. Most of the world's work is done by ordinary people—they couldn't stand it if they were extraordinary, and in the eyes of employers they would be "overqualified" for the jobs open to them. Television has relieved these myriads of the boredom of being alone with themselves. No doubt it would be better if they were thinking great thoughts—or even little ones—or meditating—or inviting their souls—but most of them would not be doing anything of the kind anyway. It's not their fault that they were disqualified for the solace—and burden—of thought early in life. Either way, if television in its dubious form seduced them, they were ready and willing to be seduced—and we can't blame that on Sarnoff.

The opposition that counts, whether in the Catholic church or the entertainment world, comes from within. It may germinate elsewhere, but significant change cannot develop outside alone. In the entertainment world tripe eventually leaves a partial vacuum, which eventually is filled.

With the advent of television the criticism became harder to brush off. The standard rebuttal—that the critic was a Red—obviously could not be applied to Edward R. Murrow when he told the Radio and Television News Directors Association that their instrumentalities had been good to him beyond his due; but he predicted future historians would find in the annals of television "evidence of decadence, escapism, and insulation from the realities of the world in which we live." Another cogent comment of Murrow's was that "if television and radio are to be used for the entertainment of all the people all of the time, we have come perilously close to discovering the real opiate of the people."

Now that television is predominant, the situation has grown no better, the attacks have not ceased, and David Sarnoff, from his mausoleum in Scarsdale, cannot reply. On November 15, 1974, Chief Judge David L. Bazelon of the U.S. Court of Appeals for the District of Columbia, which ranks just below the U.S. Supreme Court, made a blistering frontal attack on the television industry. Speaking at a dinner of the Federal Communications Bar Association, Judge Bazelon called on the industry leaders to stop "prostituting the medium for profits" and decried "the abuse of the immense power of television for the private profit of a few." Although of course Bazelon was speaking as an individual, Warren Weaver Jr. pointed out in *The New York Times* that "the blunt tenor of his speech raised some question as to how hospitable a forum his court (which hears appeals from the Federal Communication's Commission's decisions) would provide for television in the days ahead."

At about the same time the late Rod Serling, a prominent TV writer and producer, spoke before Ithaca College's School of Communication to the same effect, or worse. Serling told the students:

> For some twenty-five years, I've been laboring in the vineyards of television and motion pictures, and I am forever struck by our mediocrity, our imitativeness, our commercialism and, all too frequently, our deadening and deadly lack of creativity and ingenuity and courage.
>
> God, how this multibillion-dollar industry can labor so mightily and produce a mouse—and sometimes programming that even a self-respecting mouse would find difficult to swallow and keep down! There are things on the screen that defy reason, logic, and taste.

Cultural TV suffered a severe loss when Serling died after heart surgery in June 1975.

Even the *Reader's Digest,* which among magazines is about at the same intellectual level as television, condensed some well-mannered strictures on the latter from an interview with Alistair Cooke in *U.S. News & World Report,* April 15, 1974. Especially among engineers, however—not that they count for much when it comes to content of radio or television—was a statement by Vladimir K. Zworykin, whom Sarnoff rightly regarded as the engineer most responsible for the technical basis of modern television. Zworykin hoped that his inventions "would be used for educational purposes, especially so that different cultures could learn to understand each other." In 1974 he said publicly that the part of a TV set he liked best was the "off" switch.

There has been so much discussion of children's television that it is hardly necessary to rehash it here. Nor has it had much effect on what appears on the screen during the childrens' hours. Several years ago, on the basis of thorough research, Robert B. Choate emerged as a convincing critic of nutritionally worthless cereal compositions sold largely by means of TV advertising for children. The first response of the networks and sponsors was the standard one of denying that a problem existed. When the problem would not go away, they appointed special vice-presidents and tried to mollify the critics. Some concessions were made, but the children were still being induced by premium offers and all sorts of hornswoggling attuned to the juvenile mind. The children continued to importune their mothers for cereals rich in sugar and poor in nourishment, and most of the mothers complied. *Consumer Reports* (February 1975) summed up the then current situation: "Four years after the big flap, more often than not, parents are still feeding their children high-priced junk food. . . ."

However, the critics received support from within—a possible harbinger of more of the same. James E. Duffy, president of ABC, condemned the rating system applied to Saturday-morning television. "During these specific hours when our chief concern must be for the welfare of our children," Mr. Duffy said, "we are far too concerned with outrating the competition."

Children's diet and nourishment are important; even more important is the effect of TV violence on their own inherent propensity to violence, which we are told is on the increase, to the extent that it is becoming a matter of concern to the more farsighted advertisers and broadcasters. In his advertising column in *The New York Times* (November 21, 1975), under the title "Action on TV Violence Urged," Philip S. Dougherty suggests, "There could be a quiet revolution against violence on television brewing in powerful advertiser circles." Dougherty refers to an "impassioned speech" given by Archa O. Knowlton, media services director of General Foods, the country's fourth largest national advertiser, disposing of some $80 million in network television a year. Mr. Knowlton called for unified action on the part of the advertising industry, which amounted to an appeal for an agreement among the sponsors to cut down on violence as a group, rather than to let those who wish to continue to cash in on the easy way while their competitors take the hard way of scrounging around for entertainment that entertains by other means than bang-bang-bang today and bang-bang-bang tomorrow. "We should do this," Mr. Knowlton said before the Association of National Advertisers, "not only because of our concern for the fabric of our society, but also on a hard-nosed business basis. It is entirely possible that a commercial will work harder in a program that reflects positive social interaction as opposed to one dealing with blood and guts."

Mr. Knowlton also suggested that while the evidence was only speculative, there was reason to believe that violence "is contagious and that depicting crime or publicizing crime can stimulate criminal minds to follow suit." Without going into still another voluminous survey, wouldn't it be remarkable if by sheer volume of viewing such an effect did not follow? Responsible bodies like a committee of the American Bar Association have publicized research figures indicating that children who watched television have witnessed about 11,000 murders by the time they were fourteen years old. In the great majority of cases, deterrent influences prevent the kids from doing likewise, but a nation in which murder and aggravated assault are as prevalent as in the United States had better not assume that there is no connection between television depiction and crimes of violence.

The trouble with television's sporadic efforts to combat evil is that there is seldom, if ever, any follow-up. A praiseworthy documentary is shown, (not on prime time, naturally) is duly acclaimed by the critics; then it goes into the archives and is heard of no more. In the meantime, unless Mr. Knowlton's proposals should have a decisive effect, the murders—on television and on the streets—will go on and on—at a time when the Republic's institutions are in deep trouble generally.

This is just one example of the hiatus between commercial radio-TV and the social services the electronic media might be rendering if business considerations were not paramount. Another case is cited by Les Brown in the July 1, 1975 *New York Times:* "Clinic Is Losing Cable-TV Link to Doctors." The fact that a cable link is involved is incidental; the principle is the same. The connection was between a child-care center in East Harlem and the Mount Sinai School of Medicine a mile and a half away. Nurse practitioners at the clinic worked with pediatricians at the hospital, who were on call over the circuit while attending to their regular duties at the hospital.

But the service was being terminated for what, to the rational mind, would seem the strangest of reasons. The Department of Health, Education and Welfare had initiated the system as a research project. Convinced that the system worked efficiently, HEW was not empowered to keep it working as a service. The cable link had been provided free by the Teleprompter Corporation, the doctors donated their services, but there were bureaucratic obstacles to converting a research project into a regular service. An official referred to the termination as "really a tragedy. . . . What we have proved is that a lot of good can come from cable-TV, but we're a long way from home and the reason, of course, is money."

This was after David Sarnoff's time, but the principle goes back fifty years, and at the present rate of progress can continue for another fifty.

Of course you can look at it as only a trivial incident involving kids, mostly black, in Harlem. Nothing to get excited about, really.

David Sarnoff's life was his and not yours or mine. He lived it according to his lights, which varied from brilliant to dim. He was great as a creative businessman; on that all can agree. We know—or do we? —his views through the innumerable speeches he made; but these were largely inseparable from his executive capacity in RCA, hence often contradictory.

He was not an ordinary businessman—even of the highest caliber. There was something behind the commanding presence and the brusque decisions which Lilienthal saw, and Mandelbaum, and many others who are haunted by it five years after his death. Indefinable, impalpable, it does not exist in the same sense as radio, and television, and all the material struggles that preoccupied David Sarnoff throughout a long life. But so long as it exists, hope for a more civilized use of electronic communications exists, too.

INDEX